Digital Activism in Asia Reader

Digital Activism in Asia Reader

edited by
**Nishant Shah, Puthiya Purayil Sneha,
and Sumandro Chattapadhyay**

µ meson press

Bibliographical Information of the German National Library
The German National Library lists this publication in the Deutsche Nationalbibliografie (German National Bibliography); detailed bibliographic information is available online at http://dnb.d-nb.de

Published by meson press, Hybrid Publishing Lab,
Centre for Digital Cultures, Leuphana University of Lüneburg
www.meson-press.com

Design concept: Torsten Köchlin, Silke Krieg
Cover Image: The photograph is taken by Gigi Ibrahim on November 29, 2011; and is shared via her Flickr account under the Creative Commons Attribution 2.0 Generic license (https://www.flickr.com/photos/gigiibrahim/6428279173/)

The print edition of this book is printed by Lightning Source,
Milton Keynes, United Kingdom

ISBN (Print): 978-3-95796-050-4
ISBN (PDF):   978-3-95796-051-1
ISBN (EPUB): 978-3-95796-052-8
DOI: 10.14619/013

The digital editions of this publication can be downloaded freely at:
www.meson-press.com

Funded by the EU major project Innovation Incubator Lüneburg

See the section "Publication Details and License Information" (p. 265) for detailled license information on the texts assembled in this book.

Contents

Foreword   9
Nishant Shah

From Taboo to Beautiful: Menstrupedia   15
Denisse Albornoz

  Annotated by *Nandini Chami*

Keeping Our Voices Loud: The Evolution of CrowdVoice.org   31
Esra'a Al Shafei

  Annotated by *Puthiya Purayil Sneha*

Digital Natives' Alternative Approach to Social Change   37
Maesy Angelina

  Annotated by *Sarah Mckeever*

We Come from an Activist Background   55
An Interview with Htaike Htaike Aung, MIDO

Digital Natives and the Return of the Local Cause   63
Anat Ben-David

  Annotated by *Padmini Ray Murray*

Greatfire.org   79
Sumandro Chattapadhyay

Taiwan's Sunflower Protest: Digital Anatomy of a Movement   87
Tracey Cheng

  Annotated by *Puthiya Purayil Sneha*

Digital Revolution in Reverse: Syria's Media Diversifies Offline 99
Armand Hurault

   Annotated by *Puthiya Purayil Sneha*

India Calling 105
Rachel Jolley

   Annotated by *Puthiya Purayil Sneha*

Digital Populism in South Korea? Internet Culture and the Trouble with Direct Participation 113
Youngmi Kim

   Annotated by *Sumandro Chattapadhyay*

Many Clicks but Little Sticks: Social Media Activism in Indonesia 127
Merlyna Lim

   Annotated by *Nishant Shah*

Rising Voices: Indigenous Language Digital Activism 155
Subhashish Panigrahi

   Annotated by *Padmini Ray Murray*

Towards 2 Way Participation 159
Prabhas Pokharel

   Annotated by *Padmini Ray Murray*

Wikipedia, Bhanwari Devi and the Need for an Alert Feminist Public 173
Urvashi Sarkar

   Annotated by *Shobha S.V.*

Digital Natives in the Name of a Cause: From "Flash Mob" to "Human Flesh Search" 179
YiPing (Zona) Tsou

   Annotated by *Nandini Chami*

Three Forces Acting behind the Development of the Internet 197
Hu Yong

   Annotated by *Puthiya Purayil Sneha*

Old and New Media: Converging During the Pakistan Emergency (March 2007 – February 2008) 205
Huma Yusuf

　Annotated by *Shobha S.V.*

Redefining Youth Activism through Digital Technology in Singapore 235
Weiyu Zhang

　Annotated by *Sarah McKeever*

Acknowledgements 257
Contributors 259
Publication Details and License Information 265

Foreword

Compiling this Reader on Digital Activism in Asia is fraught with compelling challenges, because each of the key terms in the formulation of the title is subject to multiple interpretations and fierce contestations. The construction of 'Asia' as a region, has its historical roots in processes of colonial technologies of cartography and navigation. Asia was both, a measured entity, mapped for resources to be exploited, and also a measure of the world, promising an orientation to the Western World's own turbulent encounters. As Chen Kuan-Hsing points out in his definitive history of the region, Asia gets re-imagined as a 'method' in cold-war conflicts, becoming the territory to be assimilated through exports of different ideologies and cultural purports. Asia does not have its own sense of being a region. The transactions, interactions, flows and exchanges between different countries and regions in Asia have been so entirely mediated by powers of colonisation that the region remains divided and reticent in its imagination of itself. However, by the turn of the 21st century, Asia has seen a new awakening. It finds a regional identity, which, surprisingly did not emerge from its consolidating presence in global economics or in globalised structures of trade and commerce. Instead, it finds a presence, for itself, through a series of crises of governance, of social order, of political rights, and of cultural productions, that binds it together in unprecedented ways.

The digital turn might as well be marked as an Asian turn, because with the new networks of connectivity, with Asian countries marking themselves as informatics hubs, working through a circulated logic of migrant labour and distributed resources, there came a sense of immediacy, proximity, and urgency that continues to shape the Asian imagination in a new way. In the last decade or so, the rapid changes that have emerged, creating multiple registers of modernity, identity, and community in different parts of Asia, accelerated by a seamless exchange of ideas, commodities, cultures, and people have created a new sense of the region as emerging through co-presence rather than competition and conflict. Simultaneously, the emergence of global capitals of information, labour and cultural export, have created new reference points by which the region creates its identities and networks that are no longer subject to the tyranny of Western hegemony. Alternative histories are marking new routes of traffic and uncovering local and contextual histories which have otherwise been subsumed under a postcolonial West versus the Rest rubric, where the rest was always imagined as a monolithic whole. Ironically, the recognition of this diversity, is what allows for an Asian turn to come into being, reshaping the borders of negotiation and boundaries of exchange in the region.

While the digital remains crucial to this shaping of contemporary Asia, both in sustaining the developmental agenda that most of the countries espouse, and in opening up an inward looking gaze of statecraft and social organisation, the digital itself remains an ineffable concept. Largely because the digital is like a blackbox that conflates multiple registers of meaning and layers of life, it becomes important to unengineer it and see what it enables and hides. The economic presence of the digital is perhaps the most visible in telling the story of Asia in the now. Beginning with the dramatic development of Singapore as the centre of informatics governance and the emergence of a range of cities from Shanghai to Manilla and Bangalore to Tehran, there has been an accelerated narrative of economic growth and accumulation of capital that is often the global face of the Asian turn. However, this economic reordering is not a practice in isolation. It brings with it, a range of social stirrings that seek to overthrow traditional structures of oppression, corruption, control, and injustice that have often remained hidden in the closed borders of Asian countries. However, the digital marks a particular shift where these questions are no longer being excavated by the ICT4D logic, of the West's attempts to save Asia from itself. These are questions that emerge from the ground, as more people interact with progressive and liberal politics and aspire not only for higher purchase powers but a better quality of rights. The digital turn has opened up a range of social and political rights based discourses, practices, and movements, where populations are holding their governments and countries responsible, accountable, and culpable in the face of personal and collective loss and injustice.

From flash-mobs in Taiwan to organised political demonstrations in India, from Twitter campaigns in Indonesia to cultural protests in Thailand, the range of activities that have emerged, changing the citizen from being a beneficiary of change to becoming an agent of change, have been bewildering and wonderful. The digital interfaces of interaction, peer-2-peer networks of connectivity, real-time documentation and evidence building in the face of crises, and the ability to build autonomous networks of resistance and dialogue have all resulted in extraordinary demonstrations and political movements which shape Asia from within. Additionally, boundaries which were once built to separate, have now become borders that are porous and people learn through viral connections. Thus, one form of protest and organisation immediately takes up a replicating form that gets exercised within different contexts to adapt to specific situations, and bring about dramatic changes that are no longer contingent upon traditional practices of activism. Asian countries that are constantly being challenged by these forms of collectivity that emerge with the digital are caught in a quandary where they invest in the very infrastructure that is used against the neoliberal and developmental logic. The impulse of development and economic growth that the public private partnerships in India had pinned upon the digital is being met with a strong critique and resistance by the widespread use and penetration of digital technologies. What the digital shall be used for, and what its consequences will be, are both up for speculation and negotiation.

In the face of this multiplicity of digital sites and usages that are reconfiguring Asia, it is obvious then, that the very nature of what constitutes activism is changing as well. Organised civil society presence in Asia has often had a strong role in shaping modern nation states, but more often than not these processes were defined in the same vocabulary as that of the powers that they were fighting against. Marked by a strong sense of developmentalism and often working in complement to the state rather than keeping a check on the state's activities, traditional activism in Asia has often suffered from the incapacity to scale and the inability to find alternatives to the state-defined scripts of development, growth and progress. In countries where literacy rates have been low, these movements also suffer from being conceived in philosophical and linguistic sophistry that escapes the common citizen and remains the playground of the few who have privileges afforded to them by class and region. Digital Activism, however, seems to have broken this language barrier, both internally and externally, allowing for new visualities enabled by ubiquitous computing to bring various stakeholders into the fray. The participants in activist movements, the roles that people play in engaging with political protests, and the very forms of organisation and structure of activism has undergone a significant change.

At the same time, the digital itself has introduced new problems and concerns that are often glossed over, in the enthralling tale of progress. Concerns around digital divide, invasive practices of personal data gathering, the nexus of markets and governments that install the citizen/consumer in precarious conditions, and the re-emergence of organised conservative politics are also a part of the digital turn. Activism has had to focus not only on digital as a tool, but digital also as a site of protest and resistance. New activism, shaped by the presence of pervasive technologies, recognises the technological domains as equally mired in processes of inequality and inequity and are developing tools that make the digital transparent and accountable. Activism of the digital has become as important as activism through the digital, and there is a need to combine the two, so that the human right and the technological right come together to form better modes of living.

Given these polymorphous concepts that we deal with, a Reader on Digital Activism in Asia can always only be a fragmentary and tentative snapshot. This is not an attempt to give a comprehensive overview of the diversity of the region, the multiplicity of practices or the different scales, scopes and temporalities of the changes that Asia is experiencing. The Reader does not offer an index of the momentous emergence with the growth of the digital or a chronological account of how digital activism in Asia has grown and shaped the region. Instead, the Reader attempts a crowd-sourced compilation that presents critical tools, organisations, theoretical concepts, political analyses, illustrative case-studies and annotations, that an emerging network of change makers in Asia have identified as important in their own practices within their own contexts. In 2014, the Dutch development aid agency Hivos, in collaboration with the Centre for Digital Cultures at the Leuphana University in Germany and the Centre for Internet and Society in Bangalore, India, initiated a project titled 'Making Change' that conceived of a production sprint that brought together 30 activists, artists, theorists, policy actors and other stakeholders from around Asia to reflect on new processes, vocabularies and ideas of making change. Each participant represented wider networks of change making in their regions and brought together expertise and experience that draws from the past to imagine the futures that we live in.

This Reader emerges from the exchanges that were initiated in this production sprint, working with these change makers as they guided us to local, contextual, specific, and particular resources that would help understand their current concerns as well as the ways in which they envision their next steps. The essays in this Reader, then, need to be seen, not as academic resources, but as tools that might help distil lessons and ideas that are in use, with life, in circulation with the change makers that we have been working with. Similarly, as you scan through the book, you will realise that these essays do not have just one vision or one particular usage. A range of editors have read and annotated these essays, to think through what the strengths are and how they would enable new thought and practice in their own contexts. In many ways, this reader is an academic equivalent of a crowd-mapping exercise where multiple on-the-ground participants have provided important snapshots and then a variety of experts have contextualised and framed these snapshots to make them usable and intelligible to their own practice.

Additionally, we were faced with the challenge of what a Reader should include, when it has to account for the multiplicity of practices and the diversity of intentions. If there is one thing that emerges in thinking about Digital Activism, it is the understanding that Digital Activism can only be understood as a 'Wicked Concept'. It remains incommensurable when confined to certain kinds of knowledge systems, and ineffable when not distributed across multiple stakeholders. The power of the digital has been in opening up the silos within which change and activism discourse and practice have often been pushed into, and it was necessary for us to reflect this multi-stakeholder knowledge ecology that helps present a connected, even if not comprehensive view of the field. Thus, unlike traditional Readers which depend on tertiary scholarship and academic publishing, both of which have their valid and important role to play in the knowledge ecosystem but can often be lagging in their interventions and post-facto analyses, this

Reader sees at its core, a variety of different material. Academic scholars and researchers provide leading annotations and critical questions as entry points to all the material. However, the material itself is varied. It includes snapshots of platforms and practices that are not yet analysed in scholarship but stand as strong instances of how digital activism is being shaped and shaping the region. It brings together policy reports and manifestos as they betray the aspirational intersections of activism and governance. It consolidates websites and applications that become symptomatic of the interfaces and interactions of change. It also invites critical scholarship in the field, but the scholarship is also examined as a tool of thought rather than as evidence of knowledge performance. The Reader is imagined as a Swiss Army Knife, with different formats and forms of knowledge producing new functions that a Reader like this can contribute to the very change practices it draws upon.

It gives me great pleasure to present you with this Digital Activism in Asia Reader and hope that it continues to catalyse new conversations and accrue iterative annotations as it enters into new networks of circulation and exchange.

Nishant Shah
Co-Founder, The Centre for Internet and Society, India.
Knowledge Partner, 'Making Change Project', Hivos, The Netherlands.
Visiting Professor, Centre for Digital Cultures, Leuphana University, Germany.

From Taboo to Beautiful: Menstrupedia

Denisse Albornoz

CHANGE MAKER: Tuhin Paul, Aditi Gupta and Rajat Mittal
ORGANIZATION: Menstrupedia
METHOD OF CHANGE: Storytelling and comics
STRATEGY OF CHANGE: To shatter the myths and misunderstandings surrounding menstruation, by delivering accessible, informative and entertaining content about menstruation through different media.

[Image 1] Menstrupedia is a guide to explain menstruation and all issues surrounding it in the most friendly manner. Credit: Menstrupedia, http://menstrupedia.com/.

Most of us think we know what menstruation is; except…we don't. Many of my male friends still cringe at the mention of the phrase "I'm on my period", or use it as a derogatory justification for my occasional cranky mood at the office: "It's that time of the month, isn't it?" Poor menstruation has been the culprit of femininity; always bashful, tiptoeing for five days straight, trying its best to remain incognito. The social venture Menstrupedia is committed to change this. Aditi, Tuhin and Rajat want to shift how we look at menstruation and remove the stigma that haunts the natural, self-regulation process women undergo to keep their bodies healthy and strong to sustain life in the future.

Now, if you are already wondering what menstruation has to do with internet and society, just wait for it. This post manages to bring art, punk, menstruation *and* technology together, all within the scope of the Making Change[1] project! Before though, we shall start with some definitions. Let us first lay conceptual grounds about menstruation and Menstrupedia, to then locate and unpack their theory of change.

What is Menstruation?

It can be defined as:

> *Menstruation*[2] is the periodic discharge of blood and mucosal tissue (the endometrium) from the uterus and vagina. It starts at menarche at or before sexual maturity (maturation), in females of certain mammalian species, and ceases at or near menopause (commonly considered the end of a female's reproductive life).

But, I believe, most women will agree the following image 2 is an accurate depiction of the spectrum of thoughts, emotions and sensations that menstruation spurs.

The Beauty of RED

Red was beauty, was love, was passion, was dreams…

[Image 2] Red was beauty, was love, was passion, was dreams… Credit: Menstrupedia and mypromovideos.

My Periods: a Blessing or a Curse
by Naina Jha[3]

My periods
Are a dreadful experience
Because of all the pain.
Myths and secrets make it a mystery
What worsens it most though, are members of my family
Especially my mother, who always make it a big deal
They never try to understand what I truly feel
I face all those cramps and cry the whole night long
None of which is seen or heard or felt by anyone.
Instead of telling me, what it is,
They ask me to behave maturely instead.
Can somebody tell me how I am supposed to
Naturally accept it?
My mother asks me to stay away from men
And a few days later, she asks me to marry one!
When I ask her to furnish
the reason behind her haste
She told me that now that I was menstruating,
I was grown up and ready to give birth to another.
I don't know whether to feel blessed about it
Or consider it to be my curse.
For these periods are the only reason for me to be disposed.
Since my childhood, I felt rather blessed to be born as a girl
But after getting my periods now,
I'm convinced that it's a curse...

Despite all this, it is still perceived as a social stigma in society. There is clearly a dissonance between the definition, experience and perceptions around menstruation, that calls for a reconfiguration of the information we are using to define it.

Stigma as a Crisis

However, re-defining 'menstruation' is no popular or easy task. The word belongs to a group of contested terminology around womanhood and is the protagonist of its own breed of feminist activism: *menstrual activism*.[4] Although I would consider many of the stigmas surrounding menstruation to be quite self-explanatory (we've all experienced and perpetuated them in one way or another -and if they are not, then you are the product of an obscenely progressive upbringing for which I congratulate your parents, teachers and all parties involved), I will still outline the main reasons why menstruation is a source of social stigma for women, and refer to scholarly authority on the subject to legitimize my rant.

Ingrid Johnston-Robledo and Joan Chrisler use Goffman's definition of stigma on their paper: "The Menstrual Mark: Menstruation as a Social Stigma"[5] to explain the misadventures of menstruation:

> Stigma: [S]tain or mark setting people apart from others. it conveys the information that those people have a defect of body or of character that spoils their appearance or identity.

Among the various negative social constructs deeming menstruation a dirty and repulsive state, this one made a particular echo: "[menstruation is] a tribal identity of femaleness". Menstruation is the equivalent of a rite of passage marking the lives of girls with a 'before' and an 'after' on how the world sees them and how they see themselves. From the dreaded stain on the skirt and the 5-day mission to keep its poignant color and smell on the down low, to having to justify mood and body swings to the overly inquisitive; menstruation is imagined as inconvenient, unpleasant and unwelcome. As Johnston-Robledo and Chrisler point out: the menstrual cycle, coupled with stigmas, pushes women to adopt the role of the "physically or mentally disordered" and reinforce it through their communication, secrecy, embarrassment and silence.

Why Does it Matter?

Besides from strengthening attitudes that underpin gender discrimination and attempting against girls' self-identity and sense of worth, there are other tangible consequences for their development and education. I'm going to throw some facts and figures at you, to back this up with the case of India.

An article published by the WSSCC, the Geneva based Water supply and Sanitation Council, shows the Menstruation taboo, consequence of a "patriarchal, hierarchical society"[6], puts 300 million women at risk in India. They do not have access to menstrual hygiene products, which has an effect on their health, education (23% of girls in India leave school when they start menstruating and the remaining 77% miss 5 days of school a month) and their livelihoods.

In terms of awareness and information about the issue, WSSCC found that 90% didn't know what a menstrual period was until they got it. Aru Bhartiya's research on Menstruation, Religion and Society, shows the main sources of information about menstruation come from beliefs and norms grounded on culture and religion.[7] Some of the related restrictions (that stem from Hinduism, among others) include isolation, exclusion from religious activities, and restraint from intercourse. She coupled this with a survey where she found: 63% of her sample turned to online sites over their mothers for information, 62% did not feel comfortable talking about the subject with males and 70% giggled upon reading the topic of the survey. All in all, a pretty gruesome scenario.

Here's Where Menstrupedia Comes in

The research groundwork attempted above was done in depth by Menstrupedia back in 2009 when the project started taking shape. They conducted research for one year while in NID and did not only find that awareness about menstruation was very low, but that parents and teachers did not know how to talk about the subject.

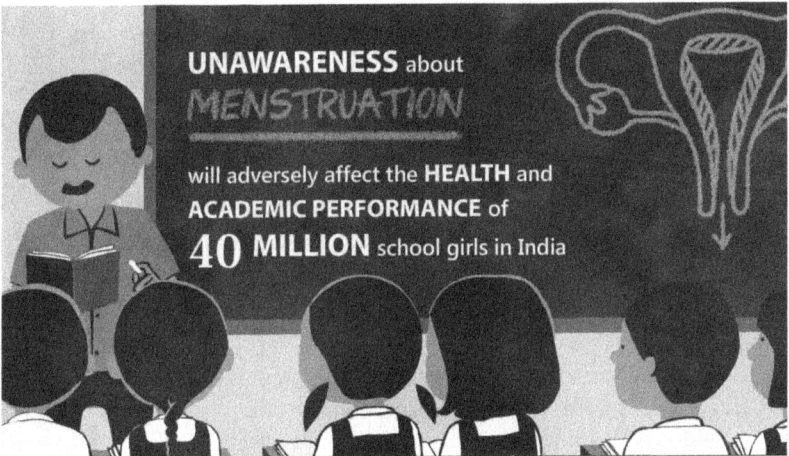

[Image 3] Facts about menstruation awareness in India. Credit: Menstrupedia.[8]

Their proposed intervention: distribute an education visual guide and a comic to explain the topic. They tested out the prototype among 500 girls in 5 different states in Northern India and the results were astonishing.

> To my surprise, they [the nuns] all agreed that until they read the information given in the Menstrupedia comic, even they were of the opinion that Menstruation was a 'dirty' and 'abominable' thing and they wondered 'why women suffered from it in the first place'? But after reading the comic book, their view had changed...now they felt that this was a 'vital' part of womanhood and there's nothing to feel ashamed about it! The best part was while this exercise clarified their ideas, beliefs, concepts about menstruation, it also helped me to get over my innate hesitancy to approach such a sensitive issue in 'public' and boosted my confidence for taking this up as a 'mission' to reach out to the maximum possible girls across the country. (Ina Mondkar, on her experience of educating young

nuns about menstruation. Testimonial shared after a workshop held in two Buddhist monasteries in Ladakh)

Their mandate today reads: *'Menstrupedia is a guide to explain menstruation and all issues surrounding it in the most friendly manner.'* They currently host a website with information about puberty, menstruation, hygiene and myths, along with illustrations that turn explaining the process of growing up into a much friendlier endeavour than its stigma-laden alternatives.[10]

[Image 4] A workshop conducted by MJB smriti sansthan to spread awareness about menstruation. Credit: Menstrupedia.[9]

Through the comic and the interactions around it, Menstrupedia strives to create a) *content* that frame menstruation as a natural process that is inconvenient, yes; but that should have no negative effects on their self-esteem and development; and b) *an environment* where girls can talk about it openly and clarify their doubts.

Technology's Role in the Mix

We want to reach out to as many girls as possible. (Tuhin, Menstrupedia)

The role of digital technologies basically comes down to *scalability*. Opposite to The Kahani Project's views on scaling up,[12] Menstrupedia makes emphasis on using technology *to reach a larger audience*. Currently they have a series of communication channels enabled by technology that include: a visual quick guide[13], a Q&A forum[14] (for both men and women), a blog[15] (a platform of self-expression on menstruation), a YouTube channel[16] (where they provide updates on their progress) and the upcoming comic.

Upon the question of the digital divide and whether this expands the divide between have and have nots, Tuhin was very set on the idea of producing the same content in both its digital and print form. "Parents or schools should be able to buy the comic and give it to their daughters, so whenever they feel like it, they can refer to it". The focus is on making this material as readily available as possible, in order to overcome the tension between new and old information: "workshops are conducted but the moment they go back home, their mothers impose certain restrictions. It becomes a dilemma. But if you provide [The girl] with a comic book, she has something she can take home and educate her mother with."

[Image 5] Menstrupedia Comic; the first chapter of the comic can be read for free on the Menstrupedia website.[11]

And Here's Why it Works

More than the comic book itself, what is truly remarkable about Menstrupedia is Tuhin, Rajat and Aditi's guts to pick up such a problematic theme in the Indian social imaginary and challenge the entrenched, stubborn beliefs surrounding the issue. The comic book, asides from being appealing to the eye and an accessible format of storytelling (a method we have unpacked in previous posts[17]), fits right into the movement of menstrual activism and what it stands for.

> We thought of creating something: a tool that can help girls understand menstruation without having to rely on anybody else. (Tuhin, Menstrupedia)

First, it is a *self-reliant resource*. Once the comic book leaves Menstrupedia's hands and lands on those of kids and adults, it takes its own journey. The format of the comic is accessible enough for someone to pick it up and learn about menstruation without the intervention or the support of a third party. This makes Menstrupedia's comic *highly flexible and mobile*. It can be shared from teacher to child, from mom to daughter, from peer to peer: "[it should teach] how to help your friends when they get their period" (Tuhin) However, it has the autonomy to also take roads less travelled: from mom to dad, from child to teacher, from boy to girl. The goal at the end of the day: a self-reliant, solidarity-based community where information circulating about menstruation highlights its capacity to give life and overshadows its traditional stigmatized identity.

This self-reliance is characteristic of previous manifestations of menstrual activism. Back in the 80s, the feminist movement, tightly linked to punk culture, embraced the *Do It Yourself movement*,[18] that enabled women to materialize personalized forms of resistance. They published zines[19] promoting "dirty self-awareness, body and menstrual consciousness and unlearning shame" through "raw stories and personal narratives".[20] According to Bobel using the *self as an example* is a core element in the "history of self-help" within the DIY movement. The role of the Menstrupedia blog is then crucial to sustain the exposure and production of "raw narratives". Tuhin adds: "We don't write articles on the blog. It is a platform where people from different backgrounds write about their experiences with menstruation and bring in a different perspective."

For example:

Red is My Colour
by Umang Saigal[21]

Red is my colour,
To make you understand, I endeavour,
Try to analyse and try to favour.
It is not just a thought, but an attempt,
To treat ill minds that are curable.
When I was born, I was put in a red cradle,
I grew up watching the red faces for a girl-children in anger,
Red became my favourite,
But I never knew,
That someday I would be caged in my own red world.

Red lover I was,
All Love I lost,
When I got my first red spots,
What pain it caused only I know,
When I realized, Red determined my 'class'
I grew up then, ignoring red,
At night when I found my bedsheet wet,
All day it ached,
All day it stained,
And in agony I would, turn insane.

At times I would think,
Does red symbolize beauty or pain?
But when I got tied, in the sacred knot,
I found transposition of my whole process of thought,
When from dirty to gold, Red crowned my bridal course.
As I grew old,
All my desires vanished and got cold,
My mind still in a dilemma,
What more than colour in itself could it unfold?
What was the secret behind its truth untold?
Is Red for beauty, or is it for beast?
It interests me now to know the least,
All I know is that Red is a Transition,
From anguish to pride
Red is a sensation.
Red is my colour, as it is meant to be,
No matter what the world thinks it to be,
No love lost, one Love found,

Red symbolizes life and also our wounds,
I speak it aloud with life profound,
That red is my colour, and this is what I've found.

'Self-expression' is not a concept we usually find side by side with 'menstruation'; however, if we look at what has been done in the past, we find that Menstrupedia is actually contributing to a much larger tradition of resistance. For instance, Menstrala[22], by the American artist Vanessa Tiegs. Menstrala is the name of a collection of 88 paintings "affirming the hidden forbidden bright red cycle of renewal."

[Image 6] Menstrala. Credit: Vanessa Tiegs.[23]

Another interesting example is American feminist Gloria Steinem's[24] text "If Men Could Menstruate"[25]:

> What would happen, for instance, if suddenly, magically, men could menstruate and women could not?
> The answer is clear:
> Menstruation would become an enviable, boast worthy, masculine event:
> Men would brag about how long and how much.
> Boys would mark the onset of menses, that longed- for proof of manhood, with religious and stag parties.

Opportunities like these, enable Menstrupedia's community to actively participate in the reconfiguration of 'menstruation' as a concept and as an experience. By exposing new narratives and perspectives on the issue and by disseminating menstrual health information, the community is able to crowd source resistance and dismantle the stigma together.

Making Change through Menstrupedia

The case of Menstrupedia reminds us of Blank Noise[26] because of its approach to change. Both locate their crises at *the discursive level* and seek to resolve them by creating new forms of meaning-making. They advocate for a reconsideration of 'givens', for a self-reflection on our role perpetuating these notions and for resistance against conceptual status quos: be it socially accepted culprits like 'eve-teasing', or more discrete rejects like 'menstruation'. Both seek to dismantle power structures that give one discourse preference over others, and both count with a strong gender dynamic dominating the context where these narratives unfold. They are producing a revolution in our system of meaning making, yet only producing resistance in the larger societal context they inhabit.

On the question of where is Menstrupedia's action located, Tuhin replied by pinning it at the *individual level*: "if a person is aware of menstruation and they know the facts, they are more likely to resist restrictions and spread awareness". However, they still acknowledge the historicity behind menstrual awareness (as knowledge passed down from generation to generation) that precedes the project. While the introduction of Menstrupedia, to an extent, does shake up household dynamics in terms of content, it also provides tools and resources to sustain the traditional model of oral tradition and knowledge sharing within the community.

In terms of their role as change-makers, Tuhin stated that the possibility to intervene was a result of their socio-economic status and the resources they had at hand as "educated members of the middle class with access to information and communication technologies". Is this the role the middle class should play? I asked. To which he gave a two fold answer: First, in terms of *responsibility of action*: "it is a role that anyone can play depending on what kind of expertise they have. It comes to a point where [intents of change] cannot be sustained by activism if you want to achieve long term impact" And second, in terms of setting up a *resilient infrastructure*: "I believe we can create an infrastructure people can use and create models that can help low income groups overcome their challenges and become self-sustainable." Both answers highlight the need for sustainability in social impact projects, hinting a retreat from wishful thinking upon the presence of technology and a more strategic allocation of skills and resources by middle class and for-profit interventions.

As far the relationship between art, punk, menstruation and technology goes; that was just a hook to get you through the unreasonable length of my blog post, but if anything, it represents an effort to portray the importance of *contextuality and interdisciplinary* we have been exploring throughout the series. Identifying the use of various mediums and language systems, such as different art forms and modes of self-expression, as well the acknowledgement of the theoretical and social contexts preceding and framing the project, as is feminist activism and the cultural and religious backdrop in India, contribute immensely to fill gaps in the stories of how we imagine change making today; especially at the nascence of new narratives, as we hope is the case for menstruation in a post-Menstrupedia era.

Endnotes

1. Shah, Nishant. 2013. "Whose Change is it Anyways? Towards a Future of Digital Technologies and Citizen Action in Emerging Information Societies." Hivos Knowledge Program. April 30. http://cis-india.org/digital-natives/blog/whose-change-is-it-anyway.pdf.
2. 2015. "Menstruation." Wikipedia. June 04. https://en.wikipedia.org/wiki/Menstruation.
3. Jha, Naina. 2014. "My Periods: A Blessing or a Curse." Menstrupedia Blog. January 13. http://menstrupedia.com/blog/my-periods-a-blessing-or-a-curse/.
4. Refer to Chris Bobel's work including, Bobel, Chris. 2010. New Blood: Third-Wave Feminism and the Politics of Menstruation. Rutgers University Press.
5. Johnston-Robledo and Chrisler made reference to Erving Goffman's 1963 work *Stigma: Notes on the Management of Spoiled Identity*: "According to Goffman (1963), the word stigma refers to any stain or mark that sets some people apart from others; it conveys the information that those people have a defect of body or of character that spoils their appearance or identity Goffman (1963, p. 4) categorized stigmas into three types: "abominations of the body" (e.g., burns, scars, deformities), " blemishes of individual character" (e.g., criminality, addictions), and "tribal" identities or social markers associated with marginalized groups (e.g., gender, race, sexual orientation, nationality)". Johnston-Robledo, Ingrid & Joan C. Chrisler. 2013. "The Menstrual Mark: Menstruation as Social Stigma." *Sex Roles*. Volume 68, Issue 1-2. January. Pp 9-18.
6. Mollins, Julie. 2013. "Menstruation Taboo Puts 300 Mn Women in India at Risk." Water Supply and Sanitation Collaborative Council. http://www.wsscc.org/resources/resource-news-archive/menstruation-taboo-puts-300-mln-women-india-risk-experts-0.
7. Bhartiya, Aru. 2013. "Menstruation, Religion and Society." International Journal of Social Science and Humanity. Volume3, Number 6. November. http://www.ijssh.org/papers/296-B00016.pdf.
8. Menstrupedia. 2014. "Menstrupedia: Friendly Guide to Healthy Periods." YouTube. https://www.youtube.com/watch?v=2caqzHWk2r8.
9. Menstrupedia. 2015. "Menstrupedia Comic being Used in Different Part of India." Facebook. https://www.facebook.com/media/set/?set=a.538044002975089.1073741837.277577839021708&type=3.
10. Menstrupedia. http://menstrupedia.com/.
11. "Menstrupedia Comic." Menstrupedia. http://menstrupedia.com/comic/english.
12. "Scaling Up." SoundCloud. https://soundcloud.com/user742107957/scalingup.
13. "Quick Guide." Menstrupedia. http://menstrupedia.com/quickguide.
14. "Questions." Menstrupedia. http://questions.menstrupedia.com/.
15. "Menstrupedia Blog." Menstrupedia. http://menstrupedia.com/blog/.
16. "Menstrupedia." YouTube. https://www.youtube.com/user/menstrupedia.
17. http://cis-india.org/@@search?SearchableText=storytelling.
18. For a short run through on DIY as part of the Punk Subculture, refer to Ian P. Moran's paper: "Punk - The Do-it-Yourself culture." He states: "Punk as a subculture goes much further than rebellion and fashion as punks generally seek an alternative lifestyle divergent from the norms of society. The do-it-yourself, or D.I.Y. aspect of punk is one of the most important factors fueling the subculture." Moran, Ian P. 2010. "Punk: The Do-It-Yourself

Subculture." *Social Sciences Journal.* Volume 10, Issue 1. http://repository.wcsu.edu/ssj/vol10/iss1/13.
19 2015. "Zine." WIKI 2. https://en.wiki2.org/wiki/Zine.
20 Bobel, Chris. 2006. "'Our Revolution Has Style:' Contemporary Menstrual Product Activists 'Doing Feminism' in the Third Wave." *Sex Roles.* Volume 54, Number 5-6. Pp. 331-345.
21 Saigal, Umang. 2014. "Red is My Colour." Menstrupedia Blog. February 4. http://menstrupedia.com/blog/red-is-my-colour/.
22 Tiegs, Vanessa. "Menstrala." http://menstrala.blogspot.in/.
23 Tiegs, Vanessa. 2009. "Vanessa Tiegs: Menstrala." YouTube. https://www.youtube.com/watch?v=KJ5-_zegKSU.
24 Gloria Steinem is a journalist, and social and political activist who became nationally recognized as a leader of, and media spokeswoman for, the women's liberation movement in the late 1960s and 1970. Visit her official website: http://www.gloriasteinem.com/.
25 Steinem, Gloria. 1978. "If Men Could Menstruate." Ms. Magazine. October. http://www.mylittleredbook.net/imcm_orig.pdf.
26 Albornoz, Denisse. 2013. "Public Art, Technology and Citizenship - Blank Noise Project." The Centre for Internet and Society. November 30. http://cis-india.org/digital-natives/making-change/blank-noise-citizenship.

Annotation

Nandini Chami

Denisse Albornoz, in her essay on Menstrupedia, an India-based initiative that has focused on addressing prevailing myths and taboos surrounding menstruation, explores the new possibilities opened up by digital spaces in furthering 'menstrual activism'. Menstrual activism is a movement in the tradition of 'intersectional feminism', as revealed by its emphasis on everyday struggles of emancipation (in this case, the politics of choice exercised in menstruation management), and its willing accommodation of extremely divergent feminist identities—from gyno-centrics to queer feminists (Bobel 2010).

Considering that intersectional feminism is flourishing in social media and other spaces of the online public sphere (Subramanian 2014), the essay can be used as a springboard to dive into the broader debates on the implications of digital mediation for feminist activism.

Firstly, the current, intersectional avatar of feminism emphasises the fluidity of identity and plurality of discourse; and therefore, it is no surprise that its advocates are comfortable with the post-ideological online public sphere characterized by a complete horizontalisation of communications (Frissen 2002).

In fact, some commentators have described this development as the 'rise of a new fourth-wave of feminism' marked by the emergence of multiple feminist publics whose combined weight poses a formidable challenge to all discursive hegemonies, including that of the valorisation of a single type of feminism (Cochrane 2013). Of course, these interpretations are in no way a glib endorsement of digital spaces being havens for free and unfettered feminist expression and articulation; and they do recognise the numerous limits that one comes up against (such as the threat of state surveillance; censorship at the hands of the state and Internet intermediaries; and the self-censorship spawned by the prevailing cultures of gender and sexuality; and the threat of gender-based violence in online spaces). But on the whole, this trend of analysis emphasises the amplification of voice, and the gains with respect to the 'politics of presence', enabled by the online public sphere. Needless to say, in and of themselves, these gains do not automatically enable a challenging of the underlying structures of gender power and exclusion (Gurumurthy 2013).

A complete realisation of the transformatory potential of digital feminist activism is possible only if the following two caveats are met:
- Digital feminist activism needs to move beyond a preoccupation with the politics of recognition and questions of identity, and pay equal attention to struggles for redistribution (Fraser 2012) – especially pertaining to the ownership, management and control of technological architectures underpinning the network society we inhabit (APC 2014).
- The competing and sometimes contradictory feminist articulations opened up by emerging digital publics need to be acknowledged as marking the transition to a new, fluid, 'issue-based' idiom of feminist politics with less institutional coherence. In this context, it is vital for feminist activists to decipher the challenge of building movements that combine 'flexibilities of horizontalism with structures for coherence (in decision-making)', in the right proportion – as without this, they could degenerate into the tyranny of structurelessness, and be easily co-opted for the consolidation of existing power structures (Gurumurthy 2013).

References and Further Readings

APC. 2014. "Feminist Principles of the Internet." GenderIT. August 20. Accessed June 10, 2015. http://www.genderit.org/node/4097/.

Bobel, C. 2010. *New Blood. Third Word Feminism and the Politics of Menstruation*. Rutgers University Press.

Cochrane, K. 2013. "The Fourth Wave of Feminism: Meet the Rebel Women." The Guardian. Accessed June 10, 2015. http://www.theguardian.com/world/2013/dec/10/fourth-wave-feminism-rebel-women

Gurumurthy, A. 2013. "Participatory Citizenship: Tracing the Impact of ICTs on the Social and Political Participation of Women." In *Global Information Society Watch 2013—Women's Rights, gender and ICTs*. Accessed June 10, 2015. http://www.giswatch.org/en/womens-rights-gender/tracing-impact-icts-social-and-political-participation-women.

Fraser, N. 2012. "Feminism, Capitalism, and the Cunning of History: An Introduction." FMSH-WP-2012-17. Fondation Maison des sciences de l'homme. Accessed June 10, 2015. http://www.ssnpstudents.com/wp/wp-content/uploads/2015/03/Feminism-Capitalism.pdf

Frissen, P. H. A. 2002. "Representative Democracy and Information Society: A Postmodern Perspective." *Information Polity*. Volume 7, Number 4. Pp. 175-183.

Subramanian, S. 2014. "From the Streets to the Web: Feminist Activism on Social Media." Submitted Report. Centre for the Study of Culture and Society. April. Accessed June 10, 2015. http://cscs.res.in/dataarchive/textfiles/from-the-streets-to-the-web-feminist-activism-on-social-media-sujatha-subramanian-tata-institute-of-social-sciences

Keeping Our Voices Loud: The Evolution of CrowdVoice.org

Esra'a Al Shafei

The importance of information has always been at the engine of all the operations of Mideast Youth.[1] The nature of information is that it evolves as the situation on the ground changes, and in addition to that, the means through which that information is shared has changed just as rapidly. The history of CrowdVoice[2] has been a reflection of that change, and of its dedication to providing not just the information, but the story that lies at the heart of social movements and current events.

From its earliest days between 2005 and 2009, Mideast Youth was running various human rights campaigns online. We shared information with our team of supporters and volunteers constantly as it was the only way we could follow issues closely enough to write about them in an engaging way, in a way that raised awareness about abuses that were typically ignored by the mainstream. This information was shared exclusively through e-mail updates, which was not only time consuming, but it was also ineffective and non-transparent. By its nature it was a single-sided information sharing mechanism, where we controlled the flow of information in a way that limited engagement. Articles, images and videos that provided evidence of human rights abuses or simply tracked news coverage were important, but the delivery was weakening the message.

Mideast Youth set out to develop a system that aggregated information collectively, in an environment that invited public engagement through crowdsourcing while at the same time making it easier for us to share information.

Our aim was to create a visually dynamic interface that gave users an overall idea of what they were clicking on.

CrowdVoice was launched in 2010 as an internal experiment within our team, and within a matter of a few years, it grew to accommodate thousands of users around the world with topics from sexual violence in India, to forced labor in China, to police brutality in the United States.

[Image 1] CrowdVoice homepage: https://crowdvoice.org/.

Between 2010 and 2013, the presence of social media in general multiplied exponentially. CrowdVoice had global access and unprecedented engagement, but we realized that it wasn't enough for us to just curate information. We were faced with a different problem; giving people links to curated media feeds was useful to current issues and recent protests and movements, but it fell flat as a way of conveying a long term, useful narrative.

By 2013, we realized the new challenge wasn't just in providing media, but in placing that media into an understandable and accessible context. At this stage of social media and information aggregation, users faced the opposite problem that they had faced a few years before – being so overly inundated with information that they couldn't focus on what was going on. The next phase of CrowdVoice began, and we began to build infographics for major or ongoing issues that helped people understand what was happening generally. Infographics that explained history, casualty rates, and other key general information reminded users that the thousands of videos that they have access to are still connected to a central struggle. The voices of the people involved in these movements stayed relevant and human, rather than disappearing into an unconnected web of videos and articles.

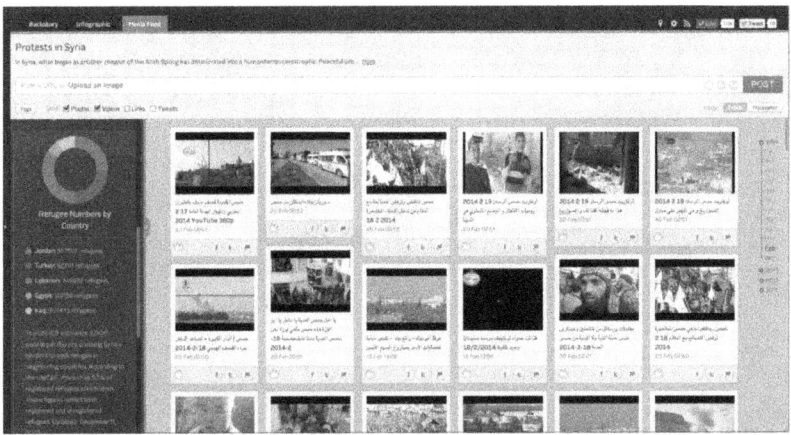

[Image 2] Protests in Syria. Credit: CrowdVoice, https://crowdvoice.org/.

Ultimately, I was pushed to keep working on CrowdVoice by this drive to maintain connections. A recent article about news coverage of conflict zones asked:

> As builders of these online networked spaces, how do we make sure we optimize not only for traffic and engagement, but also for an informed public?[3]

At CrowdVoice, we came to the realization early on that information alone didn't make for an informed public, and thus we pushed for the third layer to CrowdVoice that provided an even more engaging story to the public. The "backstory" that we developed is essentially a timeline that explained the roots of a conflict or movement, whether it was 3 months, 3 years or 30 years ago or more. The timelines drew from the information on the pages and from our own curated information to give a thorough understand of the issue to users before they are met with a media feed that contains evidence of those events and issues – videos, eyewitness reports, news coverage, and anything else people help curate into one place.

Today, CrowdVoice balances these multifaceted functionalities to give one of the most comprehensive explanations of social movements available online. The complexities of current and past issues have proven that news reports are not enough, and neither is mere curation. To truly do justice to struggles around the world, people need to be presented with the story, then the numerical facts and their relevant sources, then they need to be able to engage with the media feed and have the ability to add more information so that more primary sources and raw videos can be taken into account.

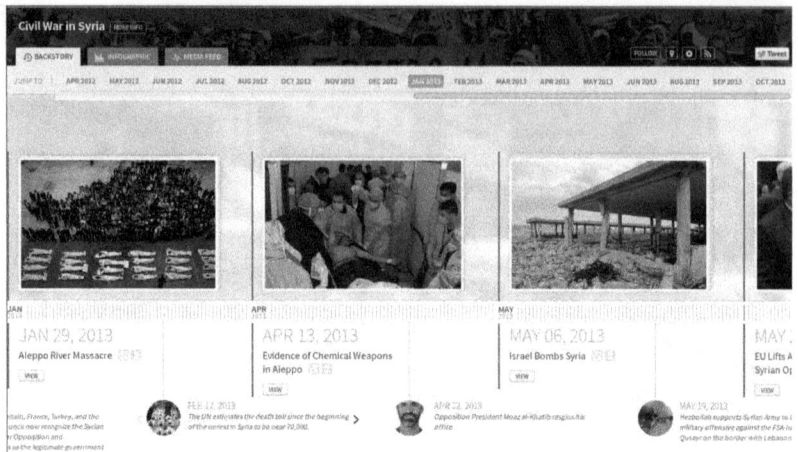

[Image 3] Civil War in Syria Timeline on CrowdVoice. Credit: CrowdVoice, https://crowdvoice.org/.

CrowdVoice is a work in progress – it has to be, because our world is as well. As social movements redefine our societies and tech innovations redefine how we relate to our societies, CrowdVoice is important because it fits right in the intersection between these two dynamics. Whatever the future holds, CrowdVoice will be prepared for it – informing the public, building information into stories, and making sure people's voices are heard.

Endnotes

1   Mideast Youth. http://www.mideastyouth.com/
2   CrowdVoice. http://crowdvoice.org/
3   Lotan, Gilad. 2014. "Israel, Gaza,War and Data: Social Networks and the Art of Personalising Propaganda." Medium. August 4. Accessed June 18, 2015. https://medium.com/i-data/israel-gaza-war-data-a54969aeb23e

Annotation

Puthiya Purayil Sneha

In the last couple of decades, the use of the Internet and other digital tools and platforms for activism has increased greatly, owing to better access to and diversity in the use of the Internet, among other reasons. The online space has also seemingly become one where voices of dissent can be freely heard, although there have been several efforts to curb this freedom. CrowdVoice.org was started in 2010 by Bahraini civil rights activist Esra'a Al Shafei as part of her non-profit organization Mideast Youth, which actively campaigns for freedom of expression through the use of open source software and development of various digital and online tools and platforms. Apart from CrowdVoice.org, Mideast Youth has several initiatives such as Mideast Tunes, which connects underground musicians, and Ahwaa, a discussion tool for Arab LGBT youth. In addition to this, it has also launched several apps for smartphones, and focuses on 'amplifying voices of change' through these diverse platforms. CrowdVoice rose to prominence during the Arab spring, when it documented the widespread protests by crowdsourcing material from different parts of the world in the form of news feeds, blogs, comments, images, videos and tweets, among others. Due to the sensitive and very political nature of the content, and the heavy censorship on media in several countries in the Middle East, CrowdVoice.org was banned in Bahrain, Yemen and Iran during the Arab Spring; it continues to be banned in Bahrain even today. Indeed, with the Bahraini uprising that began in 2011, post the Arab Spring protests, media censorship by the present regime has been high, and violence and torture against media persons and citizen activists is rampant. This is the case with many other parts of the MENA region as well, thus making the exercise of building and sustaining such an initiative fraught with very real dangers of persecution.

The growth of Internet and digital technologies in the last decade has also meant an unprecedented increase in information – its production and modes of dissemination. While the advent of the digital brought with it the problem of the digital divide and the need to examine levels of access to information, tools and resources across geographical and social barriers, the issue of access becomes contoured differently also due to the problem of 'excess' – the availability of too much information, and the absence of ways to curate and utilize it well. CrowdVoice.org essentially performs this function, of aggregating material in a single place and facilitating collaborative annotations around a particular topic, so that it is presented from multiple perspectives. As the write-up mentions, the platform is an effort to respond to situations on the ground, and make media flexible and more accessible to different groups of people. While information has always been a key aspect of social movements, never before has its curation been more imperative, given the sheer volume of its availability, and the ways in which it travels and evolves online, which become all the more important in this context. Curation by a larger public comes with its own challenges and problems, but the notion of voice itself is important, in whatever fragmented, diverse forms it is made available through this platform. CrowdVoice.org also functions as an archive of material generated around issues, thus creating a backstory as such to current events, and making this content available to the public at large. The use of open source software and platforms is also part of its activism, in terms of making technology openly available to encourage its use in different ways and promote innovation. The understanding and methods of digital activism also therefore changes through the use of these technologies and the Internet in diverse and innovative ways.

References and Further Readings

Chan, Siobhan. 2010. "Q&A: Middle Eastern Web Technology for Social Change, with Esra'a Al Shafei." SciDev.Net. Accessed June 9, 2015. http://www.scidev.net/index.cfm?originalUrl=-global/human-rights/feature/q-a-middle-eastern-web-technology-for-social-change-with-esra-a-al-shafei-1.html.
CrowdVoice. http://crowdvoice.org
Wise, Monica. "How CrowdVoice Collects Data On Underreported Protests Around The World." The Toolbox. Accessed June 9, 2015. https://www.thetoolbox.org/articles/2301-how-crowd-voice-collects-data-on-underreported-protests-around-the-world#.VQ1lyvyUf5M.

Digital Natives' Alternative Approach to Social Change

Maesy Angelina

Digital natives with a cause: Between champions and slackers[1]

My first encounter with the idea of new media technologies' crucial role in contemporary youth movements was when I read the United Nations World Youth Report in 2005. The report stipulated that emerging youth movements are characterised by the use of such technologies in organising, communicating, and campaigning (UN DESA, 2005:125). The interest on this topic has since considerably escalated among academics, policy makers, and other practitioners.

Studies have progressed from an initial pre-occupation with the instrumental role of technology (see, for instance Kassimir, 2006; Brooks and Hodkinson, 2008, and Shirky, 2008) to an inquiry on emerging new actors, politics, and forms of activisms enabled by such technologies. At the centre of this new line of research are digital activisms conducted by young people whose lives are significantly shaped by the ubiquitous internet technologies – the 'digital natives'[2].

They are hailed as the new actors who are defining the potential future directions of activism – one that focuses more on issues related to everyday democracy and favours self-organised, autonomous, and horizontal networks (for examples, see Bennett, 2003; Martin, 2004; Collin, 2008). However, the emergence of this hopeful narrative is also accompanied by one of doubt. It questions the extent to which internet activism can contribute to concrete social change (Collin, 2008; Kovacs, 2010). Some proponents of this view insist that digital activism can only be effective if accompanied with rigourous real-life activism, to the extent of calling those who engage solely in digital activism as 'slacktivists' (Morozov, 2009; Gladwell, 2010).

The current debates were propelled by the question on the impact of youth digital activism. The problem with this question lies in the inherent assumption that the researcher's idea on activism is universally shared, including by the digital natives. History has shown that new forms of activism have emerged along with the structural transformation of societies (Offe, 2008; Touraine, 2008). Hence, it is valid to presume that youth in the 21st century 'network society' (Castells, 1996) also give birth to alternative approaches to activism.

Instead of impact assessment, I argue that the effort to understand digital natives' activism should start by asking how youth imagine and approach social change to give room for alternative approaches to emerge. Inspired by Claus Offe's (2008) method to identify the "newness" in new social movements, I attempt to address the question by looking at the issue, strategy, site of action, as well as the internal mode of organising of a movement.

The framework will be first used to confront existing assumptions on activism and social movements, which will also serve as a point of comparison to a digital natives' movement chosen as a case study. As a response to the Global North focus in studying digital natives, the case study chosen is Blank Noise, a youth-led collective that has been addressing the issue of street sexual harassment in urban India through street interventions and online campaigns since 2003.

Activism with a capital 'A'

What do we mean by activism? Literatures have acknowledged that it is a difficult concept to pin down, since it has been used in many different ways by a variety of actors. Broadly speaking, activism has been meant to refer to collective action for social change as one of the forms of civic and political engagement, such as protest events and direct actions, advocacy to change policies of powerful institutions, consumer boycotts, or public awareness raising campaigns (Kassimir, 2006; Sherrod, 2006).

The aforementioned understanding seem to be the lens with which the majority of researches on youth digital activism have been conducted (see, for instance, Juris and Pleyers, 2009), resulting in two problems. Firstly, most researches tend to only discuss the concrete and action aspects of activism, ignoring the intangible aspects that also determine activism as a practice: the underlying ideology, articulation of issue, the profile of actors, and how the movement organises itself.

Secondly, there seems to be some underlying assumptions on the established form of activism (Angelina, 2011). Referring to Offe's framework, the issue chosen relates to structural changes, manifested in making concrete demands for policy reforms or behavioural change. The demand is made to an identified 'opponent', formal entities such as the state or major corporations. The *strategies* include policy advocacy, campaigns, or marches with the streets or physical space as the *site of action*. As for the *internal mode of organising*, the movement consists of highly-committed individuals who are involved full time in the movement. To paint a picture, for many of us activism on women's rights might refer to a group of extremely dedicated people who have spent years advocating for a Domestic Violence bill to be passed by the government and attempt to raise public awareness by marching on the streets with placards saying "Stop violence against women!"

While activism in common understanding definitely plays an important role in today's society, is this approach the only form of activism? More importantly, is this approach to social change also employed by digital natives with a cause?

Despite the digital divide, it has been widely acknowledged that to some extent all of the current generation of young people is a part of a "network society" (Feixa et al, 2009), one in which technology is deeply embedded in social structures (Castells, 1996). This results in a number of shifts in our societies, most notably the interconnection between the physical and the virtual as public space, where "ideas and values are formed, conveyed, supported, and resisted; space that ultimately becomes the training ground for action and reaction" (Castells, 2009: 301). Other shifts include the decreased influence of the state, whose power is challenged by globalisation, and the significance of major corporations and mass media as power holders. These shifts provide ground to believe that young people who grow up in this societal structure may have different approaches to social change as opposed to the assumptions held by many current scholars and practitioners – a proposition we will explore through the case of Blank Noise.

Blank Noise: A digital natives' movement

Blank Noise started in 2003 as a final year art project of Jasmeen Patheja, then a design student in Bangalore, as a response to the experience of many women around her, including herself, facing street sexual harassment on a daily basis. It was initially known for its street interventions, but what distinguished Blank Noise from similar initiatives is its prominent use of the web, with four blogs, a YouTube channel, as well as a Flickr, Facebook, and Twitter account. Today, Blank Noise exists in nine cities in India and consists of over 2,000 volunteers, most of whom are women and men between 16 to 35 years old. The collective has received national and international media attention and was named as one of the most outstanding citizen activism in India (Mishra, 2010).[3]

The issue: A new kind of articulation

Blank Noise was born to address prevalent acts of sexual harassment against women in public spaces in India, which ranges from staring, catcalls, to groping. The harassment is widely ignored by the society and called 'eve-teasing'.[4] The term, an Indian–English euphemism, both trivialises the issue by calling it "teasing" and places the blame on women through its play on the biblical Eve, a temptress who lures men into teasing her. Eve-teasing as a term is not formally recognised in the Indian Penal Code, but women could file a report under Sections 292 and 298 that criminalise any actions that make women targets of obscene gestures or violate women's modesty (Baxi, 2001). However, police rarely takes action unless it leads to violent death or fatal injury, and eve-teasing is often portrayed as being a romantic gesture as shown in Bollywood films (Natarajan, 2008).

Based on my conversations with 13 people in the collective, I discovered that Blank Noise shares similar characteristics with women's movements that focus on violence against women. Both identify the internalisation of patriarchal mindset as the root cause and the struggle to redefine cultural patterns regarding women's presence and engagement with the public space. Indeed, the Indian women groups of the 1970s laid the ground for Blank Noise's work by raising public awareness on the many forms of violence against women (Kumar, 1993). Although they acknowledge eve-teasing as a form of violence, the Indian women's movement has only done occasional, sporadic interventions, perhaps due to the choice of dedicating their limited resources to the more serious forms of violence - such as rape, bride burning, or dowry murder (Gandhi and Shah, 1992).

Blank Noise is the first one to systematically address street sexual harassment, but it differs from the usual women's movement in other respects as well. Most women's movements do identify patriarchal mindset as the source of violence, but they also make structural, tangible demands and identify opponents to make the demands to (Taylor and Whittier, 1995). New legislation criminalising domestic violence or service provision by the state are often advocated for an indication of concrete progress towards their overarching goal. The battle is for women; men are welcomed mostly only as far as signing petitions or joining the protests (Gandhi and Shah, 1992).

In apposition, the participants in the Blank Noise collective, all named spreading public's awareness on street sexual harassment as its overarching goal, but there were no intermediary tangible demands articulated. The collective did not even offer a rigid guideline of what constituted street sexual harassment. Instead, it opened up the space for a collective vocabulary building through polls on its blog and the streets to explore, question, and trigger debates around the ambiguous forms of eve-teasing, like staring.

Furthermore, they unanimously refused to identify an opponent because all members of the society are deemed equally responsible. While many scholars might read this as a sign of youth's faltering trust in the state, it is actually more based on the grey nature of the issue itself. Hemangini Gupta, a Blank Noise coordinator, asked, "*Should we be allowing the state to legislate an issue like street sexual harassment where there is so much grey even with how it is understood and defined - from 'looking' to physical violence?*"

I would argue, however, that Blank Noise has a conceptual, intangible opponent: the mindset that normalises street sexual harassment. This is reflected in their strategy to create public dialogue, both in the physical and virtual public spaces. The expectation is to make the collective as inclusive as possible, including for men because this is also an issue of their concern. Blank Noise also has a significant number of men volunteers and a specific intervention for men called Blank Noise Guys that asks for men's perspective and experiences on the issue (Blank Noise, 2009). This is where Blank Noise differs from the general picture of activism in terms of the issue articulation.

The strategies: Public dialogue and culture jamming

Blank Noise is a form of public art meant to provoke thoughts on a deeply normalised issue in a society that is already de-sensitised with the more established forms of protest, like street marches and petitions. Aarthi Ajit, a 25-years-old volunteer, explains this as: "*Maybe they don't have the same effects anymore and we need to look for new ways. Perhaps the more direct, playful ones will make people think and want to be a part of your movement.*"

Art interventions to provoke thoughts on street sexual harassment can be exemplified by a poster made by Rhea Daniel, a Mumbai-based self-employed design consultant. Rhea, who has been following and commenting on Blank Noise blogs and Facebook group since 2008, was tired of the representation of women only as victims of street sexual and one day got the inspiration to draw a different image: Women who are not afraid to take action, or in Blank Noise's vocabulary, "Action Heroes."

She explained to me that the poster was influenced by the 1950s pin-up and Indian calendar art. "*I deliberately wanted to attract attention with established art forms, however kitsch or sexist, and turn it into an instrument for empowerment... I know sexist imagery influences people and I was trying to reverse it, using the same instrument for my purpose.*"

What Rhea described is called culture jamming, a technique of raising awareness by subverting an element of a well-known cultural object and causing people to think critically about the message behind the twisted object (Cox, n.d.). The poster was provocative because it subverts the internalised popular notion of women in eve-teasing. She is dressed in a *salwar kameez*5 with a *dupatta*6, not Western clothes; she is feisty and winks as she smacks the hand that groped her belly, not looking afraid or humiliated by the harassment. This re-appropriation of mainstream cultural symbols is currently used by many consumer-based social movements and is especially popular among urban youth who distribute their work virally through the internet (*Ibid*). Although Blank Noise does not explicitly claim culture jamming to be its strategy, this is indeed its entry point to open up the space for dialogue in public spaces.

While the playfulness of Blank Noise differentiates itself from the protest approach employed by activism in general, what can be achieved from such a strategy?

I discovered the answer while studying one of its most popular street interventions, the 'I Never Ask for It' clothes collection campaign, which is a street exhibition of various clothes contributed by women who have been harassed by wearing them. It tackles the notion that women are to blame for the way they dress, for the clothes collected have ranged from tight shirts to a *saree*. There is no slogan like 'Stop Eve Teasing" or definitive messages of the type, but volunteers engage passers-by in conversations about the clothes gallery and the issue of street sexual harassment.

The twist of gender dynamics in this intervention is a form of culture jamming. While commonly culture jammers leave the viewers to think about the message, Blank Noise helps them process the message by taking the space opened by this thought-provocation and having volunteers engage passers-by on a conversation about street sexual harassment. Going back to the issue articulation, Blank Noise embarks on a dialogue in the streets without defining street sexual harassment or prescribing solutions. The people engaged are diverse in gender and class, a sign of 'everyone' being included.

What kind of impact is created by such an intervention? It is fair to assume that not many passers-by will change their behaviours after witnessing only one event and Blank Noise does not have the means to contact and check with them. The members admitted that they do not know how to measure tangible impacts generated for the people who saw the intervention, but this is not their main concern. "*This is an issue nobody talks about, so the very act of doing something about it seems to be enough right now*," said Apurva Mathad (28, male). This indicates that Blank Noise's most significant impact is not external (the public), but rather internal (the activists). This is echoed by all the other interviewees, all of whom felt that they were changed by their experience with the collective regardless of the length and intensity of their involvement. Some people realised how much their bodies have been disconnected from the public space; others felt empowered to deal with street sexual harassment.

This is when I understood the other, more central objective of Blank Noise that was verified later only by the founder and coordinators: To empower people through their experience with the Collective. The discussions and debates raised through the public dialogue help the volunteers themselves to learn more about the issue, reflect on their experiences and opinions, as well as to give meaning to their involvement. This is when I also understood the point of "no target group": People in Blank Noise also learn and become affected by the interventions they performed. Influencing 'others' is not the main goal although it is a desired effect, the main one is to allow personal empowerment of those within the Collective.

In this sense, Blank Noise is again very similar with grassroot feminist collectives whose main objective is to empower its members and do artistic interventions on the streets. However, when they raise public awareness, there are usually clear verbal messages through protests or street theatres and the main intention is to attract media attention – a clear separation between the activists as content providers and the public as the target audience. This separation is not as clear in Blank Noise, where the performers and the audience are mutually dependent for them to create meanings from the intervention.

The site of action: The streets and the cyber

Like so many other movements, Blank Noise started by taking its interventions to the streets, an example of which is already elaborated in the previous section. While Blank Noise shares most movements' current use of the Web, which are mostly for communication and coordination purposes (Juris and Pleyers, 2009), it differs from existing movements in its engagement with the cyber public and its inception to its cyber public campaigns.

Blank Noise started its online presence with a blog that was used to announce upcoming street interventions. The nature of its web presence changed when it shifted from one-way communication using Web 2.0 tools, as what older activists mostly do.[7] The previous one-way communication in the Blank Noise blog changed after two events that I call the digital tipping points, the points where the communication shifts into an interactive joint content-production with other internet users. This mode of communication has been noted by scholars, such as Manuel Castells (2009) and Clay Shirky (2010), as being the characteristics of the network society – where people are used to being producers and not only consumers of content.

The first was when Jasmeen started uploading photos of her harasser, taken by her mobile phone, to the blog in 2005. Comments immediately flooded in, raising questions about the nature of the violation, whether such actions are warranted, and the ethics of the action given that the man is of the lower class and has no access to the internet. The discussion resulted in Blank Noise deciding to blur the photos. This is when Blank Noise first realised that the cyber space is also a kind of public space that can give shape to the public conversation it imagines.

The second was the blogathon proposed by one of Blank Noise volunteers to commemorate the International Women's Day in 2006, which asked bloggers around India to write about their experiences with street sexual harassment and link it to the Blank Noise blog. The blogathon received massive responses, perhaps both due to the frustration on the silence around the issue and because blogging had just recently become a major trend at that time in India. Eve-teasing became an urgent topic on the cyber space and the success triggered the creation of Blank Noise's community blogs, in which the contents are contributed by other internet users. The tipping point was when the nature of Blank Noise's web presence changed due to its interaction with other web users. It took place when Blank Noise jumped into actions entirely dependent on the public response to be successful.

Now Blank Noise engages with the virtual public through comments in its main blog[8], virtual campaigns, and the community blogs. The most famous of the community blogs is the Action Hero blog[9], which hosts the stories of women's encounters with street sexual harassment and how they reacted. After speaking with a woman who contributed a post in the blog, I discovered that the anonymity granted by the internet and the supportive environment in Blank Noise's blog compelled her to write. She further shared that reading others' stories and receiving comments for hers made her feel less alone and helped her healing process. Blank Noise's cyber presence became a virtual support group for many women affected by street sexual harassment.

Kelly Oliver (in Mitra-Kahn, unpublished)[10] argued that writing experiences of a trauma, in this case street sexual harassment, helps the self heal by using speech and text to counter their emotions and exercise their agency; the process of empowerment that occurs hence establishes Blank Noise as a (cyber)feminist praxis.

Other than engaging with the virtual public through community blogs, Blank Noise also started conducting online campaigns. One of them is the online version of the same 'I Never Ask for It' campaign in February 2010, which asked Twitter users to tweet about their experiences with street sexual harassment and provide posters that can be used as a Profile picture or on Twitter background. These interventions are forms of culture jamming: breaking the existing silence on street sexual harassment in the virtual public space.

Internal mode of organising: One full-timer among thousands

In the words of Kunal Ashok, one of the male volunteers, the collective consists not only of, *"people who volunteer or come to meetings, but anyone that has contributed in any way they can and identify with the issue."* In this sense, Blank Noise today consists of over 2,000 people who signed up to their e-group as volunteers.

How does a collective with that many people work? Firstly, although these people are called 'volunteers' for registering to the e-group, I would argue that a majority of them are actually what I call casual participants – those who comment on Blank Noise interventions, retweet their call for action, promote Blank Noise to their friends through word of mouth, or simply lurk and follow their activities online. In the offline sense, they are the passers-by who participate in their street interventions or become intrigued to think about the issue afterwards. These people, including those who do the same activities without formally signing up as volunteers, are acknowledged to be a part of Blank Noise as much as those who really do volunteer.

Blank Noise is open to all who share its concern and values, but its volunteers must go beyond articulating an opinion and commit to collective action. However, Blank Noise applies very little requirement for people to identify themselves with the collective. The main bond that unites them is their shared concern with street sexual harassment. Blank Noise's analysis of the issue is sharp, but it also accommodates diverse perspectives by exploring the fine lines of street sexual harassment and not prescribing any concrete solution, while the latter is rarely found in existing social movements. The absence of indoctrination or concrete agenda reiterated through the public dialogue approach gives room for people to share different opinions and still respect others in the collective.

Other than these requirements, they are able to decide exactly how and when they want to be involved. They can join existing activities or initiate new ones; they can continuously participate or have on-and-off periods. This is reflected in the variety of volunteers' motivations, activities, and the meaning they give to their involvement. For some people, helping Blank Noise's street interventions is exciting because they like street art and engaging with other young people. Many are involved in online campaigns because they are not physically based in any of the cities where Blank Noise is present. Others prefer to do one-off volunteering by proposing a project to a coordinator and then implementing it. There are people who started volunteering by initiating Blank Noise chapters in other cities and they gradually have a more prominent role. Some stay for the long term, some are active only for several times before going back to become supporters that spread Blank Noise through word of mouth. The ability to personalise volunteerism is also what makes Blank Noise appealing, compared to the stricter templates for volunteering in other social movements.

Any kind of movement requires a committed group of individuals among the many members to manage it. The same applies to Blank Noise, who relies on a group of people who dedicate time and resources to facilitate volunteers' and think of the collective's future: The core team. Members of the core team, about ten people, are credited in Blank Noise's Frequently Asked Questions page and are part of a separate e-group than the volunteers. In its seven years, the core team only went for a retreat once and mostly connected through the e-group. In this space, they raise questions, ideas, and debates around Blank Noise's interventions, posters, and blog posts. Consequently, for them the issue is not only street sexual harassment but also related to masculinities, citizenship, class, stereotyping, gender, and public space. However, there are also layers in the intensity of the team members' engagement.

The most intense is Jasmeen, the founder and the only one who has been with Blank Noise since its inception until today. Jasmeen is an artist and considers Blank Noise to be a part of her practice; she has received funds to work for Blank Noise as an artist. Thus, she is the only one who dedicates herself to Blank Noise full time and becomes the most visible among the volunteers and the public eye. According to Jasmeen, she is not alone in managing the whole process within Blank Noise. Hemangini Gupta who joined in 2006 has slowly become the other main facilitator.

Hemangini, a former journalist who is now pursuing a PhD in the United States, explains her lack of visibility, *"Blank Noise could never be my number one priority because it doesn't pay my bills, so I can only do it when I have free time and my other work is done."* The same is true for others in the core team: students, journalists, writers and artists. Unlike Hemangini who still managed to be intensively involved, they have dormant and active periods like the volunteers. The core team functions as coordinators that facilitate the volunteers' involvement in Blank Noise and ensure that the interventions stay with the values Blank Noise upholds: confronting the issue but not aggravating people, creating public dialogue instead of one-way preaching. This role emerged in 2006 when the volunteer applications mounted as the result of the aforementioned blogathon. They have also initiated or facilitated the growth of Blank Noise chapters in other cities. Although some of them have also moved to other cities for work, they remain in touch online. Together, the core team forms the de-facto leadership in Blank Noise.

A strong nucleus of committed people is crucial in any form of social movement. However, Blank Noise is unique in its accommodation of people who cannot make Blank Noise a priority in their lives.

Understanding Blank Noise

Returning to the prevailing assumptions on the concepts and practice of activism, it is clear that Blank Noise cannot be understood using the lens of these assumptions. Blank Noise shares most feminists' analysis of harassment, naming normalisation, internalisation, and patriarchal mindset as the root causes. Their standpoint of street sexual harassment being a societal issue that concerns women and men are the same, but they part ways when Blank Noise does not identify an opponent or propose a concrete structural solution.

Its aim to raise public awareness and enable people's empowerment through involvement with the collective are not new; neither is their use of art and performances. It is new in the translation of the objectives. Instead of a structural change, Blank Noise interprets social change it desires as a cultural change which can be seen in concrete at an individual level as well as in the increase of media and public attention on the issue of street sexual harassment.

The method of achieving this is not through clearly articulated messages that can be written on a placard and carried to street marches, but by exploring the ambiguity through public conversation and culture jamming through street interventions and online campaigns alike. Instead of having a clear distinction of content producer and audience, both performers and audience are interdependent in creating the meaning for the interventions. These are not the result of "slack", as proponents of the aforementioned doubt narrative would contend, but a critical deliberative process.

Speaking of "slack", Blank Noise also defies the stereotypical dichotomy of full-time activists and slacktivists. As a collective, there are many roles and degrees of intensity that are needed for it to sustain and expand itself. Many of them are 'everyday activists' (Bang, 2004; Harris et al, 2010), young people who are personalising politics by adopting causes in their daily behaviour and lifestyle, for instance by purchasing only Fair Trade goods, or being very involved in a short term concrete project but then stopping and moving on to other activities.

A collective of everyday activists means that there are many forms of participation that one can fluidly navigate in, but it requires a committed leadership core recognised through presence and engagement. As Clay Shirky (2010: 90) said, the main cultural and ethical norm in these groups is to 'give credit where credit is due'.

Since these youth are used to producing and sharing content rather than only consuming, the aforementioned success of the movement lies on the leaders' ability to facilitate this process. The power to direct the movement is not centralised in the leaders; it is dispersed to members who want to use the opportunity.

Alternative approaches to social change

Current studies on the intersections of youth, activism, and new media technologies have begun to leave the techno-centered paradigm and use activism as a conceptual lens. Nevertheless, activism as a concept is currently loaded with assumptions on the kind of social change desired and how it can be manifested. By identifying these biases and putting the case of Blank Noise into the picture, I have demonstrated that today's digital natives may have an alternative approach to social change and organising a movement that cannot be understood through the current stereotypes.

Many youth movements today aim for social and cultural change at the intangible attitudinal level. Consequently, they articulate the issue with an intangible opponent (the mindset) and less-measurable goals. Their objective is to raise public awareness, but their approach to social change is through creating personal change at the individual level through engagement with the movement. Hence, 'success' is materialised in having as many people as possible involved in the movement. This is enabled by several factors.

The first is the internet and new media/social technologies, which are used as a site for community building, support group, campaigns, and a basis to allow people spread all over the globe to remain involved in the collective in the absence of a physical office. However, the cyber is not just a tool; it is also a public space that is equally important with the physical space. Despite acknowledging the diversity of the public engaged in these spaces, youth today do not completely regard them as two separate spheres. Engaging in virtual community has a real impact on everyday lives; the virtual is a part of real life for many youth (Shirky, 2010). However, it is not a smooth 'space of flows' (Castells, 2009) either. Youth actors in the Global South do recognise that their ease in navigating both spheres is the ability of the elite in their societies, where the digital divide is paramount. The disconnect stems from their acknowledgement that social change must be multi-class and an expression of their reflexivity in facing the challenge.

The second enabling factor is its highly individualised approach. The movement enables people to personalise their involvement, both in terms of frequency and ways of engagement as well as in meaning-making. It is an echo of the age of individualism that youth are growing up in, shaped by the liberal economic and political ideologies in the 1990s India and elsewhere (France, 2007). Individualism has become a new social structure, in which personal decisions and meaning-making is deemed as the key to solve structural issues in late modernity (*Ibid*). In this era, young people's lives consist of a combination of a range of activities rather than being focused only on one particular activity (*Ibid*). This is also the case in their social and political engagement. Very few young people worldwide are full-time activists or completely apathetic, the mainstream are actually involved in 'everyday activism' (Bang, 2004; Harris et al, 2010).

The way young people today are reimagining social change and movements reiterates that political and social engagement should be conceived in the plural. Instead of "activism" there should be "activisms" in various forms; this is not a new form replacing the older, but all co-existing and with the potential to complement each other. A more traditional movement focusing on changing legislations would benefit greatly from the existence of a digital natives movement aiming at empowering individuals and transforming attitudes, since they are addressing different stakeholders with different strategies but intending to achieve the same overarching goals. In cases where digital natives are taking an issue where no tangible opponent or goals can be identified, it can still be harmonious with the larger goals of a movement, the way Blank Noise's efforts to address street sexual harassment is still in line with the spirit of the wider women's movement. Hopefully, this will be a beginning to wider acknowledgement of digital natives' alternative approach to imagining and achieving social change.

Endnotes

1 The paper is based on the author's 'Beyond the Digital: Understanding Digital Natives with a Cause' research project, documented through a series of blog posts and position paper on the Centre for Internet and Society (CIS) website as well as a Master's thesis. The author would like to thank Blank Noise, especially Hemangini Gupta and Jasmeen Patheja, as well as Nishant Shah of CIS and Fieke Jansen and Josine Stremmelaar of Hivos for their support for the research.
2 I use the term 'digital natives' while being fully aware of the debates related to the name, which I could not address given the limitations of this essay.
3 For more details on Blank Noise, visit: http://blog.blanknoise.org
4 Editors' note: For us what the Blank Noise project has in common with other digital native actions that we have encountered is that individuals who are directly or indirectly affected by an event, societal experience, taboo or distrust try to tackle these issues in the public sphere. For them it is clear that issues like eve-teasing or in Ivet Piper's contribution (Book 4, To Connect), child abuse can only be de-stigmatised if it is discussed in the open. To do this one needs to challenge existing power structures. There need not be tangible results, but once these issues are brought into the public domain, they find others affected by the same issues and the community of participants and supporters grows.

5   Loose shirt and pants popular in South Asia.
6   A scarf women wear with salwar kameez.
7   Based on an interview with Anja Kovacs, a researcher on the Centre for Internet and Society in Bangalore who is documenting forms of digital activism in India.
8   http://blanknoise.org
9   http://actionheroes.blanknoise.org
10 Mitra-Kahn, Trishima (unpublished) *Holler back, Girl!: Cyberfeminist praxis and emergent cultures of online feminist organizing in urban India*. Quoted with permission.

Bibliography

Bennett, W.L. 2003. "Communicating Global Activism: Strengths and Vulnerabilities of Networked Politics." Information, Communication & Society, Vol. 6:2, pp. 143-168.

Blank Noise. 2005. 'Frequently Asked Questions'. Accessed on 21 September, 2010. http://blog.blanknoise.org/2005/03/frequently-asked-questions.html

Blank Noise (2009) "Your Attention Please." Accessed on 6 November, 2010. http://blog.blanknoise.org/2009/07/your-attention-please.html

Brooks, R. and Hodkinson, P. 2008. "Introduction." Journal of Youth Studies Vol. 11:5, pp. 473 – 479

Castells, M. 1996. The Rise of the Network Society: Information age, economy, society and culture Vol. 2. Malden: Blackwell Publishing.

Castells, M. 2007. "Communication, Power, and Counter-power in the Network Society." International Journal of Communication Vol. 1, pp. 238-266.

Castells, M. 2009. Communication Power. New York: Oxford University Press.

Collin, P. 2008. "The internet, youth participation policies, and the development of young people's political identities in Australia." Journal of Youth Studies Vol. 11:5, pp. 527 - 542

Cox, D. (n.d.) Notes on Culture Jamming. Accessed on 21 September, 2010 http://www.sniggle.net/Manifesti/notes.php

Feixa, C., Pereira, I., and Juris, J,S. 2009. "Global citizenship and the 'New, New' social movements: Iberian connections." Young: Nordic Journal of Youth Research Vol. 17:4, pp. 421-442.

France, A. 2007. Understanding Youth in Late Modernity. Berkshire: Open University Press.

Gandhi, N. and Shah, N. 1992. The Issues at Stake: Theory and Practice in the Contemporary Women's Movement in India. New Delhi: Kali for Women

Gladwell, M. 2010. Small Change: Why the revolution will not be tweeted. Accessed on 7 November, 2010 http://www.newyorker.com/reporting/2010/10/04/101004fa_fact_gladwell

Harris, A., Wyn, J., and Younes, S. 2010. "Beyond apathetic or activist youth: 'Ordinary' young people and contemporary forms of participation." Young Vol. 18:9, pp. 9-32

Juris, J.S. and Pleyers, G.H. 2009. "Alter-activism: Emerging cultures of participation among young global justice activists." Journal of Youth Studies Vol. 12 (1): pp. 57-75.

Kassimir, R. 2006. "Youth Activism: International and Transnational." Sherrod, L.R., Flanagan, C.A. and Kassimir, R. (eds.) Youth Activism: An International Encyclopedia, pp. 20-28. London: Greenwood Press.

Katzenstein, M. F. 1995. "Discursive Politics and Feminist Activism in the Catholic Church." Ferre, MM. and Martin, P.Y. (eds.) Feminist Organizations: Harvest of the Women's Movement, pp. 35-52. Philadelphia: Temple University Press.

Kovacs, A. 2010. "Inquilab 2.0? Reflections on Online Activism in India." Accessed 7 April 2010. http://www.cis-india.org/research/cis-raw/histories/netactiv/topics/Digital%20Activism

Kumar, R. 1993. The History of Doing: An Illustrated Account of Movements for Women's Rights and Feminism in India 1800 – 1990. New Delhi: Zubaan.

Martin, G. 2004. "New Social Movements and Democracy." Todd, M.J. and Taylor, G. (eds.) Democracy and Participation: Popular protests and new social movements, pp. 29-54. London: Merlin Press.

Mishra, G. 2010. "The State of Citizen Media in India in Three Short Ideas." Accessed on 19 May 2010. http://www.gauravonomics.com/blog/the-state-of-citizen-media-in-india-in-three-short-ideas/

Morozov, E. 2009. "The brave new world of slacktivism." Accessed on 19 May 2010. http://neteffect.foreignpolicy.com/posts/2009/05/19/the_brave_new_world_of_slacktivism

Natarajan, M. 2008/ Women Police in a Changing Society: Back Door to Equality. Hampshire: Ashgate.

Sherrod, L.R. 2006. "Youth Activism and Civic Engagement." in Sherrod, L.R., Flanagan, C.A. and Kassimir, R. (eds.) Youth Activism: An International Encyclopedia, pp. 2-10. London: Greenwood Press.

Shirky, C. 2008. Here Comes Everybody: How Change Happens and People Come Together. New York: Penguin Books

Shirky, C. 2010. Cognitive Surplus: Creativity and Generosity in a Connected Age. London: Penguin Press

Taylor, V. And Whittier, N. 1995. "Analytical Approaches to Social Movement Culture: The Culture of Women's Movement." Johnston, H. and Klandermans, B. (eds.) Social Movement and Culture, pp. 163-187. Minneapolis: University of Minnesota Press.

United Nations Department of Economic and Social Affairs / UN DESA (2005). 'World Youth Report 2005: Young People Today and in 2015'. Accessed 7 April 2010 http://www.un.org/esa/socdev/unyin/documents/wyr05book.pdf x

Annotation

Sarah McKeever

As the digital age continues to shape and alter the way individuals interface with the world, new challenges to previously understood definitions and theories have begun to appear in recent scholarship. The idea of what constitutes "activism" in the age of easy clicks and digital signatures signifying support of a cause has been described both as "slacktivism" and as the powerful rise of a globally connected network society. Each notion of the digital masks realities on the ground, and rarely contextualizes how so-called "digital activists" choose to define themselves and their actions on the digital and physical ground.

The notion that digital activism is somehow fundamentally different from past histories of activism has challenged scholars and practitioners to rethink how online protest and digital practices work in practice. Case studies, such as the one in question on Blank Noise, a collective created in Bangalore, India in 2003 by design student Jasmeen Patheja, allow "activists" to speak for themselves, to self-define their actions and provide crucial depth and context.

Before engaging with a case study, a sense of history and place lends nuance and provokes questions that the study itself may not address. Within India, a cursory overview of the women's rights movement reveals, at the risk of essentializing, a movement dedicated to objective-driven change through legal action and protest; a movement which calls for intense dedication and has been charged with being overly textual and locked in closed academic circles (for an overview of feminism in India, see Chaudhuri: 2005). This contextualises

Blank Noise's rejection of the activist label - they define themselves as "Action Heroes" - and their choice to be an awareness campaign rather than to be defined as an activist movement. It also allows the reader to critically question their stated rejection of these labels and histories, and place it within a historical legacy of feminist activism in India.

Within the article, several points spring to mind while engaging with this piece. The first is to always remain critically aware of the history and context of a locality. While it's clear that Blank Noise was and remains incredibly innovative in its approach as a public awareness campaign, can it be so easily divorced from and dismissed by the long and rich history of the feminist movement in India? The post-feminist move away from textual to visual mediums, from offline to online, is a conscious decision to bypass these very histories and the theoretical assumptions made when applying these labels to a movement. While the founder utilizes the tools and frameworks available to her, one cannot simply negate the history that came before. Instead this conscious shift represents an acute awareness of the disconnect between the feminist movement of the past and the "new" movements of the digital age.

The second point is to always keep the audience in mind. Who is the Blank Noise movement engaging with and for? By engaging with youth previously labelled apathetic to "activism," it made feminism palatable to an urban middle class through manipulations of cultural iconography. It also successfully leveraged the considerable affordances of the Internet as the movement evolved from an art project into an awareness campaign and pan-Indian collective. Other movements, including the Pink Chaddi campaign in 2009, have successfully used the aesthetics of the visual to draw attention in a visceral way, and once more highlight the departure from historical textual discourse and shift into the realm of the digital visual spectacle.

As a final take away, it is always important to be aware of what movements speak to and who the intended audience is. This allows us to critically examine whose voices are not heard and who is perhaps denied access to certain avenues of digital empowerment. The struggle and disconnect between the offline and the online can lead to extreme generalisation. In a country as diverse in language, experience, and technological access as India, it is crucial to limit the generalizations made from any case study.

To engage with any case study, an awareness of history, locality, and generalisations made within a field of study generates a deeper engagement with the study's strengths and potential limitations. Placing a case study within an enhanced context can lead to new avenues of inquiry and enriches the wider academic field. The complicated social, technological, and cultural nature of digital activism requires us to push beyond our primary observations into deeper intellectual observations.

References and Further Readings

Buckingham, D., S. Bragg & M.J. Kehily. (Eds.) 2014. *Youth Cultures in the Age of Global Media*. New York: Palgrave Macmillan.

Chaudhuri, M. (Ed.) 2005. *Feminism in India*. London: Zed Publishing.

Donner, H. (Ed.) 2011. *Being Middle Class in India: A Way of Life*. Abingdon: Routledge.

Ferree, M.M. & C.M. Mueller. 2007. "Feminism and the Women's Movement: A Global Perspective." In D.A. Snow, S.A. Soule & A. Kriesi. (Eds.) *The Blackwell Companion to Social Movements*. Malden, MA: Blackwell Publishing. Pp. 576-607.

Jaffrelot, C. & P. van der Veer. (Eds.) 2008. *Patterns of Middle Class Consumption in India and China*. New Delhi: Sage Publications Ltd. DOI: http://dx.doi.org/10.4135/9788178299976.

We Come from an Activist Background

An Interview with Htaike Htaike Aung, MIDO

Myanmar ICT for Development Organization, or MIDO, is a Myanmar based, non-governmental and non-profit organization. It collaborates globally and acts locally. MIDO is linked with both International as well as local organizations in order to help people deploy ICTs as a tool to meet core development goals. It is run by a board of directors, full-time staff, part-time staff and volunteers, all of whom are both committed and experienced. It also has an Advisory Board from various sectors that extend and guide to achieve the vision set by MIDO.

The following is the edited transcript of an interview with Htaike Htaike Aung, Programme Manager at MIDO, conducted by Sumandro Chattapadhyay in Yangon, Myanmar, on May 15, 2015.

Sumandro Chattapadhyay: Let us begin by asking you what you think of the term 'digital activism'?

Htaike Htaike Aung: Simply as using digital tools for activism. Digital tools may be online or offline.

SC: Do you use this term? Is it a term that is prominent in everyday usage?

HHA: Digital activism? Not really, they are words that are combined together... the word digital itself and activism itself are totally not new but then combining together is actually a new thing.

SC: Can you talk a little about the history of 'digital activism' in Myanmar?

HHA: In Myanmar we have always said that there are generations of activists. So the first activists (that we know of) are from way back, during 1964-1965, during the start of the military regime. The second generation, we call them the 88 generation. And then the third generation, we called them the 2007 Saffron Revolution generation. I myself am much more from the Saffron Revolution generation. So during the time [of the Saffron Revolution] the public already had some access to the Internet. At that time people were starting to use blogs because in the offline world there was a lot of scrutiny. People [could] actually write anything but on the other hand getting information from the outside was difficult, so people were very interested in blogging and the whole blogosphere. So I find that [that] was the first instance of using these digital tools for activism. I remember many bloggers in the country using these blogging tools to voice what was happening in the country. That was one [instance] that I remember and experienced as well.

SC: In 2007 during the Saffron Revolution, with various kinds of digital tools, especially the Internet being available, and as you were saying with blogs as an important medium of expression in general, did you also experience significant intervention by the government? A kind of counter attack by the government in the digital sphere?

HHA: Of course. During the Saffron Revolution, for our generation it is the first thing that we kind of witnessed in our lives… I mean it did happen in 88 too but people were too young to know what was happening… That one was the first [experiences of media censorship by government that] we witnessed. But what is different from the 88 generation is that we now have some noticeable tools and ICT tools that we can use to [send our] voice out. So many of the bloggers [were] actually going underground, working with the protestors, taking pictures and videos, and uploading them on their blogs. That is when the main big media for example like CNN and other main media take all that content and then publish it online. Just after a day or two the government shut down the full Internet so people weren't able to use it… That [happened] just like that.

SC: So the taste of the benefits of digital tools and the dangers [were experienced] simultaneously almost?

HHA: Yes, exactly so! After that many bloggers that we know of were under watch by the government. One of our colleagues Nay Phone Latt was dragged from his home and put behind bars.

SC: On that note, can you talk about the formation of MIDO, [in the context of the Saffron Revolution]?

HHA: We come from very [much an] activist background. Before MIDO, we self-organized as Myanmar Bloggers Society. It was a self-help group. We propagated blogging so that people can use these tools to know and share knowledge, or share what is happening, and so on. After Nay Phone Latt got detained, and when he got released, we [and] some of the blogger friends that we met [through] this Myanmar Blogger Society thought that we should do something: not only on blogging, or not only on freedom of expression on Internet, but on the whole ICT and Internet as a whole. So we formed MIDO together with some of our like-minded friends. We come from [these] activist roots. Not only development but also activism.

SC: This question of activism and activism that uses digital technology have thus been central to MIDO's work. Can you [speak briefly about the different] things MIDO does?

HHA: Mainly there are three things that we are doing. One is capacity building, another one is dissemination, and the third one is research. In capacity building we previously did a lot of digital literacy training and social media training because we think making people digitally literate can help them to maybe get information or disseminate information. In dissemination we did research and advocacy work as well. For example, we are highly involved in this campaign called the Panzagar campaign. It's all about using social media to combat hate speech. Also, we do research on hate speech, Internet and [work on] some of the ICT related things in the country.

SC: How do you understand digital literacy, because that is the key idea here, right?

HHA: There are many, not necessarily high-tech but also low-tech, digital tools that have been introduced to the world and to our country as well. The people who want to use it, or who *have* to use it, need to have the knowledge of not only digital literacy but also media literacy. These digital tools are like a knife: you can use it to kill people or use it to help people too. So not only digital literacy but we give media literacy training to them as well.

SC: What does this digital literacy training involve?

HHA: In digital literacy training, we teach very basic concepts of how to use the mobile phone, how to use the computer, what is the Internet, how to search for information on the Internet, how to find reliable information on the Internet. i.e. introducing them to reliable media and sources on the Internet. We also give training on social media, and a little bit of privacy, security and also media literacy.

[Image 1] Poster for the Panzagar campaign. Credit: Myanmar ICT for Development Organization.

SC: Often with new forms of social movements, mostly urban ones, which use digital media as a central tool for coordination ... and also to grab the media spotlight ... there is a [possibility] of being dependant on particular social media channels. And this is a difficult question because on one hand activism needs to happen where the people are, and the people are often in social media networks… [While,] social media is an important place for activists to be in, [it also] has its own logic and own constraints. For example, it may make people easier to spot for the government…

HHA: Yes, it is a concern. It depends on the kind of activism what we are doing. In some kinds of activism we just need to crowdsource and get more people to believe in the cause or to [contribute to] the cause. So for [those] cases… we definitely need the power of social media. But on the other hand some activism tools we might not [use], [especially] if [high media visibility makes us] vulnerable… It depends on the kind of activism actually. For example in Myanmar a year ago there was this blogger who was [writing about the functioning of the parliament]… [T]he parliament [started] trying to shut the [blogger] down by using various means, for example setting up a committee to search him,… [and] asking for help from Google, because the blogger was using a Blogspot platform… In this case if you are using a specific social media platform, which would not be safe for you, then you get captured very easily. It still depends on the type of activism.

SC: Earlier you mentioned that MIDO is interested in both online and offline digital activism. Can you please talk a bit about that?

HHA: Sure. In offline digital activism, we are a big supporter of using a low-tech approach. For example, using SMSs for campaigning, SMSs for advocacy too, shooting videos with your mobile phone, and then coming up with an advocacy video as well. So it does not necessarily need to be online. Also creating very [effective] messages and illustrations as print material. For online [activism, we] of course [talk about] using Internet, Facebook, and so on.

SC: Can you please talk about hate speech in Myanmar, and how MIDO [thinks of] addressing it?

HHA: In Myanmar we do have [a] history of religious groups having a [presence] in the country. After the Internet [becomes available] to the public, and everybody has a mobile in their hand, it is becoming much easier to spread hate speech. For example, Facebook is a hotbed of extremism here. You can see all types of hate speeches and extremist messages passing around. That is also because people are not digitally literate. When you buy a mobile phone, as a service the mobile shop installs Facebook for you and even creates an account and helps you to like some of the popular pages… This often includes many viral news pages, and many kinds of nationalist pages. Now people with the [new] mobile phone [already] have Facebook installed and, all these things that they did not voluntarily [subscribed for appearing] on the mobile.

They see these things, they share things, and it is much more easily spread. We were trying to find a way not to stop, because it is very difficult to stop, but to tone down these messages. So we came up with this campaign called the Panzagar movement, which starts online by [posting] a message that we will not be the one who incite hate... We started Panzagar with very nice illustrations, [messages, and stickers] and ... people who support Panzagar began to use our messages, began their campaigns, and also [distributed] the Panzagar messages and campaign materials offline as well. We can say that [the movement] creates a difficult situation for some pages, and high profile people on Facebook, who create hate speech. This is how Panzagar is trying to make the online space a bit safe from hate speech. ...

SC: On the one hand, you are saying there is fresh [public] memory ... [of people facing imprisonment] due to the lack of privacy on internet, in the sense that when you write something ... it is possible for the government to find out who you are. On the other hand, in the hate speech world you see that this [online] visibility does not necessarily prevent people from saying hateful things. Do you see a kind of paradox in how the government reacts to these two things: the criticisms of the government and the [online] hate speech?

HHA: The government takes very fast and firm action upon [anyone posting or sharing] criticism of itself. But on the other hand the government will not pay much attention to all these anonymous accounts on Facebook that are spreading hate speech. That is why the grassroots and civil society organisations are trying to take up actions against it. For example, in Panzagar we have this online campaign, and some groups are trying to set up small monitoring efforts on what the people who are living in their region are saying [on Facebook], what are the rumours being spread, and how to limit, verify or take action against them.

SC: Do you see a difference in doing activism in Myanmar today from say 2007?

HHA: Definitely the space has opened up a little bit, but it does not mean that it is open to what you want... We are becoming much more visible as you can see lots of campaigns going on. For example, around Sule [Pagoda] you can see the people whose lands have been grabbed, and they have spent almost a year [protesting against] this and occupying the street there. But nothing has been done. Previously you could not [even] do that: if you just go on the streets and shout, then you could get behind bars. But now you [are not immediately imprisoned] but still you are not getting the things you ask for.

SC: With the government [developing] significant interest in digital [infrastructure and] tools for [purposes of governance]..., how do you see MIDO's role in this [situation] where digital activism is not only about using digital tools to [express yourselves], but also doing activism about how the government is planning to use digital tools?

HHA: Exactly. There are many steps that the government is going to take [towards using digital tools in governance], they are talking much about e-government, e-participation, e-citizenship, and e-everything. [However,] they are not building the capacity of the citizens [simultaneously]. So we find that one [side] is very powerful and has all those resources, but the other [side] does not... [Also, to realise] e-participation, there [is] still a lot of things involved. It is not only the e-participation part, but also that the digital rights and fundamental human rights that apply to the Internet, or to ICT... [W]e need to get laws and policies that address this issue.

SC: What is MIDO's experience in working with other activist organisations, whose work does not necessarily focus on digital activism but who may benefit from learning about it or knowing about it?

HHA: There are a lot of civil society organisations coming up online but they are really not using it to the fullest. They may have pages online or may organise their discussions online, but there are still many other things that they can do. So when we conduct training or when they ask for help, we always offer them the idea of 'online marketing' to apply to their campaigning: having a kind of social media activities calendar for their campaigns, and so on. We find that these civil society organisations are interested in learning but then they are actually doing their work [at the same time] and do not have the time or the capacity to do [social media communications]. Sometimes that is true for us as well!

SC: My last question: what do you think of 'ICT for development'?

HHA: ICT for development... That is also something that we are trying to understand and study. You know, when people talk about development from the government sector, they often talk about basic economic development, socio-economic development. But in our understanding of development, we also have in mind the development of rights. We think development is not only for the economy, or for the social, but also for the rights, and for the citizens' ability to engage [with the government].

Interviewer's Note: *Throughout the transcription, '...' is used to mark pauses in the conversation and deleted unfinished sentences (which usually have been restated by the interviewee afterwards), and '[ ]' is used when either the actual word used by the interviewee has been replaced by a word that may convey the meaning more effectively given the context of the conversation, or to insert additional words so as to convey the meaning of the sentence more clearly. The text above also includes simple grammatical and language changes (for example, from 'are having' to 'organising') that are unmarked.*

References and Further Readings

2014. "Blogging in Burma." Wikipedia. February 20. Accessed June 10, 2015. https://en.wikipedia.org/wiki/Blogging_in_Burma.

2014. "Myanmar." Freedom House. https://freedomhouse.org/report/freedom-net/2014/myanmar.

Aung, San Yamin. 2014. "'Hate Speech Pours Poison into the Heart.'" The Irrawaddy. April 9. Accessed June 10, 2015. http://www.irrawaddy.org/interview/hate-speech-pours-poison-heart.html.

Calderaro, Andrea. 2014. "Connecting Myanmar: Telecom Reform and Political Transition." OpenDemocracy. February 06. Accessed June 10, 2015. https://www.opendemocracy.net/andrea-calderaro/connecting-myanmar-telecom-reform-and-political-transition.

Human Rights Watch. 2013. *Reforming Telecommunications in Burma. Human Rights and Responsible Investment in Mobile and the Internet.* Accessed June 10, 2015. http://www.hrw.org/reports/2013/05/19/reforming-telecommunications-burma

Myanmar ICT for Development Organisation. Accessed June 10, 2015. http://myanmarido.org/.

Myanmar ICT for Development Organisation. 2014. *Myanmar Internet Freedom Forum Report.* Accessed June 10, 2015. http://myanmar-startups.com/wp-content/uploads/2014/03/MIFF-report.pdf

Oye, Mari Michener. 2014. "Using 'Flower Speech' and New Facebook Tools, Myanmar Fights Online Hate Speech." Rohingya Blogger. December 26. Accessed June 10, 2015. http://www.rohingyablogger.com/2014/12/using-flower-speech-and-new-facebook.html.

Snaing, Yen. 2013. "In Burma, Facebook is Increasingly Used for Social Activism." The Irrawaddy. December 28. Accessed June 10, 2015. http://www.irrawaddy.org/burma/burma-facebook-increasingly-used-social-activism.html.

York, Jillian C. 2014. "Internet Freedom in Myanmar: A Curse or an Opportunity?" Al Jazeera. April 11. Accessed June 10, 2015. http://www.aljazeera.com/indepth/opinion/2014/04/internet-freedom-myanmar-curse--201441095932371441.html

Digital Natives and the Return of the Local Cause

Anat Ben-David

Prologue

In December 2010 I attended a conference titled Digital Natives with a Cause? Thinkathon. It was organised by Hivos and the Centre for Internet and Society (CIS) in The Hague.[1] During the event there was much debate amongst the participants around the current definition of a digital native. This got me thinking. Is a definition necessary? If yes, does it encompass the current phenomenon of young people who are engaged with digital technologies for promoting social change? Do all digital natives care about social change? Does it exclude other types of actors who share similar practices but are not considered digital natives? Does the definition entail that there are practices unique to digital natives, which justify this distinct ontological and epistemological group ? When the Thinkathon concluded, some of these questions remained unsolved, and I was still puzzled by them. A few weeks later, an idea of a possible answer came from an unexpected quarter.

I was walking in our neighbourhood in Tel-Aviv with my four-year-old daughter, when she suddenly asked me why there was so much graffiti on the streets. "Graffiti?" I asked, puzzled, since I had not noticed any graffiti in our neighbourhood before. She had noticed the graffiti as the small fences were just her height. From a taller point of view of an adult, I had only noticed the blooming hibiscus bushes that grew above them. Then she asked, "Don't you think graffiti makes our streets very ugly and dirty?" "Yes, it's very ugly," I replied, amused by her environmental concerns. Then she asked me to post a message on the internet on her behalf, calling for people to demonstrate against graffiti. At first I laughed, but she was very serious about it. Amused by her request, I took her picture standing next to the graffiti and posted her cute request on Facebook, which received 'Likes' and comments from the usual suspects in my immediate social network .

But she was more serious than that. When we arrived home, she started preparing signs for demonstration, asking if people were already coming and if the roads will be blocked with traffic. At that point it was clear that it would be difficult for me to realise her fantasy for social change. I explained that in order to organise a mass demonstration we have to ask for a permit from the police. "Ok," she said, and together we wrote a letter to the police (which I never sent, of course). Days passed and nothing happened, but she kept on asking whether they had replied and when the demonstration was going to take place. She is still waiting for it to happen.

To me, this story serves as a frame of reference for understanding digital native practices. As uncomfortable as I may feel about the current definition of digital natives and the connotations attached to it, I follow Nishant Shah's position that it might be better to accept the "found name", rather than to replace it, while at the same time attempt to unpack the baggage of presumptions attached to the current definition and reload it with new meanings (Shah, 2010, pp. 18-25). If we must accept the term as such and the demographic dichotomies it alludes to (i.e., natives as opposed to non-natives, digital as opposed to analogue, young versus older users of digital technologies), then the story about my daughter is a story about an "everyday Digital native", who is, as Shah described, "not perhaps just a user of digital technologies, but a person who has realised the possibilities and potentials of digital technologies in his/her environments" (emphasis mine) (Shah, 2010, p. 19). The emphasis on the immediate environment , or the situated location— the granular cause, as seen through digital native eyes—is perhaps one of the lacunae often ignored in the current discourse about digital natives. Accordingly, this chapter conceptualises the term 'digital natives' in a way that attempts to reload it with new meanings about digital native practices as such that have a commitment to grounded places and situated knowledges. By tracking the parallel developments both in digital technologies as well as digital activism in relation to place, this chapter wishes to reintroduce the meaning of 'the native place' into the discourse on digital natives.

Introduction

The term 'digital natives' consists of an adjective and a noun, whose connotations, taken both separately or together, periodise the point in time in which the term emerged. It was coined by Marc Prensky in 2001 to refer to a young generation of students who "are 'native speakers' of the digital language of computers, video games and the internet (Prensky, 2001, p. 1).[2]

In its original context, thus, both 'digital' and 'native' refer to language – the language of these technologies is digital, and those native to it speak it fluently. However, the choice of words has broader implications. The 'digital' in digital natives also refers to the current evolutionary phase of Information and Communication Technologies (ICTs). Had Prensky coined the term ten years earlier, digital native would have probably been called 'Cyber Natives', 'Virtual Natives', much alike other prevalent terms of that time, such as 'Cyber Activists' or 'Virtual Communities'.[3] Similarly, the 'native' in digital natives connotes things other than fluency in a native language and the natural process of acquiring it. The literal definition of the noun, rather, refers to being born in a specific place.[4]

The purpose of this chapter is to conceptually unfold the broader meaning of the term 'digital natives' both by a historical contextualisation of the 'digital', as well as by a discussion of the geopolitics of the 'native'. The terminological analysis, grounded by a historical contextualisation of digital activism and the history of digital technologies in the past decade, serves to argue that in its current form, the term 'digital natives' may represent a renewed dedication to the native place in a point in time when previous distinctions between 'physical' and 'digital' places no longer hold (Rogers, 2008). As claimed by Palfrey and Gasser (2008), digital natives no longer distinguish between the online and the offline and relate to both as a hybrid space. This definition relates to older debates about the introduction of ICTs that questioned the differences between the 'virtual' and the 'real', the 'online' and the 'offline' (Rogers, 2009). The claim made by Palfrey and Gasser is ontological and epistemological; since digital natives do not differentiate between online and offline realities, the definition implies a new spatial epistemology. If this is the case, how does a digital native – spatial epistemology manifest itself in various forms of digital native activism?

Before attempting to answer this question in the following part of the chapter, I return to the terminological analysis of the existing definitions of digital natives. If the 'nativeness' of digital natives relates to their fluency in 'digital language' and their 'being at home' in digital spaces, how are their predecessors defined? Prensky, for example, contrasts digital natives with a previous generation of 'digital immigrants' – "those of us who were not born into the digital world but have, at some later point in our lives, become fascinated by and adopted many or most aspects of the new technology" (Prensky, 2001, pp. 1–2). Palfrey and Gasser add a third category to describe the predecessors of digital natives – 'digital settlers', those who grew up in an analog world but have helped shaping the contours of the digital realm, but unlike digital natives, they "continue to rely heavily on traditional, analog forms of interaction" (Palfrey & Gasser, 2008, p. 4).

The distinction between 'native', 'settler' and 'immigrant' does not only separate chronological generations; it also re-awakens the debate between the offline and online realities that preceded the emergence of the term. From a spatial point of view, it also distinguishes between the places of birth of different generations. As inferred from Palfrey and Gasser's definition, digital natives are presumed to be born into a hybrid space comprised of enmeshed digital and physical components, while digital settlers and digital immigrants are perceived as having travelled to those spaces from the offline world. The terminological premise is that natives are better acquainted with their place of birth than immigrants, or settlers, and refers to the extent to which they are "at home" with digital technologies. However, it would not be far-fetched to assume that the imagery of the native, the immigrant and the settler also borrows from colonial history, or any other history of territorial disputes for that matter. The chronology of such demographic developments entails that a space is first inhabited by natives, the 'indigenous inhabitants', who are later joined by settlers (often times not without struggle), and much later eventually joined by immigrants. In the digital context, however, the chronological order is reversed. For digital natives were not born into a digital 'terra nullius'; digital spaces were conceived, shaped and already inhabited by those referred to as 'settlers' and 'immigrants'. Ironically, it is the settlers who set the grounds for natives, and whose practices precede those of the natives.

This chronological paradox of being native to a place already created and inhabited by others may explain the tension between other connotations of 'digital natives' that arose as the term evolved. As Shah claimed (Shah, 2010, p. 15), the naming of a group as "natives" entails an act of "othering" and in the case of digital natives, the "othering" was loaded with expectations to have unique, "indigenous" characteristics that would ontologically justify their classification, while at the same time adopt and continue the practices of their predecessors, the "settlers".

As a consequence, the mystification or laments about the new generation of digital activists were performed vis-à-vis what was already performed digitally, which explains terms such as "slacktivists" (Shah, 2010, p. 17), or Bennet's explanation of digital natives' politics as "self-actualizing citizens" versus "old century dutiful citizens" (Bennett, 2008). As proclaimed by Shah, to better understand digital natives, a fresh look at what digital natives do may be more useful than the constant (and often failed) attempt to define who digital natives are (Shah, 2010, p. 20).

Perhaps one way of doing so is by shifting the weights in the definition of digital natives from "being digital" to "being native", focusing on the geographies and places digital natives are native to – not as being surrounded by a media-rich environment, but as operating in a hybrid geography of physical and online spaces. In the following, I argue that digital natives have a granular dedication to their local places and local causes, a dedication that can be seen as a form of counter-practice to previous forms of cyber-activism, shaped by transnational activist networks using ICTs for promoting global causes. To make the case for digital native practices as a renewed dedication to the local, I now turn to a historical account of previous practices of digital activism for social change led by Civil Society Organisations (CSOs).[5]

By comparing two key-events of social protests and large-scale mobilisation of activists using ICTs, one marking early forms of digital activism in the late 1990s, the other marking one of the most recent forms of digital activism to date, it shows that both digital technologies and agents of social change have structurally changed from the transnational to the local, and from the institutional to the individual. I then claim that the current discourse about digital natives can be better understood by placing it in a specific point in time, and a specific place in the constantly-changing digital space.

From Seattle to Tahrir Square

The anti-globalisation protests against the WTO summit in Seattle in 1999 marked the beginning of an era of what was then termed 'cyber-activism' led by CSOs.[6] During the protests, a diverse range of activists, groups, organisations and social movements coordinated actions against the WTO summit using laptops and mobile phones. Some of the actions were directed at coordinating protests on the streets; others were directed at disseminating information about the demonstrations and the anti-globalisation movement on the Web. The media took up the stories put together by the various organisations, which eventually led to the establishment of www.indymedia.org, the alternative media outlet for social activists (van Laer & van Aelst, 2009).

Twelve years (and many other digital campaigns and protests) later, the masses took on the streets of Cairo to protest against President Mubarak's regime. They too used the internet and mobile phone technologies to coordinate the protests. People from all over the world watched the events through Al Jazeera's satellite TV channel as the Egyptian authorities first switched off the internet in Egypt to prevent the protests, then saw Mubarak step down.[7]

Are these events comparable? Do they represent a 'generational gap' between public protests facilitated by ICTs in the 'digital settlers' era, and their current manifestation in a digital age inhabited by 'digital natives'? If we accept for a moment the dichotomous demographic definitions of older versus younger inhabitants of the digital space, then an analytical comparison of the events may highlight the differences between older and younger generations of digital activists, to better understand what is unique to digital native activism that was not already performed before.

At first sight, however, the differences between Seattle and Cairo do not seem significant: both are events of public protest facilitated by ICTs, both were propelled by a loose network of activists working on a joint cause , both are examples of civic initiatives that proved effective and powerful in promoting a cause against well-established institutions such as governments, inter-governmental organisations, or the mainstream media. Such similarities question the extent to which current forms of digital activism are unique practices that justify the dichotomous definitions of older versus younger users of digital technologies. Yet an examination of the differences between the events reveal that in a decade's time, technological and social factors are responsible for a gradual shift in the types of actors, the types of causes involved in the process, and the digital spaces in which they operate.

Although the internet and mobile phones played a role in both the cases, what was called 'The Internet' in 1999 was slightly different from its current form . Within a decade, digital technologies have transformed from a decentralised network of computers connected to the internet and a parallel-but-separate network of cellular communication devices, to enmeshed networks that combine both. Taking into account that in 1999 there were few, if none, wifi hotspots, the activists in Seattle had to use laptops with a LAN or modem connection to the internet to coordinate their actions (mobile phones were only used for voice communication, not for uploading data or seeking information). The Web was less social, too. While current protests in the Middle East and North Africa were mostly coordinated through social media platforms, Twitter and Facebook especially, in 1999 most of the coordination of actions was performed using email distribution lists, e-bulletin boards and NGO's websites. The actors were different, too, since the main level of coordination of actions in Seattle was performed by a core network of CSOs, with a loose network of other CSOs and individuals attached to them (Clark & Themudo, 2003, p. 116). The activists in Egypt, on the other hand, were not necessarily mobilised by civil society organisations, but by a critical mass of citizens, individuals, who communicated with their immediate social networks to mobilise and coordinate the demonstrations.

One other difference relevant to the case I wish to make for digital natives is that both the actors as well as the causes in the two instances represent a shift from the transnational to the local. While Tahrir square has become both the physical site and symbolic location of the Egyptians' liberation from their local regime, Seattle had transformed into a battle site only because it hosted the WTO summit and attracted a network of transnational activists to protest against it. Put differently, while the protests in Cairo were about

Egypt, the protests in Seattle were not about Washington; they were about anti-globalisation.

The scholarly literature on social transformation facilitated by ICTs that spurred in the aftermath of the 'Battle of Seattle' highlighted the importance of the structural fit between ICTs and social movements. This 'perfect match' has been given many names, one of them was "the dot cause", coined by Clark and Tehmudo (2003: 110):

> The term 'dot cause' can apply to any citizen group who promotes social causes and chiefly mobilises support through its website. Such group fit Keck and Sikkink's (1998:2) definition of 'transnational advocacy networks' as including 'those relevant actors working internationally on an issue, who are bound together by shared values, a common discourse, and dense exchanges of information and services'. In social movements, dot causes can be important mobilising structures, attracting new support, coordinating collective action and producing and disseminating new framings.

In many ways, the new technology, perceived as decentralised, global, and flattening time and space, only facilitated the already-existing structures of transnational networks of civil society organisations. Thus, the "settlement" of civil society organisations in cyberspace and their transnational networking on the Web was perceived as a 'natural move'. However, digital technologies did not transform civil society organisations' modus operando: their networked structure has remained the same (albeit greatly facilitated by the new technologies), their causes have not changed, and their actions are still directed at the same institutions (government, inter-governmental institutions, and the mass media) (Garrett, 2006).

To contextualise the current discourse on digital natives, I suggest a rhetorical 'thought experiment', by applying the terminology used today to refer to Digital Natives versus Immigrants or Settlers on the various stakeholders that used ICTs for social change in the late 1990s. In such a case, transnational networks of CSOs were the 'natives' since their networked, transnational structure was not alien to the transnational and networked structure of the new technologies. Other institutional stakeholders, such as governments, inter-governmental organisations, or mass media corporations, had difficulties adjusting their fixed structures and business models to emerging ICTs in the same way the current discourse about 'digital natives' refers to the generation of 'digital immigrants' or 'digital settlers'.

Over time, however, the paradigms hailed for the structural fit between CSOs, transnational advocacy and ICTs have started to collapse. Transnational collaboration was effective, but in certain cases it hit a wall, especially when local issues and causes were addressed by the international community. As Garrett points out: "Protests occur regularly around the world, but activity generally doesn't continue at a single location for extended periods, and a particular location is unlikely to see more than a few protests a year" (2006:210). Rogers and Marres (2008), for example, report how NGO-Web involvement in the controversy around the Narmada Dam in Gujarat, India resulted in the abstraction and generalisation of the issue to the extent that it no longer addressed the situated problem. In a different study on the involvement of transnational network advocacy in the Palestinian–Israeli conflict, we found that local Israeli NGOs involved in objecting Israel's construction of the structure between Israel and the Palestinian territories were left out of the debate (Rogers & Ben-David, 2008). Local issues, then, remained less well-treated by the transnational community, using the global structure of ICTs.

At the same time, the World Wide Web has become less and less wide. Very much following the logic of "daily me" Web cultures described by Cass Sunstein in Republic.com 2.0 (Sunstein, 2007), Ethan Zuckerman speaks of an "imagined cosmopolitanism" effect of digital technologies, reflecting on the need to tune into local reports from all over the world in order to widen the potential of the Web as a global technology (Zuckerman, 2010). Zuckerman is especially referring to Global Voices Online[8], the blogging platform he co-founded in 2004, hosted at the Berkman Center for Internet and Society at Harvard Law School. Global Voices Online shares and translates local citizen media and blog posts from areas in the world which usually do not make it to the global news.[9] Yet, a study of Global Voices Online, performed in 2006 by the Govcom.org Foundation, which examined the extent to which the local reports are discussed in other places, showed that the conversations did not travel far—they were rather clustered regionally (Rogers & Govcom.org Foundation, 2006).

From a technological point of view, the effect of the narrowing Web described by Zukerman is explained by a gradual process of localisation of Web-based and mobile communications technologies. Richard Rogers (2008) describes the evolution of the politics of Web-space by dividing it into four periods, starting from the perception of the Web as a global, hyperlinked space, followed by a period in which the Web was perceived as a public sphere, then transformed into isolated islands of content that marked the "Web as social networks" period, followed by its current politics of localisation, what he also terms "the revenge of geography", where the Web's organising mechanisms, such as search engine algorithms and IP-based Web-services no longer distinguish between Web-spaces and geographical spaces. From a Web-space perceptive, then, the 'Battle of Seattle' is placed in the "Web as public sphere" period, whereas current events in Egypt, Tunisia, and other countries in the Middle East and North Africa represent the "revenge of geography" period. The rapidly localising digital technologies, characteristic of the period in which the discourse about digital natives emerged, is also characterised by increasing control of nation-states on digital technologies (as evident in Egypt's Internet shut-down, to name one example), as well as by the increase in access to the Internet through mobile phones which in many developing countries is now more prevalent than access from PCs (International Telecommunications Unit, 2010).

Arguably, the growing localisation of ICTs has transformed the structural fit between transnational advocacy networks and ICTs. Until recently, civil society organisations have been the hegemonic agents for social change using ICTs. They were quicker than governments and other institutions in adopting digital technologies, and thus changed power relations between them. Alternative media outlets such as the Independent Media Center (Indymedia)[10] which was established in the aftermath of the 'Battle of Seattle' successfully competed with the traditional hegemony of mass media outlets such as newspapers and broadcast electronic media, and were effective in mobilising and informing sympathisers of various causes from around the world. However, as ICTs became more local, the hegemony of transnational networks and organisations withered, and the agency of change shifted from the organisational level, to the individual (Angelina, 2010). In the same way that institutions such as governments and mass media corporations have had to adjust to the new digital spaces a decade ago, civil society organisations now need to rethink their paradigms to adapt to the current developments in digital technologies. Last decade's natives, then, become 'settlers', or 'immigrants', in contemporary digital space, while at the same time new actors need less adaptation in using the new technologies for social change. In the short history of the Web and of digital spaces, then, this is perhaps the moment in time when the discourse about digital natives comes into the picture.

New forms of digital activism are less reliant on existing structures of organisation, fund-raising, and framing of campaigns. Instead, activism for social change by actors termed as 'digital natives' is characterised by individuals and groups promoting immediate, local causes, relaying information and mobilising for action through their immediate social networks.

Such activities changed the ways 'campaigns' were thought of so far. Current debates on whether launching a Facebook group may or may not attract a critical mass of members that will eventually lead to social revolutions have not yet been resolved, but the spontaneity of action, the granular level of the causes, as well as the lowered threshold of the agents and initiators, are typical of the current trends in digital activism that are different from previous practices from a decade ago.

Examples from all over the world abound. Among the less-celebrated of the countless examples is a digital initiative called Gaza Youth Breaks Out (GYBO).[11] What started as a provocative manifesto posted on Facebook by individuals who knew they should remain anonymous for the durability of their cause,[12] became a youth-movement of young Palestinians who wished to break out the current situation in Gaza, being critical not only of Israel's closure policy, but also of the fracture between Hamas and Fatah. Their concern was to make a specific place – Gaza – a better place to live in. The manifesto was circulated outside Facebook and has reached audiences from all over the world ; it both enabled the local mobilisation of youth in Gaza as well as raised support for the humanitarian situation in Gaza in ways that reached beyond the well-worn political debate about Gaza. When Facebook eventually froze their account, GYBO moved to Twitter, Youtube and other digital spaces, but their geographical cause has remained the same.

In less than six months, GYBO transformed from a digital initiative to a social movement, without adapting the structure of a civil society organization. It did not have a media strategy, did not have accountability commitments to funders, it did not launch a planned campaign.

Rather, they made use of their situated knowledge—both of their life in Gaza, and of the digital tools they have at hand, to promote social change in their local place.

The historical contextualisation of digital activism does not serve to claim that current practices replace previous ones. Digital natives do not replace previous actors for social change such as CSOs and transnational advocacy networks. Rather, it sketches the spaces in which digital natives operate, one that is both digital and geographical and that is populated not only by natives, but by other types of actors and stakeholders characterized by their respective practices. With these renewed meanings loaded into the concept of digital natives, the following part concludes this chapter by returning to the conceptual discussion of digital natives and their digital places of birth.

Conclusions: Hybrid Spaces, Situated Knowledges

This chapter attempted to reintroduce a spatial context to the term 'Digital natives'. The shift from focusing on 'native actors' to 'native places' enables bypassing some of the problems and ambiguities attached to the term. Instead of struggling with the problems of ontological dichotomies and exclusions that come with the characterisation of a group of actors and users, it treats the 'digital native space' as a continuous space that is constantly evolving and that simultaneously hosts a complex network of actors and practices, digital natives among them. As Palfrey and Gasser claimed, and as described by Rogers from a Web space point-of-view, this space is characterised by hybridity, both of digital and geographical spaces, of various digital mechanisms and technologies and of a heterogeneous set of actors.

This is very much in line with Shah's conceptualisation of a digital native space as a flatland, a "free floating space, which is at once improbable and real, and where the elements that constitute older forms of change processes, are present but in a fluid, moving way, where they can reconnect, recalibrate and relate to each other in new and unprecedented forms" (Shah, 2010, p. 30). As demonstrated in the previous part of this chapter, forms of public protests facilitated by digital technologies may not be completely new, but they introduced an unprecedented dedication to the local place. This dedication, however, does not entail that the knowledge produced by local forms of actions are confined to local spaces. The protests in Egypt were inspired and influenced by the events which took place in Tunisia a month earlier, where digital technologies also played a significant role in disseminating information and mobilising action. The GYBO initiative in Gaza started more or less at the same time and had similar characteristics, but the type of action and knowledge about the local issues was adjusted to the situated place. In that sense, knowledge produced by current forms of digital activism travels from one place to another, but is constantly localised and transformed to fit the local actors and their causes.

This type of knowledge is very different from the previous dominant use of digital technologies by transnational networks. As described above, transnational networks of activists often times failed to effectively address, or even see, the situated causes and issues of local places. The current dedication to the local place can be thus interpreted in terms of a counter practice, one that alludes to Donna Haraway's concept of situated and subjugated knowledges (Haraway, 1991). Transnational advocacy networks on the Web may be described as adopting "the view from above, from nowhere, from simplicity" (Haraway, 1991, p. 195), while granular activism dedicated to local places may be described in terms of the grounded knowledge, that albeit its partiality, encompasses greater complexity.

This brings me back to the anecdote about the hibiscus flowers and the graffiti which I described in the prologue to this chapter. Despite my commitment to environmental issues which I try to pass on to my daughter, my taller gaze was a 'gaze from nowhere' and failed to notice the graffiti that she found so disturbing and demanded an immediate action for change. Admittedly, my response to her dedication entailed an act of 'othering', of treating her devotion to remove the graffiti from the streets as something that is by all means very cute, but incapable of understanding the complexities involved in the real politics of change. The conceptualisation of digital natives as a young generation of users may entail a similar act of 'othering' that views their politics of change as different, while at the same time failing to notice that despite their difference, they are very real. I suggest that by shifting our 'othering' gaze from the indigenous actors called digital natives, to the indigenous landscapes in which various types of actors operate, we can benefit from learning about the complexity, heterogeneity and multiplicity of situated knowledges and practices that take place in hybrid geographical and digital spaces.

I conclude by returning to the terminological problem of digital natives. Consider, for example, how the current generation of digital natives would behave ten or twenty years from now, when they are no longer 'young' and when digital technologies and spaces would probably be very different from the way we know them today . Would they still be considered 'natives' in these future spaces? Would they rather become 'immigrants' or 'settlers' in the spaces considered their place of birth, as is the case now with CSOs having to adapt their campaigns and strategies to social media platforms? It may very well be so that the paradigm of the 'native', with its connotations of subjugation of power and chronological orders attached to it, will be abandoned in the future. For now, the term is here to stay. As Shah claimed, we would rather treat the concept of digital natives as an umbrella term, or a "placeholder" (Shah, 2010, p. 13). Following Shah, and by focusing on the return to the local cause, this chapter treated the concept of digital natives as "a holder of place".

Acknowledgements: I express my gratitude to Nishant Shah, Fieke Jansen, and the staff at Hivos and CIS for hosting the *Digital Natives with a Cause? Thinkathon* conference in The Hague in December 2010. I also thank Noah Efron, Anat Leibler, and the book's editors for providing valuable comments on a previous version of this text.

Endnotes

1. Jansen, Fieke. 2010. "Digital Natives with a Cause? Thinkathon. Organized by Hivos and the Centre for Internet and Society on the 6-8 December 2010." Hivos. http://www.hivos.net/Hivos-Knowledge-Programme/Themes/Digital-Natives-with-a-Cause/News/Digital-Natives-with-a-Cause-Thinkathon.
2. Note that the 'nativity' referred to originally is that of a language, rather than a place of birth, a point to which I return.
3. The turn from the 'cyber' and 'virtual' to the 'digital' is based on Rogers (2009). For an overview of the umbrella of terms related to 'digital natives' see Shah, 2010.
4. See, for example, the Merriam Webster Dictionary definition for 'Native'. http://www.merriam-webster.com/dictionary/native .
5. This chapter does not map all forms of Digital Native activism, but focuses mostly on forms of public protests facilitated by digital technologies.
6. This is not to claim that cyberactivism was 'born' in Seattle. Older practices of cyberactivism date back to the 1980s. See, for example, Rheingold 1993.
7. See, for example, ("Can Egypt's Internet Movement Be Exported?" 2011) and ("Social Media, Cellphone Video Fuel Arab Protests," 2011).
8. Global Voices Online. http://globalvoicesonline.org/. Accessed May 2, 2011.
9. In March 2011, for example, Global Voices Online reported that the Cameroonian government banned access to Twitter via SMS, an issue that did not travel outside Cameroon in the news space. See Global Voices Online. 2011. "Cameroon: Netizens React

to SMS-to-Tweet Ban". March 10. http://globalvoicesonline.org/2011/03/10/cameroon-netizens-react-to-sms-to-tweet-ban/. Accessed May 2, 2011.
10   Independent Media Center. http://www.indymedia.org/en/index.shtml. Accessed May 2 2011.
11   "Gaza Youth Breaks Out" (GYBO). Facebook. http://www.facebook.com/pages/Gaza-Youth-Breaks-Out-GYBO/118914244840679. Accessed May 2 2011.
12   The Manifesto was eventually removed from Facebook. But it is still blogged on the group's Wordpress platform. http://gazaybo.wordpress.com/about/. Accessed May 2, 2011.

Bibliography

2001. "Can Egypt's Internet Movement Be Exported?" *The Nation*. February 18.
2011. "Social Media, Cellphone Video Fuel Arab Protests." *The Independent*. February 27.
Angelina, M. 2010. "Towards a New Relationship of Exchange." *Digital Natives with a Cause(?)* Position Papers. The Hague, Museum of Communication, The Netherlands: Hivos and the CIS. Pp. 105-129.
Bennett, W. L. 2008. "Digital Natives as Self Actualizing Citizens." In A. H. Fine, M. L. Sifry, A. Rasiej, & J. Levy (Eds.) *Rebooting America: Ideas for Redesigning American Democracy for the Internet Age*. Personal Democracy Forum. Pp. 225-230)
Clark, J. D., & N. S. Themudo. 2003. "The Age of Protest: Internet-Based 'Dot Causes' and the 'Anti-Globalization Movement.'" In J. D. Clark (Ed.), *Globalizing Civic Engagement. Civil Society and Transnational Action*. London: Earthscan publications LTD. Pp. 109-126.
Garrett, R. K. 2006. "Protest in an Information Society: A Review of Literature on Social Movements and New ICTs." *Information, Communication & Society*. Volume 9, Number 2. Pp. 202-224.
Haraway, D. J. 1991. Simians, Cyborgs, and Women : the Reinvention of Nature. New York: Routledge.
International Telecommunications Unit. 2010. *The World in 2010. ICT Facts and Figures*. Accessed June 10, 2011. http://www.itu.int/ITU-D/ict/material/FactsFigures2010.pdf
Marres, N., & R. Rogers. 2008. "Subsuming the Ground: How Local Realities of the Fergana Valley, the Narmada Dams and the BTC Pipeline are Put to Use on the Web." *Economy and Society*. Volume 37, Number 2. Pp. 251-281.
Palfrey, J., & U. Gasser. 2008. *Born Digital: Understanding the First Generation of Digital Natives*. New York: Basic Books.
Prennky, M. 2001. Digital Natives, Digital Immigrants Part 1. *On the Horizon*. Volume 9, Number 5. Pp. 1-66.
Rheingold, H. 1993. *The Virtual Community* (28 ed.). Reading, MA: Addison Wesley.
Rogers, R. 2009. *The End of the Virtual: Digital Methods*. Amsterdam: Amsterdam University Press.
Rogers, R. 2008. *The Politics of Web-Space*. Unpublished MS.
Rogers, R., & A. Ben-David. 2008. "The Palestinian-Israeli Peace Process and Trans-National Issue Networks: The Complicated Place of the Israeli NGO." *New Media and Society*. Volume 10, Number 3. Pp. 497-528.
Rogers, R., & Govcom.org Foundation. 2006. *Public Media Projects and their Publics: Global Voices Online*. Center for Social Media, American University. Accessed May 2, 2011. http://www.centerforsocialmedia.org/sites/default/files/documents/pages/Global_voices_maps.pdf
Shah, N. 2010. "Knowing a Name: Methodologies and Challenges." *Digital Natives with a Cause (?) Position Papers*. The Hague, Museum of Communication, The Netherlands: Hivos and the CIS. Pp. 11-34.
Sunstein, C. R. 2007. *Republic.com 2.0*. Princeton and Oxford: Princeton University Press.

van Laer, J., & P. van Aelst. 2009. "Cyber-Protest and Civil Society: The Internet and Action Repertoires in Social Movements." In Y. Jewkes, & M. Yar (Eds.) *Handbook on Internet Crime*. Willan Publishing. Pp. 230-254.

Zuckerman, E. 2010. "A Wider Web, a Wider World." SIGUCCS '10. Proceedings of the 38th Annual Fall Conference on SIGUCCS. New York: ACM.

Annotation

Padmini Ray Murray

"The past is a foreign country; they do things differently there." The parameters of Anat's endeavor to define the digital 'native,' 'settler,' and 'immigrant' have incredibly, in merely four years, shifted radically, in a post-Snowden moment that has witnessed Facebook going public and debates over net neutrality, occasioned by the increasingly visible nexus between governments and technology corporations.

Prensky's (2001) seminal essay defines digital natives as young people who "have spent their entire lives surrounded by and using computers, videogames, digital music players, video cams, cell phones, and all the other toys and tools of the digital age." By this definition, it is undeniable that all the university students I have taught during my career, by virtue of economic privilege and access, belong to this category. However, these experiences have demonstrated to me that there is no magical osmosis of what it means to 'be' digital—in fact, the more native to the manner born these generations are, they are *less* likely to see the potential of technologies as activist tools, due to the proprietary holding pens created by technology corporations. The visible repercussion of neoliberal practices in the technological sector is an alienation of these digitally native generations from the means of production underpinning the tools they use, forcing their political engagement only at the level of interface. One of the most prominent examples of this would be the rise of the petition site, which has increased exponentially with the popularity of social networking and, I would argue, stages a further turn that has been precipitated by the shift from the transnational cause to the local that Anat discusses in her article.

These processes have now created a context that mobilises the labour of these users in the service of often hyperlocal causes that are made visible by the transnational nature of the Web, thus emptying out the category of activism, and problematizing the definition of both protest and demonstration. Is the act of digital participation still considered as an activist gesture? Or do these forms of digital participation foster a different mode of political subjecthood which can readily operate under certain conditions circumscribed by a World Wide Web that increasingly exists in corporate silos? Questions of access, education, literacy, as well as the linguistic fault lines that divide urban from rural in South Asia, somewhat undermine the efficacy of technology as a tool for protest, although the increasing penetration of feature phones and mobile networks might accelerate these processes. Given these uneven contours that shape 'the digital', maybe the condition of being a digital native is determined by making full use of the technologies that are available to one, and this in itself can be construed as Haraway's (1988) 'situated knowledge.'

Four of the founding questions at the heart of this reader are: 1) how do technologies change the way we protest, 2) how do we enact activism at the level of the digital, 3) how does the digital shape activism, and 4) how does activism shape the digital. Anat's article engages with all of these questions, and explores what it means when these questions are posed together in concert. The answers to these questions are not straight-forward.

References and Further Readings

Gunawardene, Nalaka. 2013. "Journey of a digital immigrant." *Himal Southasian*. Volume 26, Number 3. Pp. 63-78.

Haraway, Donna. 1988. "Situated Knowledges: The Science Question in Feminism and the Privilege of Partial Perspective." *Feminist Studies*. Volume 14, Number 3. Pp. 575-99.

Prensky, Marc. 2001. "Digital Natives, Digital Immigrants." *On the Horizon*. Volume 9, Number 5. Pp. 1-6.

Greatfire.org

Sumandro Chattapadhyay[1]

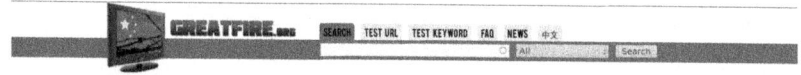

[Image 1] https://en.greatfire.org/blog/2015/mar/we-are-under-attack

Greatfire was 'under attack' in March 2015. Now how do you attack a website? As they explain above, you attack it by sending a large number of visitors to the website. It is like occupying a park or a building. With that many users visiting the website, it stops working. Of course, these visitors are non-human visitors: they are automated scripts/bots asking the website for information.

---

1   Text written and screenshots from Greatfire.org compiled by Sumandro Chattapadhyay.

But what information does the Greatfire website possess for which it got attacked?

WHAT IS GREATFIRE.ORG?

We collect data about the Great Firewall of China and share real-time and historical information about blocked web sites and searches, with a particular focus on Google and Baidu.

[Image 2] https://en.greatfire.org/faq/what-greatfireorg

WHO ARE YOU?

Due to the sensitive nature of the content on our web sites we prefer to remain anonymous at this point. You can, however, contact us on info at greatfire dot org or via @GreatFireChina on Twitter.

[Image 3] https://en.greatfire.org/faq/where-does-our-data-come

WHAT ARE YOU TRYING TO ACCOMPLISH?

There is no other real-time, up-to-date resource on what sites and searches are blocked in China. Our aim is to be the leading destination for information of this kind and our goal is to bring transparency to online censorship in China.

[Image 4] https://en.greatfire.org/faq/what-are-you-trying-accomplish

WHERE DOES OUR DATA COME FROM?

Our data comes from the following sources:

1. User additions. Anyone can add a new URL for testing and it will be continuously tested by our system.

2. Collaboration with other projects. Any URL that's marked as blocked in China by these sources is automatically imported into our system: Autoproxy, China Digital Times and Herdict. Each keyword in our system - be it on on Baidu, Google, Weibo or Wikipedia - corresponds to a URL on that website which is tested for censorship similarly to how any other URL is tested. These keywords are mainly added by users. China Digital Times have an extensive list of blocked or sensitive keywords and all of them have been integrated into our system.

You can read more about the mentioned organizations at https://en.greatfire.org/friends.

[Image 5] https://en.greatfire.org/faq/where-does-our-data-come

So how can the blocked sites and webpages in China be explored through Greatfire?

Go to the homepage first.

The Latest Stats section shows the various counts of online censorship in China maintained by the website. It monitors the global top 1000 most-visited domains according to Alexa to check if those are blocked in China or not. Similarly it monitors specific domains, sites and search result pages within Google domains, HTTPS addresses (as separate from HTTP addresses), direct IP addresses of webpages, URLs of webpages (even if the domain itself is not blocked, specific pages within it might be), search result pages on Weibo (the major Chinese social microblogging platform), and pages across Wikipedia domains.

[Image 6] https://en.greatfire.org/

Greatfire maintains a list of all these domains, webpages, IPs, search result pages, etc. that it tests periodically to see if they are blocked within China or not. You can go to the Recently Added section to check what all domains and pages and IPs have they started to monitor in recent times: https://en.greatfire.org/recently-added.

The Search bar on top also allows you to directly search for specific keywords and URLs and check if they are blocked or not.

For example, we can search for 'Tibbet' in the search bar on the top, and Greatfire will show us a result page like the following one:

[Image 7] https://en.greatfire.org/keyword/tibbet

Now how should we interpret this censorship score? The 33% value indicates that out of the three search engines that Greatfire tracks—Baidu, Google, and Sina Weibo—the search results for the term 'Tibbet' is only blocked for one search engine, that is Google.

The thing to remember here is that Baidu and Sina Weibo being Chinese companies, content that is available via them might be already subject to other forms of censorship. The critical value of this 33% score hence is in demonstrating how Chinese censorship targets digital content being produced elsewhere in the world and prevents it from being accessible to Chinese users of the Internet.

A look at the list of ' Censorship of Alexa Top 1000 Domains in China' reveals how global digital content is comprehensively stopped from being accessed by Chinese Internet users.

CENSORSHIP OF ALEXA TOP 1000 DOMAINS IN CHINA

This page lists the top 1000 sites on the web according to Alexa, and our latest data on whether they are blocked or otherwise censored in China. Domains marked as red are fully blocked and those marked as yellow are throttled, ie not blocked but very slow. This list does not include subdomains. For example, http://google.com is not blocked, but http://sites.google.com is. If you want to view all blocked websites including subdomains, check out the Blocked section.

Title	Tested Since	Censored*	Tags
facebook.com	Feb 2011	100%	Blocked, Domains, Alexa Top 1000 Domains, URLs
youtube.com	Feb 2011	100%	Blocked, Domains, Alexa Top 1000 Domains, URLs
twitter.com	Feb 2011	100%	Blocked, Domains, Alexa Top 1000 Domains, URLs
google.com	Mar 2011	99%	Blocked, Domains, Alexa Top 1000 Domains, Google Sites, URLs
google.co.in	Feb 2011	100%	Blocked, Domains, Alexa Top 1000 Domains, Google Sites, URLs
blogspot.com	Feb 2011	100%	Blocked, Domains, Alexa Top 1000 Domains, URLs
google.de	Feb 2011	100%	Blocked, Domains, Alexa Top 1000 Domains, Google Sites, URLs
t.co	May 2011	100%	Blocked, Domains, Alexa Top 1000 Domains, URLs
google.co.jp	Feb 2011	100%	Blocked, Domains, Alexa Top 1000 Domains, Google Sites, URLs
google.fr	Mar 2011	100%	Blocked, Domains, Alexa Top 1000 Domains, Google Sites, URLs

[Image 8] https://en.greatfire.org/search/alexa-top-1000-domains.

This focus on the blocking of digital content produced elsewhere from being consumed by Chinese citizens does not give us a full picture of the everyday reality of media censorship in China. Lokman Tsui highlights this point as he questions the effectiveness of the prevalent 'Great Firewall' metaphor, which even the Greatfire website employs.

Tsui writes:

> The metaphor most frequently used in describing and understanding Internet censorship in China is that of the Great Firewall... I argue that our (ab)use of the Great Firewall metaphor leads to blind spots that obscure and limit our understanding of Internet censorship in the People's Republic... To illuminate the existence of these blind spots, I use the term

Great Firewall myth (as opposed to metaphor). By using the word "myth", however, I am not denying the existence of Internet censorship in China. On the contrary. The Great Firewall myth is the belief that China's efforts to censor the Internet must ultimately fail, and that the Internet will eventually lead to the country's democratisation...

[The myth] gives the impression that censorship is practised only on information that lies outside the Great Firewall: after all, that is the purpose of the protection the wall provides. Attempts to "break down" the Great Firewall focus on countering censorship technology with more and better technology, resulting in a cat-and-mouse game between activists and censors... The image of the Great Firewall protecting China from the West thus obscures the fact that "undesirable" information often comes not from the West but from within China itself...

... [Further,] the Great Firewall metaphor hints at the difficulty only of receiving information, not sending it. Censorship prevents the barbarians from coming in, but does it also prevent the Chinese from going out? The concept of free speech has two aspects: the right to receive information, but also the right to impart it. (Tsui 2007)

Greatfire, however, effectively creates entry points to understand various kinds of censorship activities of the Chinese government. The pattern of blocking of Wikipedia pages in China, for example, offers interesting insights.

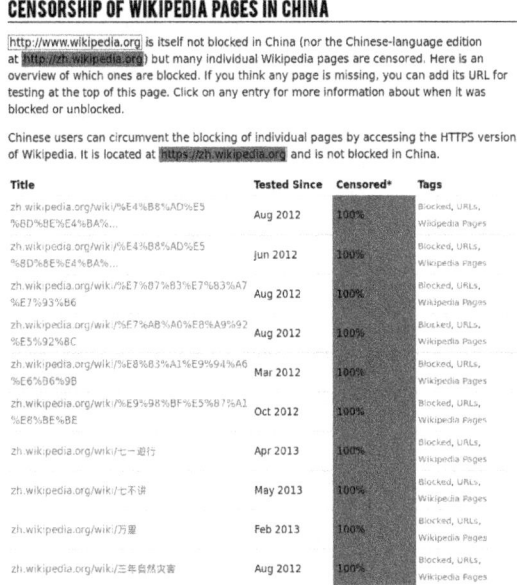

[Image 9] https://en.greatfire.org/search/wikipedia-pages.

When interpreting the censorship of Wikipedia pages, there are two things that must be given attention. Firstly, the focus of the censorship is clearly on pages in the Chinese language Wikipedia project, and not the English language Wikipedia project. And secondly, Wikipedia is as much a site of information consumption, as it is of information production. Blocking Chinese Internet users from accessing specific pages on the Chinese language Wikipedia project is hence not only about preventing them from accessing Chinese language content created elsewhere in the world, but also about preventing them from creating and sharing Chinese language content within and outside China.

Production and digital distribution of content by Chinese users is also censored by the Government of China through the 'Self-Censorship' mechanism.

WHAT DOES SELF-CENSORSHIP MEAN?

All websites hosted in China are required to exercise self-censorship. This takes many forms and is more complex to track than censorship of foreign websites. Some websites admit to self-censorship by displaying a certain message when searching for certain keywords. One example is Baidu, as shown above, which presents the following message for particularly sensitive searches:

根据相关法律法规和政策，部分搜索结果未予显示。

This roughly translates to:

In accordance with relevant laws, regulations and policies, some search results were not displayed.

However, this does not mean that searches without this message are not censored. A more realistic interpretation is probably that the search is particularly sensitive and perhaps subject to a higher level of censorship than other searches.

Our system concludes that a website is subject to Self-Censorship if:

1. The URL is a Baidu search result page, and
2. The result page contains the following text: 根据相关法律法规和政策，部分搜索结果未予显示。

[Image 10] https://en.greatfire.org/faq/self-censorship.

Let us take a step back now and remember that various forms of censorship are not that uncommon even for the *global open Internet*.

Google serves maps with different political boundaries for different countries.

Facebook conducts psychological experiments based upon its ability to algorithmically manipulate what status updates a user sees on her/his Facebook wall.

The Tempora programme of Government Communications Headquarters (GCHQ) of the Government of the United Kingdom, taps into the submarine cables carrying the global Internet data traffic, and undertakes mass interception of data passing through Bude, a small coastal town. GCHQ also runs EdgeHill, a massive-scale decryption exercise of digital communication flowing through HTTPS protocol (targeting digital certificates provided by three main authorities).

The rush for surveillance, monitoring, and censorship of global Internet transactions is a rather global phenomenon - neither being done only by government agencies, nor taking place only in Asian countries.

A key question, hence, is if the Chinese government is one of the first movers in the space of Internet censorship. Did it initiate the competition, and thus shape a global situation of acts and counter-acts of surveillance and censorship?

Evgeny Morozov disagrees.

> ...[T]he US government insists that it should have access to data regardless of where it is stored as long as it is handled by US companies. Just imagine the outcry if the Chinese government were to demand access to any data that passes through devices manufactured by Chinese companies – Xiaomi, say, or Lenovo – regardless of whether their users are in London or New York or Tokyo. Note the crucial difference: Russia and China want to be able to access data generated by their citizens on their own soil, whereas the US wants to access data generated by anybody anywhere as long as American companies handle it...

> ...Whatever motivates the desire of Russia and China to exert more control over their digital properties – and only the naive would believe that they are not motivated by concerns over domestic unrest – their actions are proportional to the aggressive efforts of Washington to exploit the fact that so much of the world's communications infrastructure is run by Silicon Valley. One's man internet freedom is another man's internet imperialism (Morozov 2015).

References and Further Readings

2015. "Denial of Service Attack." Wikipedia. June 11. Accessed June 15, 2015. https://en.wikipedia.org/wiki/Denial-of-service_attack.

2015. "Great Firewall." Wikipedia. May 20. Accessed June 15, 2015. https://en.wikipedia.org/wiki/Great_Firewall.

2015. "Internet Censorship in China." Wikipedia. June 13. Accessed June 15, 2015. https://en.wikipedia.org/wiki/Internet_censorship_in_China.

2015. "Internet Censorship in the United States." Wikipedia. April 12. Accessed June 15, 2015. https://en.wikipedia.org/wiki/Internet_censorship_in_the_United_States.

2015. "Sina Weibo." Wikipedia. June 14. Accessed June 15, 2015. https://en.wikipedia.org/wiki/Sina_Weibo.

Cox, Joseph. 2014. "The History of DDoS Attacks as a Tool of Protest." Motherboard. October 1. Accessed June 15, 2015. http://motherboard.vice.com/read/history-of-the-ddos-attack.

Dempsey Morais, Caitlin. 2012. "The Politics of Google's Mapping." GIS Lounge. May 18. Accessed June 15, 2015. http://www.gislounge.com/the-politics-of-googles-mapping/.

Morozov, Evgeny. 2009. "The Internet: A Room of Our Own?" *Dissent*. Summer. Pp. 80-85. Accessed June 15, 2015. http://www.evgenymorozov.com/files/09Summer-MorozovInternet.pdf.

Morozov, Evgeny. 2015. "Who's the True Enemy of Internet Freedom—China, Russia, or the US?" The Guardian. January 04. Accessed June 15, 2015. http://www.theguardian.com/commentisfree/2015/jan/04/internet-freedom-china-russia-us-google-microsoft-digital-sovereignty.

Reporters without Borders. 2014. "United Kingdom: World Champion of Surveillance." In *Enemies of the Internet 2014: Entities at the Heart of Censorship and Surveillance*. March 10. Accessed June 15, 2015. http://12mars.rsf.org/2014-en/2014/03/10/united-kingdom-world-champion-of-surveillance/

Tsui, Lokman. 2007. "An Inadequate Metaphor: The Great Firewall and Chinese Internet Censorship." *Global Dialogue*. Volume 9, Number 1–2. Winter/Spring. Accessed June 15, 2015. http://www.worlddialogue.org/content.php?id=400.

Tufekci, Zeynep. 2014. "Facebook and Engineering the Public." Medium. June 29. Accessed June 15, 2015. https://medium.com/message/engineering-the-public-289c91390225.

Taiwan's Sunflower Protest: Digital Anatomy of a Movement[1]

Tracey Cheng

On March 18th, 2014, hundreds of students occupied the "Legislative Yuan", Taiwan's parliament, to protest against the Cross-Strait Service Trade Agreement (CSSTA). A network of tech-savvy volunteers immediately began to use digital tools to broadcast their message to sympathizers and the public. Soon, thousands of citizens rallied on the streets outside the parliament to support the students inside. This movement became known as the "Sunflower Movement."

[Image 1] Credit: Gazhua Jiang.

1 Additional writing and support by Peichieh Chen, additional editing by Taylor Dalrymple, and final edit by Hanns-Peter Nagel.

In the eyes of many students, CSSTA had been hastily signed between the respective governments of Taiwan and China without fully informing the Taiwanese public of what it entails. Taiwan's government asserted that the agreement would boost Taiwan's faltering economy, but students thought it would result in Taiwan becoming too dependent on China at the expense of Taiwan's relations with other allies, and thus become vulnerable to political pressure from Beijing.

[Image 2] Students occupying the Legislative Yuan, Taiwan's parliament. Credit: Occupy Taiwan Legislature by Voice of America. Licensed under Public domain via Wikimedia Commons.

On March 23rd, protesters broke into the Executive Yuan building, the seat of Taiwan's executive branch. Riot police evicted them by force. A national uproar ensued and resentment toward the government reached another level, partly fueled by the global support for the Sunflower Movement's nonviolent protests. On March 30th, just 12 days into the movement, students organized a demonstration that saw more than 500,000 Taiwanese citizens taking to the streets in support of their cause.

The government could not withstand the pressure. In a speech, Legislative Speaker Wang Jin-Pyng accepted the demands of the protestors. The movement officially concluded on April 10th when the students who had been occupying the parliament left the premises.

The Sunflower Movement became one of the biggest political movements in the past 30 years of Taiwan history. It awoke a younger generation's awareness about politics, democracy and the identity of Taiwan as a country.

However, what most stood out about this movement was its clever use of technology and digital media. Enabled by the fast collaboration of a self-organized group of volunteers, the movement took flight in ways never seen before and immediately garnered the attention of Taiwanese citizens worldwide in record time.

[Image 3] Symbol of the #CongressOccupied movement in Taiwan, March 2014. Credit: http://dd-jack.tumblr.com/.

Having it Covered: Live Streaming the Movement

From the very first moment of the occupation, setting up an ongoing live broadcast from inside the parliament became a top priority. It was so important, a photo of a pair of flip-flops supporting the iPad used to film and live stream the event during the first hours of the occupation turned into an iconic image.

Live streaming was later taken over by gov.tw[1], a website launched in 2012 and run by more than 100 members. Their mission: create an open and transparent government so that citizens can make better informed decisions. Over the past few years the group had worked on several projects with the goal of delivering easy-to-understand information to Taiwan citizens by using simplified graphics, web pages and layman's terms.

To broadcast the unfolding event, the gov.tw team's first challenge was to set up a stable and reliable wireless internet environment – the lifeblood of the movement. At first, they tried working with existing WiMAX networks but then moved on to constructing their own servers when it became clear that they would need faster service to keep up with the amount of traffic they were receiving.

Now, instead of relying only on mainstream media, volunteers and the public had a faster and more reliable way of obtaining information. Over time, an impressive list of related links to the movement and transcripts of all the major speeches and announcements was compiled on gov.tw's official webpage for the movement.[2] The gov.tw team and their site were an important part of the success of the March 30th rally because of the technical support they were able to provide despite the massive turnout of 500,000 people.

[Image 4] A pair of flip-flops and a live-streaming iPad became to symbolize the Sunflower Movement's digital DNA. Credit: Diung Libiu / Chang Liyou.

Throughout the occupation, gov.tw and its many supporters relied heavily on Hackpad, a collective editing tool similar to Google Docs. Hackpad was adopted early on and was ultimately responsible for ensuring the successful collaboration of more than 1500 volunteers with transcript and data documentation.[3] Due to the heavy traffic on Hackpad as the movement gathered steam, its servers were completely overloaded more than five times in just three days, necessitating the addition of extra servers to keep up with the demand.

Crowdfunding Success Breaking Records

Around-the-clock live streaming and heavy social media use quickly turned the protest into a larger movement. But in order to spread the message more effectively, the movement needed something movements typically lack: money.

Crowdfunding was the natural solution. The students set up a funding project on FlyingV.cc[4], one of the leading crowdfunding websites in Taiwan. Within 12 hours, the goal of 6.3 million NTD ($210,000) was reached. This money funded full-page advertisements in one of the major newspapers in Taiwan as well as the New York Times.

The funding campaign for the Sunflower Movement became Taiwan's fastest crowdfunding project to reach its goal, despite the lack of any prior planning. The accompanying website 4am.tw[5] was designed and constructed within 24 hours by and all-volunteer force of 10 translators and four engineers.

For crowd-funding platform FlyingV, the story didn't end there. The start-up was fined 50,000 NTD ($1,700) for violating their contract with Gre Tai Securities Market by assisting in the crowdfunding for a social movement. FlyingV responded by announcing their plans to develop an alternative crowd-funding site not under contract with Gre Tai Securities Market. VDemocracy.tw[6] was launched on April 7th, 2014.

Transparency Volunteers in Action

An amazing number of people were willing to step up for the cause. In a short time, supporters became active volunteers. The driving force behind this rapid groundswell of support was the perceived lack of transparency and loss of trust in the government.

Determined to shed more light on government action, the movement put a strong focus on growing the public's awareness on the issues through a continuous supply of information.

Here are three examples of websites that were launched after the movement started to encourage Taiwanese citizens to exercise their civil rights and defend their livelihoods against the perceived threat of the CSSTA.

How Your Company will be Affected by the CSSTA (你被服冒了嗎)[7]

Enter any company's registered name to this website and it will show if and how the company will be affected by the CSSTA according to the current terms of the agreement. The use of witty graphics and layman's terms on the website aims to make this serious topic accessible to everyone.

CSSTA Battle (服冒東西軍)[8]

This website offers a compilation of both positive and negative news and opinions about CSSTA. The movement and its demands received a lot of media attention which led to a significant growth in debate around the trade agreement. Information such as the actual terms of the agreement, the process of how it was to be passed, the legitimacy of the occupation at the parliament,

[Image 5] How will your company be affected by CSSTA tells visitors what the trade agreement means to them. Credit: http://tisa.g0v.tw/.

and police actions to disperse the crowd on March 24th became hot topics once the general public took note of the whole situation. The site makes it easy for visitors to browse topics they find interesting and offers opposing arguments without censorship.

Review Our Own CSSTA (自己的服冒自己審)[9]

The Sunflower Movement started as a response to a controversial and obscure process to pass the trade agreement with China. This blatant disregard of the legal process outraged many citizens. They now want to have a hand in the oversight of the trade agreement since they no longer trust the government to do so on their behalf. This website breaks down complex regulations, rendering them clearer and easier to understand. It also provides transcripts from previous public hearings, all the related public hearing recordings, and clauses of the agreement.

[Image 6] The Appendectomy project adds a slightly disturbing medical analogy to the impeachment of legislators. Credit: Appendectomy Project, http://appy.tw/.

Aftermath: The Sunflower's Legacy

As the Sunflower Movement came to a close, the question on many peoples' minds became: "What happens now that the parliament will no longer be occupied?"

Some felt that it was the right time for the movement to end while others thought that doing so equaled surrendering their leverage over the government. In response to this vigorous debate, a new project started to gain momentum. The Appendectomy Project[10] is an online platform designed to rally supporters to impeach legislators who have lost the confidence of the public. The project is based on the premise that all citizens have the right to remove their representatives from office when they think it is necessary. Despite the fact that the requirements for impeachment are rigorous, the residents of certain electoral districts are still pursuing this course for targeted politicians.

The Legacy

The Sunflower Movement has been described as a highly technologically-oriented social movement. Since a majority of participants were students, it was only natural that the movement reflected the digital age in which this generation was born.

The movement left several important legacies behind; it notably created several successful digital strategies ready for adoption by other groups fighting for social change. Case in point: Taiwan's resurgent anti-nuclear power movement, born right after the Sunflower protests and using a similar digital playbook.

The success of the movement was underscored by the change of attitude towards politics and society by the younger generation; this transformation becomes all the more obvious when contrasted with the absence of high-tech communications in the political struggles of earlier generations.

Although it remains to be seen if the government will make good on its promise to properly review the CSSTA, the Sunflower Movement marks the beginning of a new era in Taiwan's social movements with its digital success story: the online protest that resulted in and supported a turnaround of public opinion.

Endnotes

1. gov. http://gov.tw/en-US/index.html.
2. "Congress Occupied." gov. http://gov.today/congressoccupied.
3. "gov." Hakpad. https://gov.hackpad.com/.
4. FlyingV. http://www.flyingv.cc/.
5. Democracy at 4 am. http://4am.tw/.
6. VDemocracy. http://VDemocracy.tw/.
7. "How Your Company Will be Affected by the CSSTA?" gov. http://tisa.gov.tw/.
8. "CSSTA Battle." Speaking. http://ecfa.speaking.tw/imho.php.
9. "Review Our Own CSSTA." Fumao. http://review.fumao.today/.
10. Appendectomy Project. http://appy.tw/.

Further Readings

https://zh.wikipedia.org/wiki/Gov_%E9%9B%B6%E6%99%82%E6%94%BF%E5%BA%9C
http://www.new7.com.tw/NewsView.aspx?i=TXT20131113142202RPZ
http://www.appledaily.com.tw/realtimenews/article/new/20140321/364347/
http://www.appledaily.com.tw/realtimenews/article/new/20140329/369121/
http://www.stormmediagroup.com/opencms/news/detail/7dbe7ab6-b7dc-11e3-82ad-ef2804cba5a1/?uuid=7dbe7ab6-b7dc-11e3-82ad-ef2804cba5a1
http://www.inside.com.tw/2014/04/09/appendectomy-project
http://www.ithome.com.tw/news/86022

http://www.ithome.com.tw/news/86017
http://www.cool3c.com/article/78266

Annotation

Puthiya Purayil Sneha

The Sunflower Movement is an important landmark in the history of democratic struggles in Taiwan. The movement has been lauded particularly for its scale and complexity of organization, with the use of digital technologies and the Internet being one of its key features. But the protests become particularly significant because of their immense geopolitical implications, due to Taiwan's disputed political status and its checkered history of problems with China. Taiwan, or the Republic of China (ROC) as it is officially known, was formed after the Chinese Civil War, and since then has been the subject of several debates about its sovereign status, and attempts at reunification with the People's Republic of China (PRC). The Cross Strait Services Trade Agreement (CSSTA), which is the focus of the protest, is important for the economic benefits and growth that it was deemed to bring for both states, due to increased employment and removal of trade barriers. However the manner of its negotiation and its representation in public is a matter of concern, as it is viewed as an attempt by China to exert more political influence over Taiwan and also as a cover for reunification with the mainland. The CSSTA is part of the Economic Cooperation Framework agreement signed between Taiwan and China in 2010, an agreement which has also been intensely debated due to lack of clarity over its stated objectives of economic growth. The CSSTA was therefore proposed for a clause-by-clause review in the legislature, a move supported by the Democratic People's Party (DPP), and many Taiwanese citizens. The breakdown of these negotiations, and an attempt by the Kuomintang (KMT)-led government to put the agreement to vote and pass it without review, caused the final upsurge amongst protesters, leading them to occupy the Legislative Yuan on March 18, 2014.

As mentioned in the article, the Sunflower Movement has been appreciated in Taiwan and all over the world for introducing a young, neo-liberal and supposedly 'apolitical' generation to a history of political protests and democratic debates. However, Taiwanese youth are no strangers to protests or public campaigns, given the country's vibrant history of student movements, with some recent examples being the Wild Lily Movement and the Wild Strawberry movement. This movement therefore reiterates that political awareness and activity is not a generational myth. The effective use of the Internet and other multi-media tools point at the advanced digital proficiency and access of a large section of people across Taiwan. At a time when the international mainstream media was divided between covering a political crisis in Ukraine and a missing Malaysian plane, the protesters were resourceful in employing an array of technologies efficiently to process information that poured in from all quarters, and to reach out to the rest of the world. The protest demonstrated its core objective of pushing for transparency and accountability in legislation and governance by setting up a live stream of video from the Legislative Yuan, making their activities open to the public through social media and tools such as Hackpad and Google Docs, and crowd-sourcing funding for materials and resources through an online platform. Apart from the implicit reliability and speed of digital networks, the manner in which the protest was organized also indicated a network of trust that people had in the movement, and in everybody involved, which enabled such transparent and open communication. However, the network also suffered from a glitch wherein erroneous messages were sent out through Facebook and messaging apps to a large group of protesters at a critical juncture, when they were about to occupy the Executive Yuan. This glitch, which was presumably the result of attempts by outsiders or pro-CSSTA activists to misappropriate information, points to the vulnerability of online networks, wherein almost the entire strategy to occupy the Executive building was compromised. As a result of the confusion, riot police could forcefully evict protesters from the streets and areas around the Executive Yuan, this time using violence as the numbers were also much fewer than expected. The use of technology as part of these protests, which seemed to be its biggest strength, also became a big weakness at one point.

The movement ended on April 10, 2014, when Legislative Speaker Wang Jin-pyng assured protestors that their demands would be heeded, and legislation monitoring all cross-strait agreements would be passed soon. Protesters vacated the legislature, but not before cleaning the place, and assuring citizens that the movement would continue in different ways. This is seen in the form of the Appendectomy project, for example which pushes for more accountability of elected officials through campaigns to review their work and remove corrupt or incompetent people from office. The Sunflower movement is said to have been influential in spurring other protests such as the anti-nuclear movement in Taiwan, and the Umbrella Revolution in Hong Kong, all of which adopted similar digital methods. The protest is also significant in thinking about the solidarity it evoked in people across social and economic barriers and the complicated nature of sovereignty in a disputed, or 'non-state.' When there is a lack of clarity regarding the identity of the state, the notion of community and demands on democracy become even more rigorous and are defended greatly. The Sunflower movement was important as it was able to reach out to a cross section of people in Taiwan and across the world who wanted to contribute in every way possible, as seen in the case of the florist who handed out one thousand sunflowers to protesters on the first day. That act gave the movement its name, and its ultimate objective, to keep hope and the voice of reason alive in times of strife.

References and Further Readings

1990. "Taipei Spring? Anachronistic Processes but Lee Promises Reforms". Taiwan Commune. Vol 44. Accessed June 17, 2015. http://www.taiwandc.org/twcom/tc44-int.pdf.

Bush, R. 2006. *Untying the Knot: Making Peace in the Taiwan Strait*. Brookings Institution Press. ISBN: 9780815712909.

Chao, Y Vincent. 2014. "How Technology Revolutionized Taiwan's Sunflower Movement." The Diplomat. Accessed March 15, 2015. http://thediplomat.com/2014/04/how-technology-revolutionized-taiwans-sunflower-movement/.

"Democracy at 4am: What Unprecedented Protest Means for Taiwan." 2015. 4am.tw. Accessed June 9, 2015. http://4am.tw/.

Hilgers, Lauren. 2015. "Hong Kong's Umbrella Revolution isn't Over Yet." The New York Times. February 18. Accessed June 18, 2015. http://www.nytimes.com/2015/02/22/magazine/hong-kongs-umbrella-revolution-isnt-over-yet.html.

J.R. 2014. "Sunflower Sutra." The Economist. Accessed March 16, 2015. http://www.economist.com/blogs/banyan/2014/04/politics-taiwan.

Pasterich, Emanuel. 2003. "Sovereignty, Wealth, Culture, and Technology: Mainland China and Taiwan Grapple with the Parameters of 'Nation State' in the 21st Century." ACIDIS Occasional Paper Series. University of Illinois, Urbana-Champaign. Accessed June 18, 2015. http://acdis.illinois.edu/assets/docs/256/SovereigntyWealthCultureandTechnologyMainlandChinaandTaiwanGrapplewiththeParametersofNationStateinthe21stCentury.pdf.

"Sunflower Movement." The Diplomat. Accessed March 16, 2015. http://thediplomat.com/tag/sunflower-movement/.

Taiwan Wild Strawberries Movement. Accessed June 18, 2015. http://taiwan-studentmovement2008.blogspot.in/.

Yun, Fan. 2004. "Taiwan Lily: A Sociological View." Taipei Times. April 22. Accessed June 18, 2015. http://www.taipeitimes.com/News/editorials/archives/2004/04/22/2003137635.

Digital Revolution in Reverse: Syria's Media Diversifies Offline

Armand Hurault

During the first year and half of the uprising in Syria, citizen media activists used digital platforms and tools to coordinate their actions remotely – setting up efficient organisations of people who had never physically met. Skype rooms were created where hundreds of people shared and verified information before passing it to international journalists. This "all-digital" model worked as long as the objective was to leak information out of Syria and to an international audience.

Today, citizen journalists are now are making efforts to switch their audience from an international one to a domestic one. Media activists have developed autonomous Internet access through satellite modems to get around the regime's imposition of a complete Internet blackout on certain regions and widespread electricity cuts. The many citizen radio stations and magazines which have emerged since the uprising use these methods to make their make content public to the world. But these methods are too costly and dangerous for the majority of Syrians – so these radios and magazines are only available to the population living abroad.

What gone nearly unnoticed in Syria is an increase in the traditional means of media dissemination: FM radio and print.

The Association de Soutien aux Médias Libres (ASML)[1] is working to help these emerging citizen media to remedy the situation. We have installed a wide network of FM broadcasting teams with a coverage of almost the entire country, called Hawa SMART.[2] The broadcasting equipment airs radio shows of citizen media radio stations (Radio al-Kul [ar][3], Capital Radio Huna Al-Sham) which otherwise would only be accessible online (functionally, abroad), but can now be heard across the country. We are also printing hard copies of citizen-journalism-driven magazines, distributing the hard copies inside the country.

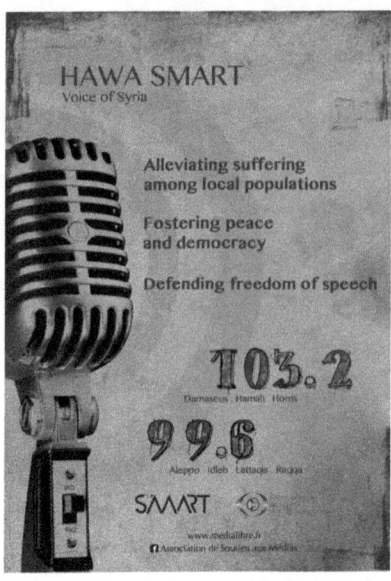

[Image 1] Poster for Hawa SMART Radio. Credit: Assocation de Soutien aux Medias, http://www.medialibre.fr/.

There are many difficulties associated with FM coverage, including physical risks to the on-location broadcasting teams by the regime's forces – calling for secrecy and tight security. But after this period of digital flourishing during the Arab Spring, radio has reemerged as the most efficient way to reach local audiences living inside Syria, requiring only a cheap receiver and a small battery. It is one of the most accessible ways for people to hear about what is going on in neighboring areas, and to hear what their fellow citizens around the country are thinking and doing.

Broadcasting team leader Amrou approves of the wide coverage:

> Now Hawa SMART covers almost un-interruptedly an area which goes from Turkey to the very south of the country... [as well as] the coastal region. This [region] is very strategic because it is populated in majority with Allawite populations, the sect of President Bashar al-Assad, and which has been mostly supporting the regime since 2011. It was very important for us to reach this region because we are working for a united Syria. It is crucial to target all segments of society to avoid the collapse of the country.

These radio stations were started by amateur citizen media who are now producing several hours of radio per day. Shows are varied – both for entertainment but also very serious issues. Radio Al-Kul, for example, features children's shows and sports, but also regional news programming focused on local concerns, and a call-in show where listeners can contribute to discuss their own worries and regional concerns.

The FM broadcasts now being heard across Syria can be streamed online through Hawa SMART, made accessible for Syrian expatriates and refugees, or anyone else wanting to hear about what is going on.[4]

To stay in touch, you can follow Radio AlKul on Facebook [arabic][5], and ASML on twitter @ASML_medialibre [arabic][6] – or get in touch with them info@medialibre.fr .

Endnotes

1   Association de Soutien aux Médias Libres. http://medialibre.fr/en/.
2   Hawa SMART. http://hawa-smart.fm/.
3   Radio al-Kul. http://radioalkul.com/#/Home.
4   "Hawa SMART." TuneIn. Accessed June 09, 2015. http://tunein.com/radio/Hawa-SMART-1032-s204859/.
5   "Radio al-Kul." Facebook. https://www.facebook.com/Radio.Alkul.
6   "@ASML_Medialibre." Twitter. https://twitter.com/ASML_medialibre.

Annotation

Puthiya Purayil Sneha

The Arab Spring has become a milestone in contemporary history not just for the manner in which it has unsettled complex equations of power and democracy in the world, but also for rethinking the way in which activism and political protest has been imagined for years before it. A key aspect of this uprising was the spotlight it shone on the role of the Internet and digital technologies, particularly social media such as Twitter and Facebook, in the mobilization of people for change. In the way that the protests were discussed and spread, both online and offline, they seemed to challenge the notion that the 'revolution cannot be tweeted'. While the jury may still be out on whether technology spurred the revolution, or whether it was the other way around, the crucial role played by the Internet and media, in all its diverse forms, cannot be ignored. This article, which is part of 'Rising Voices', an outreach project by Global Voices, illustrates the efforts taken by citizen media activists to make information available to people across Syria through a network of FM broadcasting teams and print, thus dispelling the myth of widespread Internet and mobile phone access across this part of the world. The quality of access to new communication technologies is restricted due to heavy censorship by the current regime which controls all public broadcasting services and also polices Internet and telecommunication networks. Media censorship has been strict under the Assad regime; particularly post the Arab Spring and the subsequent Syrian Civil War. According to Reporters without Borders, Syria is ranked 177 out of 180 countries in the 2015 World Press Freedom Index, with a score of 77.29. It has also featured in the Enemy of the Internet report 2014. In 2013, for the third time in a row, the Committee to Protect Journalists named Syria the deadliest country in the world for the press. Journalists have been frequently abducted, imprisoned and subjected to torture to extract passwords of social media accounts. Over 82 journalists have been killed since 1992 despite their non-combatant status; Internet censorship also puts bloggers and citizen journalists in grave peril with threats of imprisonment and torture. A pro-Government online group, the Syrian Electronic Army, hacks websites to upload pro-regime material, while the Government has been suspected of malware attacks used to curb the spread of information.

In such conditions of extreme duress and violence, citizen media, particularly in its traditional forms, has flourished, as it seems to have strangely escaped the eye of the regime. Local citizen journalists reporting for mainstream media on the unrest have been doing so with several risks, especially as foreign correspondents have been stopped from entering the country since the unrest in 2011. While it may be puzzling that the Government heavily monitors the Internet and mainstream press, but has seemingly not made any effort to muzzle the press or censor radio, this could also be an indication of censorship being applicable only to content being circulated outside of the country, and not so much within. The conflict between the local and global aspects of activism is interestingly played out in this project as seen by the selective censoring of media, and more crucially in the manner in which language forms a critical pillar of the protests. The use of the local language is important, as the target audience is domestic, and to a large extent the Syrian diaspora. It also goes against the notion of digital media being monolithic and universally accessible in some sense. Instead, it is shown to have different layers segregated in form and use. Here digital media actually works sequentially and simultaneously with traditional media, therefore also questioning these easy binaries of old and new, traditional and modern media, which segregates them into silos. As illustrated here, the technological landscape exists in many layers, and is also in transition, so information often travels through different kinds of media. This also speaks of larger questions around the choices made within activism about choosing one form over another, or addressing a particular demographic versus the rest of the world.

The intersectionality of the digital – in terms of form, language and mode – is an important aspect of understanding digital activism, as it defines the space within which it functions.

The aspect of physical space is also interesting in this discourse, as the lack of some form of materiality and 'action in the real world' has been the constant criticism of digital and specifically online activism. Here the airwaves are treated as physical space, therefore imposing some kind of materiality and limits to them. Control over the airwaves is regarded as control over an imagined community of listeners and citizens, thus here also defining a boundary at large. The manner of activists using digital technologies, and their imagination of the role played by such technology in shaping activism, is therefore a crucial point to contend with in conversations on digital activism.

References and Further Readings

2013. "Journalism in Syria, Impossible Job?" Reporters without Borders. Accessed June 9, 2015. http://en.rsf.org/syrie-journalism-in-syria-impossible-job-06-11-2013,45424.html

2015. "82 Journalists Killed in Syria since 1992/Motive Confirmed." Committee to Protect Journalists. Accessed June 9, 2015. https://cpj.org/killed/mideast/syria/

Anderson, Benedict. 1983. *Imagined Communities: Reflections on the Origin and Spread of Nationalism.* London: Verso / New Left Books.

El Zein, Dahila. 2012. "In Syria, killing the messenger hasn't killed the message." Committee to Protect Journalists. Accessed June 9, 2015. https://www.cpj.org/blog/2012/03/in-syria-killing-the-messenger-isnt-working.php

Gladwell, Malcolm. 2010. "Small Change: Why the Revolution will not be Tweeted." The New Yorker. Accessed March 19, 2015. http://www.newyorker.com/magazine/2010/10/04/small-change-3

O'Brien, Danny. 2014. "Syria's Assad gives tacit ok to online attacks on press." Committee to Protect Journalists. Accessed June 9, 2015. https://cpj.org/blog/2011/06/syrias-assad-gives-tacit-ok-to-online-attacks-on-p.php

Stern, Jason. 2014. "In Syria, fewer journalist deaths but danger has never been greater." Committee to Protect Journalists. Accessed June 9, 2015. https://cpj.org/blog/2014/12/in-syria-fewer-journalist-deaths-but-danger-has-never-been-gr.php

India Calling

Rachel Jolley

When the world needs innovation it often looks for the discovery of some cutting-edge technology to solve the problem. But sometimes something simple can provide the answer.

[Image 1] Volunteers learn how to use the news platform at Swara. Credit: Purushottam Thakur.

In central India, a journalist who wanted to change the lives of millions of people found his technical challenge solved by a simple, non-smart mobile phone.

Former BBC South Asia producer Shubhranshu Choudhary didn't have to ask the techies to pull something clever out of the box; instead, he needed a bit of technology to which millions of poor people already had access, and once he realised that, he knew where to look. He created a new kind of media service where anyone could call in and leave a message in their own language and suggest or tell a news story; alternatively, they could call and listen to stories left by others.

Many poor, rural people who live in Chhattisgarh and in the forested areas of central India do not speak Hindi or English, the main languages of the Indian media; they don't have access to newspapers or internet news; they live in remote villages, often without running water and schools. They also live at the centre of a region that the Indian government has been pouring troops into for years to tackle the "Maoist insurgency". For these people, this invention, a media platform called CGNet Swara, was a way of both telling news stories and listening to news from others, using a piece of equipment they either already owned or could get access to.

[Image 2] Women phone in to hear the news. Credit: Purushottam Thakur.

The latest Indian census (2011) reported that more people had a mobile phone than had inside toilets, with 53 per cent of households in the country owning a mobile phone, compared with only 3.1 per cent having internet access. Take into account the fact that, in addition to these 53 per cent of households, people share mobile phones with others beyond the household, and others use landlines, giving an even wider group access to telephone communication. In fact the Indian telecommunications regulator TRAI suggest that access to mobile phones stand at around 70 per cent, with this figure at 40 per cent in rural communities.

Choudhary, a Knight International Journalism Fellow, was inspired to create a news platform for this region during his time working for the BBC: "I was travelling from one war zone to another, then wars started near my home. I grew up in central India and I also covered the region for the BBC. When something happens nearer to you, nearer to your heart, it makes you think more. The difference in this case was that I grew up in that area, and the backbenchers in my school – they were the 'terrorists' that the prime minister called the 'biggest internal security threat', and it unnerved me. These were the students that never raised their voices, and how come 25 years later they had become 'terrorists'?"

So he took some time living in the forests of central India with these communities, who were being referred to as Maoists. And he was told by the local people that the system of communicating news, and communicating what was wrong in their lives, was not working for them. "This is a huge community, around 100 million people, and this is a breakdown of communication. Our communication system is still very aristocratic, where a small number of people sitting on top have too much power and the huge majority of people don't have any voice or have very little power to decide what is not heard and what should be heard. When you sit in a village in a small group of people under a tree and discuss the issues, then that discussion is democratic because the medium they use is air, which is not owned by anyone." Democracy or equality disappears when certain people own the medium that transmits the news, he argues, and when a group's voice is not being heard, grudges accumulate. He argues that the absence of those debates leads to dissatisfaction and leaves communities susceptible to groups who come to the forest claiming that they can create something better: "We call it the Maoist problem, but the number of people in the forest who are Maoist is 2 per cent or 5 per cent. They have simple problems such as water, roads, hospitals, jobs, and we didn't deliver because we didn't hear them."

Many people are adivasis, marginalised indigenous people, who often have low levels of literacy but have an oral history tradition of passing on news and traditions. "We go to these villages and ask who speaks Hindi without realising that is the language of the rich; 70 to 90 per cent of these people don't speak any language but their mother tongue," said Choudhary.

But users of the new type of news platform introduced by Choudhary don't need to speak another language – they can dial in and leave an audio message of the story they would like to tell in their own language. Areas are broken up into groups, so local people hear from other local people, and there are hundreds of these audio communities. Most of these groups primarily listen to local stories, but occasionally the moderators for the service find a story that they think other groups would be interested in, about a wider issue, and it is shared.

It is a bottom-up model, with communities electing their own moderators who are trained by CGNet on skills such as fact checking and phoning back "reporters" to check up on stories. CGNet also translates stories into Hindi and English and publishes them on its website so a wider group of people can read the stories, as well as providing audio in the original language of the contributor. They get around 500 calls per day, 50 of which they record. After checks, about five recordings are broadcast.

[Image 3] Staff work closely with volunteers at the news channel. Credit: Purushottam Thakur.

"We have a strict cross check and filtering process, including calling back to encourage them, and if it is opinion it needs to be clearly labelled," said Choudhary. He points out that the difference between this system and the traditional newspaper editor is that these moderators are elected by the community, and so actually represent them.

Stories are varied and range from one report that a forest ranger asked for bribes totalling Rs 99,000 rupees (US$1,628), to another about school dinners not arriving, while a third reports on high numbers of blind and mentally ill children in an *advasi* [sic] village. Swara is clearly having impact too: days after the report about the numbers of blind village children, a health team arrived to find out more, and the ranger has now repaid his bribes.

CGNet is carrying out a wide range of activities to enhance the smooth running of the news platform, including training young people as translators and training adults as moderators, but it is hoped that training will be devolved to the community in the longer term. It is working towards what it calls a "temple model", in which people train each other: a sort of trickle-down technique for learning. It is also publishing all its learning and knowledge about its technology so other groups can set up similar projects in other regions.

The next step is shortwave radio, which would allow them to reach much bigger audiences still, including those who cannot read. There are obstacles though. Currently there is a news radio reporting monopoly held by the government-backed national All India Radio, although there have been some suggestions that this regulation may be relaxed. So to push onwards CGNet is looking to work with an international provider such as the BBC, with whom Chaudhary has held initial conversations.

"The combination of mobile, internet and radio can really create a democracy in this country. If you can link with radio you have to do so from outside the country because India doesn't allow shortwave radio. If we want to do short-wave linkage we can only do it from outside India."

Around 104 million Indian households have access to a radio, double the number with televisions, making radio an extremely powerful communication tool.

Right now, Choudhary is looking for a partner to help make that next step happen, but he is confident that this type of news service is making a difference.

"It is not solving all problems, but you can create some hope, you can combat some problems. You can tackle the attitude of hopelessness."

Annotation

Puthiya Purayil Sneha

An example of a model of participatory democracy in the age of the digital, CGNet Swara combines the reach and potential of the mobile phone with the immense possibilities of the Internet to present an innovative platform that makes information more accessible and relevant to large but almost invisible indigenous communities in India. As this article by Rachel Jolley illustrates, CGNet Swara began as a small step to connect indigenous and tribal communities located primarily in the Gondwana region in central India (a core region which covers parts of Maharashtra, Chattisgarh and Madhya Pradesh) with each other, and now steadily with the rest of the world. The platform works through an Interactive Voice Recognition System (IVRS), wherein local news is collected, aggregated, moderated and disseminated through a network of mobile and landline phones, and a website, by a collective of trained journalists and translators. Most people of this region are economically and socially disadvantaged; many fall into the categories of scheduled tribes, such as the Adivasis, who have borne the brunt of systemic and historical marginalisation in India. Apart from a host of issues such as lack of basic amenities, employment and security, this region is also the heart of Naxalite-Maoist insurgency, an ongoing conflict between rebel groups and the Indian Government for over five decades for political control over the state. The insurgency has covered large parts of the country, and resulted in much violence and loss of lives and property, often leading to heavy militarization in many regions. Several Naxalite agitations have claimed support from the rural population, particularly the Adivasis, as well as atrocities by armed forces on civilians, and this has further complicated both the movement itself and the attempts by the state to suppress it.

The fact that CGNet Swara did not involve a lot of radically new social or technological research points towards an often ignored aspect of innovation in the development sector, which is that most breakthroughs are often the result of finding new ways to utilise existing resources. CGNet Swara makes optimum use of the ubiquitous presence of mobile phones (mostly not even of the 'smart' variety), landlines, and the Internet to effectively crowdsource information about issues that are pertinent to communities in the areas covered. The platform uses open-source software freely available online, and other minimal infrastructure in an effort to make the model replicable in diverse conditions. This so-called convergence of old and new media also in some sense questions these easy and often polarized binaries, as it makes it apparent that one may actually not be able to work without the other. The model also addresses a crucial 'last mile connectivity' problem, which has often been called the Achilles heel of all ICT-related development strategies, particularly in the Global South. The CGNet Swara model is an illustrative example of how more than being technological or technical, the problem of the last mile is really more of a conceptual one, as described by Ashish Rajadhyaksha (2011). He critiques the extant notion of techno-utopia that has framed most of the discourse around ICTs and development, wherein technology by virtue of being neutral, accessible and incorruptible, would resolve issues of governance that the state cannot, owing to its own shortcomings in this regard, thus ushering in a new era of techno-democracy propelled by increased connectivity. Apart from this imagination of technology as being value-neutral, another crucial drawback of this model of governance was that it envisaged a linear model of transmission or information/resources from the state or market-state entity to the public, in which the end-beneficiary often remained a passive recipient, which is never the case, as is made apparent by CGNet Swara.

The article also locates marginalization within and among regional languages as the cause for many insurmountable obstacles to having the voices of marginalized communities heard over privileged ones, usually the dominant English and Hindi language press and broadcast media. This demonstrates the changing contours of news media today, as the local slowly becomes at the same time invisible and over exposed through an increased emphasis on the growth of development reporting across the world.

The growth of citizen media, often posed as a counter to this hegemony of the mainstream press, and spurred by the rise of the Internet in particular, can be understood in a different context and nuance here, as the citizen reporter is not the stereotyped technologically savvy blogger, but very often a digital immigrant of sorts. The growth in citizen media and other such independent organizations also points to a decentering in the processes of communication normally controlled and regulated by the state, thus giving rise to more forms of peer-to-peer communication, as noted by Rajadhyaksha in his monograph. CGNet Swara thus raises interesting questions for us about the nature of activism today in the digital age, particularly in conditions of little or no access to technology, and the importance of making initiatives localized and relevant for greater social impact and better participation in the exercise of democracy today.

References and Further Readings

"About". CGNet Swara. Accessed June 9, 2015. http://cgnetswara.org/about.html.
Bijoy, C R. 2003. "The Adivasis of India: A History of Discrimination, Conflict and Resistance." People's Union for Civic Liberties (PUCL) Bulletin. [Digital Edition]. Accessed June 9, 2015. http://www.pucl.org/Topics/Dalit-tribal/2003/adivasi.htm.
Rajadhyaksha, Ashish. 2011. "Chapter One: Naming the Problem or Thinking like the State" in *The Last Cultural Mile*. The Centre for Internet and Society. http://cis-india.org/raw/histories-of-the-internet/last-cultural-mile.pdf.
Roy, Arundhati. 2010. "Walking With the Comrades." Outlook. February 29. Accessed June 17, 2015. http://www.outlookindia.com/article/walking-with-the-comrades/264738.
Saha, Anoop. 2012. "Cell Phones as a Tool for Democracy: The Example of CGNet Swara." Economic and Political Weekly. Accessed May 19, 2015. http://indiagovernance.gov.in/files/cgnet-swara.pdf
Subramanian, K.S.2010. "State Response to Maoist Violence in India: A Critical Response." Economic and Political Weekly. August 7. Volume XLV, Number 32. Accessed June 17, 2015. http://www.countercurrents.org/subramanian.pdf.

Digital Populism in South Korea? Internet Culture and the Trouble with Direct Participation

Youngmi Kim

The penetration of the Internet in Korean society is usually seen as a positive development, perhaps even a model for other countries; more efficient bureaucracy, more political figures making use of political blogs, and greater opportunities for citizen participation seem to connect government and citizens in a mutually beneficial way. Nevertheless the past six months have witnessed events resulting from an impersonal and seemingly uncontrolled Internet-based social mobilization that casts the shadow of the effects of unmediated online activity on social and political life: a vehement series of protests against the signing of the U.S.-ROK Free Trade Agreement in April, which led to the resignation of several senior officials and ministers in the new Lee Myung-bak administration and a number of deaths of Korean celebrities as a result of smear campaigns mounted and spread across the Web.[1] Although the latter episodes do not fall within the realm of politics, such suicides nevertheless raise the issue of whether a state should somehow regulate the free flow of information.

Discussions of the role of the Internet in politics (and society) have dominated the Korean media during the past few months. Surprisingly, the debate has yet to reach academia. In fact, the link between Internet activity and populism, as this type of behavior has been referred to in popular parlance (without proper reference to the academic use of the term) is underexplored both theoretically and empirically. To be sure, both populism and Internet-based sociopolitical action have been the objects of academic study. There is a considerable body of literature on populism, its ideological underpinning, and its empirical manifestations with regard to both West and Central Europe and Latin America.[2] Research on Internet technology has focused on the information divide between the rich and the poor and the educated and the less educated, and also on the positive or negative effects of technology on politics, namely e-government, electoral campaigns, or Internet discussions.[3]

We know surprisingly little, however, about how populist movements and leaders make use of the Internet for political ends. The issue itself is far from new, as occasional debates among netizens in East Asia over national sentiments (the dispute over the Dokdo Islands between South Korea and Japan, for example) dominate the Web. Online discussion boards are often instruments for sparking street demonstrations or even shaping electoral campaigns. This paper constitutes an explorative attempt to make sense of the type of behavior—primarily the candlelight vigils in the spring in 2008— that took place in South Korea; it is undertaken in order to understand the role that the Internet and Internet culture play in politics. By doing so, this paper also seeks to conceptualize "digital populism" as a new type of political behavior marked by the political use of the Internet as both a form of political participation and an instrument of mobilization.

There seems to be a paradox in the highly technological societies of East Asia, and in Korea in particular. On the one hand the decline of the mass party and its role in linking elites with citizens and a decreasing electoral turnout have led some to point to a lack of participation and interest of ordinary people in politics. On the other hand, with the rapid development of information technology, citizens are getting more involved in political discussions. The candlelight vigils in South Korea in the spring of 2008 well illustrate the mobilizing power of online blogs, chats, and discussion boards that sparked street demonstrations against the government policy of approval of a free-trade agreement (FTA) with the United States. The candlelight vigils[4] led to administrative shuffles (three ministers replaced) and the appointment of new presidential senior advisers (seven senior presidential secretaries out of eight were replaced). Given that most of the original appointments were fewer than three months old, this was no minor event in Korean politics. Direct participation is having an effect on representative democracy.

The April 2008 FTA Deal and the Wave of Popular Protests

In early April 2008 the United States and South Korea signed an FTA after months of intense negotiation.[5] While this was heralded by the officials of the two parties as a way to take the already significant trade volume between the two countries to a new level, reaction on the streets of South Korean cities suggested that many were unhappy with the deal.[6] On the Korean side, concerns focused on the possible resulting lack of competitiveness of South Korean businesses although the scrapping of tariffs would ensure that companies such as KIA, Hyundai, Samsung, and others would benefit from easier access to the U.S. market.

The FTA decision sparked a large wave of nationwide strikes, rallies, and demonstrations. While street protests have led to clashes with the police (which continued until late July 2008), what is interesting to note is the role played by the Internet in mobilizing ordinary people against the deal and, as a result, against the government (forcing senior aides to the president and ministers to re-sign).

South Korea is among the most wired societies in the world, and the importance of online networks has gained increased prominence not only in social relations (online games, PC rooms, online dating, cyberblogs) but even in public life. The Roh Moo-hyun administration owed a lot of its support to netizens. Political support expressed on the Web greatly contributed to the election of Roh Moo-hyun in 2002, and when the opposition sought to impeach him in 2004 the widespread popular furor hit not only the streets but especially the Internet as a thunderstorm.

The 2008 protests, the peculiarities of the current situation notwithstanding, started similarly, namely, through an Internet-fueled mobilization, with its new language (for example, 2MB and Agorians[7]). Popular participation and direct action grew as a result of the facilitating role of the Internet and online networks, which reduce transaction costs and reach wider audiences than traditional means. But is this direct democracy or is it Internet-induced street mobbing?

The lack of popular participation in public life is often lamented in modern democracies. That more and more citizens become interested in what happens in their countries should be obviously seen as a welcome development. At the same time, however, the current wave of protests and the modus operandi of the protestors have worrying implications for democratic systems. The Internet allows quicker and easier contacts among citizens of any country. More crucial (and troubling) is that the spontaneous, uncontrolled flow of information and prompt response have two important consequences: first, reliance on official sources of information dramatically decreases as people tend to rely on unverified information freely available online; second, an emotional approach to politics replaces a more rational one.

Any type of information, whatever its reliability, prompts an immediate and emotional reaction. The current FTA protests are a case in point. Compared with citizens who rely less on the Internet, netizens are less concerned about pondering the advantages or problems associated with the introduction of an FTA between South Korea and the United States, and they seem more eager to express or channel their anger against the authorities, whatever their actual faults. This targets one of the pillars of a democratic system: the fact that representatives are, in fact, just representatives—elected officials who, for a fixed period of time, govern the country and are eventually accountable to the electorate. This new type of politics, hereafter called digital populism, calls for a renegotiation of the putative contract between electors and elected.

What Is Populism?

The issues of direct representation and popular participation lie at the very center of populist appeals because "deliberations and secret elections [are] redundant impediments to a direct expression of the popular will."[8] "Populism offers a dichotomous vision of politics and society that places the people in opposition to political elites whose legitimacy is questioned. Europe and Latin America have a long history of populist leaders and parties, and even East Asia has had its fair share of populist leaders: former presidents Chen Shui-bian (of Taiwan) and Roh Moo-hyun (South Korea) and former prime minister Junichiro Koizumi (Japan) have been often characterized as such, often more because of their style of leadership than out of substance.

Scholarship on the subject of populism indicates a pre-supposition of a clear and antagonistic dichotomy between the "pure people" and the "corrupt elite";[9] as a solution, populism proposes an unmediated link between the people and the leader,[10] thus leading to unmediated popular sovereignty.[11] Abts and Rummens argue that populism is mainly concerned with direct participation of "the people." In this light, "deliberations and secret elections" are "redundant impediments to a direct expression of the popular will".[12]

Defining populism is by no means easy. The concept of populism is "difficult and slippery".[13] As a type of behavior, populism has involved various segments of the population, ranging from elites to ordinary people. Often they are not united by strong or cohesive ideological glue (values or interests). The term populism is often used to highlight movements and phenomena that occur from the extreme left to the extreme right end of the ideological spectrum. Taggart describes populism as "an episodic, anti-political, empty-hearted, chameleonic celebration of the heartland in the face of crisis".[14] For Taggart it is a combination of "a movement, leader, regime or idea",[15] and Taggart also notes that "populist movements have systems of belief which are diffuse; they are inherently difficult to control and organize; they lack consistency; and their activity waxes and wanes with a bewildering frequency".[16]

Populism can comprise both elite-driven and mass-initiated political action. For elites, populism has been actively used (or they have been accused of using it) when they tried to attract ordinary people's support. Populism has been seen in many cases in Latin America as well as in many recent popular political leaders such as Tony Blair (in the United Kingdo m), Koizumi, and Roh. Some populists do not mind being called populists.[17] Abts and Rummens identify three main characteristics of populism.[18] First, it entails an antagonistic relationship between "the people" and "the elite".[19] Mudde also defines populism as "an ideology that considers society to be ultimately separated into two homogeneous and antagonistic groups, 'the pure people' versus 'the corrupt elite,' and which argues that politics should be an expression of the volonté générale [general will] of the people".[20]

Second, populism calls for the restoration of popular sovereignty. Populism favors direct democracy, as populists believe democracy should be derived from the power of the people. This ideology based on the people guides populists to reject representative democracy and delegitimize established elites. Zaslove maintains that populist emphasis on popular sovereignty is dangerous, as this threatens "pluralism and democratic representative institutions".[21]

Finally "the people" are understood as constituting a "homogeneous unity".[22] The people are a "non-plural, virtuous, and homogeneous group[s] that are part of the 'everyday' and the 'normal' core of the country".[23] The people being one, it can only have one voice. This reinforces the us-versus-them antagonism that can even lead to overthrowing the established political order.

When Populism Meets Digital Technology

When populist activities take place in a highly developed information technology environment, populism acquires a critical tool that can ease recruitment of like-minded people and mobilize them as well as further intensify social antagonism and witch-hunting behavior. So, when populism meets digital technology, the meeting engenders three main effects that are politically relevant.

First, for the politicians or populist activists the use of the Internet as a political tool provides low-cost (or even free) access to the grassroots, the potential ordinary supporters and voters. Transaction costs are lowered (compared with costs for ordinary recruitment), and the reliance on online networks potentially yields a greater mobilizational capacity as it reaches out to more people at the same time.

Second, the unmediated nature of the means (open discussion boards, chats, and blogs) can lead people to freely and promptly respond to an event or make a comment without pausing for reflection or, more crucially, pausing for acquiring sufficient information or double-checking the information provided. The means become the source of information. Mudde has noted the crucial function of the media in populism: the media gain more independence from the state and depend on the market for their financial support when they tend to focus on "the more extreme and scandalous aspects of politics".[24] The focus on political scandals promotes exactly the type of "anti-elite sentiment" that populist actors seek to create.[25] Ordinary people can now create their own political blogs and upload films, photos, and cartoons. The emergence of influential blogs such as the Huffington Post in the United States and the use of the Internet as a recruitment tool and fund-raising instrument during the recent U.S. electoral campaign are obviously positive developments in the close relationship between Internet and politics.

Finally, immediacy and the lack of mediation—increasingly common in South Korea—allow verbal violence and witch-hunting. After netizens identify a target, a true online war against the enemy can be waged. The government's Web site may be hacked, TV celebrities can become the embodiment of all evil, and ordinary citizens accused of financial frauds true or imagined can be targeted. Moreover, the fact that at present Internet users can hide behind nicknames and hidden identities leaves these attacks mostly unsanctioned. So, how does this all translate in the Korean context?

Populism Korean Style?

The case of former president Roh Moo-hyun's presidential election in 2002 well illustrates the increasing role played by Internet in Korean politics. Roh Moo-hyun was a charismatic leader who became a leading politician despite being only a high school graduate (in a country where a university degree is a must for supporting ambition) and therefore without any university affiliation, a crucial resource in Korean society and politics. Roh Moo-hyun's ascent to prominence dates to the hearing about the corruption assessments of the Fifth Republic in 1988. His man-of-the-street style (and language) toward the formality of President Chun Doo-hwan and other high officials during the "question time" resonated with the TV audience angry at the authoritarian and corrupt government. He soon became the hearing's superstar.

As a person outside the system (no alumni ties, no party background), Roh Moo-hyun could not rely on many supporters within a party when he became a presidential candidate in 2002. His sources of support lay outside the party system, in the "Rohsamo," in other words, the society of people who love Roh Moo-hyun. Rohsamo was a movement consisting of young progressives who made widespread use of the Internet for social purposes as well as, it turned out, political goals. The Rohsamo netizens helped raise funds to support Roh Moo-hyun, and they organized meetings at their own expense. A bottom-up political campaign orchestrated through chats and online discussions contributed to elevate Roh to the presidency.

A second case illustrative of how online discussions turn into street politics occurred on the occasion of the candlelight vigils held when two junior high school students were accidentally killed by a U.S. military vehicle in June 2002. Popular anger against the U.S. military court's decision (which found the U.S. soldiers not guilty because this was an accident during their military duty) continued for several months. What started as protests by younger citizens (even teenagers) turned into political calls for renegotiating Korea's Status of Forces Agreement with the United States.

More recently, new protests started with expressions of disapproval at President Lee Myung-bak's initiative, soon after his election, to introduce a key reform in Korea's education system. The committee working on the reform announced that by 2010 most high school education would be conducted in English. Promoting English-speaking skills among pupils, their argument went, would help solve the problems of parents spending a lot of money on private-tuition education or even sending their children (along with their mothers) abroad to be educated, an increasingly common situation in Korean families. The new term for this kind of situation is *gireogi appa* (a wild goose daddy), referring to a father who travels abroad to see his family but comes back home alone to work. One effect of the policy would have been that students, teachers, and even parents would have had to spend a lot of money and time to learn English in a short period of time. This, the opponents of the initiative maintained, would reinforce the cleavage between the richer and the poorer segments of Korean society, who would inevitably lose out after the change as they could not afford private tuition.

Although protests over this policy initiative had not yet quieted, a new wave of protests broke out. In April 2008 the government announced its signing of the FTA between South Korea and the United States. While the announcement was heralded as an opportunity for Korean businesses to gain even greater access to the U.S. market, frustration and anger were boiling among the people. One of the issues at stake — and definitely the one that most captured the public's imagination and attention — concerned the implications that beef imports would have for the health of the Korean population. Korean objections were based on the possibility that the beef could have been affected by mad-cow disease.

While one may dispute the benefits or disadvantages associated with the FTA per se, what was striking was that the protests grew out of rumors such as "Korean genes are especially exposed and vulnerable to mad-cow disease," "Americans do not eat American beef; instead they import beef from Australia or New Zealand," "In the United States beef from cattle older than 30 months is not used even for dog or cat food," "Beef for domestic users in the United States is different from the beef exported to Korea," and "In the United States there are five million Alzheimer's patients; among those, 250,000 to 650,000 patients are assumed to be suffering from mad-cow disease".[26]

Rumors are common in most societies and, of course, are not alien to political affairs. However, these kinds of rumors received considerable attention (one may say support) from the Korean media in, for example, the major current affairs TV program, PD Sucheop [Producer's Note] on 29 April 2008 when it aired a broadcast on mad-cow disease. Later in 2008 the program, which included erroneous reports over the mad-cow issue, was criticized for its strongly antigovernment agenda. During National Assembly hearings on FTA-related incidents in Korea, one member of the Grand National Party accused the TV program of being a main source of rumors.[27]

The PD Sucheop broadcast led to an emotional reaction. Rumors fed other rumors, including that cheap, imported beef from the United States would be used for school lunches for children. Fear for children's health caused a panic that led to the candlelight vigils. Online discussion boards were dominated by this one issue, and Internet bloggers uploaded the PD Sucheop program on their Web sites. The program circulated more and more, gaining an even wider audience receptive of the groundless rumors. This appeared to be especially popular among teenagers, generating many satirical short movies and cartoons among youngsters.[28] A high school student suggested in an internet discussion café that there should be a presidential impeachment; within three days the Web site received a million visitors (and supporters) who signed an online call for presidential impeachment.[29] The vigils were initially peaceful and often rather like a festival, with entertainers singing and dancing. This festival-like atmosphere came to an end when protests became more violent and were met by riot police and a government crackdown.

The real origins of the rumors that stimulated the candle-light vigils (PD Sucheop; or the mainstream media such as Chosun Ilbo, Donga Ilbo, Jungang Ilbo; or even inexperienced government officials) are still disputed. MBC (Munhwa Broadcasting Corporation) and KBS (Korea Broadcasting System) are state-run companies, and many of the high officials within the companies were appointed by the previous governments and held progressive views. Thus, many current-affairs programs seemed to promote an antigovernment political agenda.

The aim of this paper is not to judge the rights or wrongs of the wave of popular protests or whether this was a democratic or even desirable way of expressing dis-satisfaction with the government. Popular protests and uprisings have played crucial roles in bringing authoritarian rules to their end, and they have contributed to democratization. The problem here is that the candlelight vigils showed strong elements of what can be termed digital populism, namely a new type of political behavior marked by the use of the

Internet as both a form of direct political participation and an instrument of social mobilization.

The three dimensions of populist behavior referred to earlier lead to the hypothesis that what happened earlier this year in the streets of Korean cities well conforms to this type of political phenomenon. Protests were articulated along a line that set into opposition ordinary citizens and elites (elites whom, incidentally, the citizens had elected a few months earlier) in a way that construed the two groups as enemies and thus available for all possible attacks. Citizens were portrayed as a homogenous group (us), allegedly representing not only common sense (Who would want to have their children poisoned by unhealthy beef?) but also the so-called true majority. Protests, online and on the streets, represented the way to restore popular sovereignty and will that had been lost to the unrepresentative government institutions. In addition, the populist narrative could count on a powerful instrument: the Internet. Spreading news and recruiting additional protesters were made easy and cheap via the popularity of blogs and chats that reduced significantly the cost of getting out the news of meetings (times and venues).

Thus, the Lee Myung-bak administration plunged into political paralysis. Support for the Lee administration after the presidential election did not last even three months. The representative system of the National Assembly and the politicians within it could not play a mediating role between the state and the citizens; the angry citizens marched to the Blue House to talk with the president directly, and police officers aligned containers on the main road leading to the Blue House as a way to fence off protesters.[30]

Conclusion

A paradox is becoming increasingly common in South Korea: the more widespread the access to information technology, the more opportunities citizens have to participate in politics, make their voices heard, and become politically active. This is certainly positive in cases where e-government links rulers and ruled and where political campaigns recruit and mobilize those who would not otherwise take part, let alone vote. However, the riots associated with candlelight vigils and the acrimony that has accompanied online debates also show a less benign face of this phenomenon.

As I noted elsewhere, the South Korean political party system suffers from a low level of institutionalization.[31] This is problematic because it affects the way in which citizens connect (or not) with political parties as the intermediary organizations between themselves and the government. Parties lose their linkage role with ordinary citizens, opening the space for alternative means for popular participation. The Internet offers such an opportunity for direct, unmediated participation.

The decline in the linkage role of representative organizations and the availability of an immediate and low-cost instrument for voicing unrestricted opinions pose a challenge to representative democracy, as Mudde notes, citing Ralf Dahrendorf when he says, "one's populism is someone else's democracy, and vice versa".[32] As digital technology allows more people to access direct political debates with politicians or even presidential blogs, home pages, and e-government facilities, digital populism seems to bring revolutionary direct participation into politics. As Abts and Rummens note, some scholars have analysed populism "as a means to reveal and even amend the shortcomings and the broken promises of the representative system".[33] Moreover, "[i]t can bring back the disruptive noise of the people and thus prevent the closure of the formal political system".[34] However this very same phenomenon is also referred to as "a pathological form of democracy"[35] or "dangerous threat to democracy"[36], given that direct participation aims to bypass the allegedly flawed representative institutions.

The Internet is playing an increasingly influential role in shaping Korean public and political life, from the campaign that led to the election of Roh Moo-hyun as president in 2002 to the candlelight vigils in the spring of 2008. This of course is not unique to Korea. What is peculiar to Korea is the scale of the phenomenon and the extent to which online political debates have become vicious and abusive, as well as the speed with which online discussions have been taken into the streets. Policy debates are now ongoing as to how to tackle the issue most effectively, but there appears to be no easy way to address the challenge that digital populism poses to a democratic society that is caught between the choices of imposing restrictions to freedom of speech and dealing with the emotional and often abusive behavior of an unchecked minority.

Endnotes

1   This includes several celebrities such as, more recently, Choi Jin-sil (in 2008) and Lee Eun-ju (in 2005), who committed suicide partly as a result of the uncontrolled rumors circulated on the Web over their personal lives. This is now called "cyber terror."
2   See Zaslove, A. 2008. "Here to Stay? Populism as a New Party Type," *European Review*. Volume 16, Number 3. Pp. 319-36. Abts, K. & S. Rummens. 2007. "Populism versus Democracy." *Political Studies*. Volume 55. Pp. 405-24. Mudde, C. 2004. "The Populist Zeitgeist." *Government and Opposition*. Volume 29. Pp. 541-63. Canovan, M. 2002. "Talking Politics to the People: Populism as the Ideology of Democracy." In Y. Mény & Y. Surel (Eds.) *Democracies and the Populist Challenge*. Houndmills: Palgrave.
3   Norris, P. 2001. *Digital Divide: Civic Engagement, Information Poverty, and the Internet Worldwide*. Cambridge: Cambridge University Press.
4   Candlelight vigils have been a regular feature of Korean politics since 2002. They were initially held to commemorate two students killed by a U.S. army vehicle that year. Online chats formed an important resource from which former president Roh Moo-hyun drew to gather support during his 2002 electoral campaign. Then, when Roh became president

and faced presidential impeachment, netizens moved beyond virtual politics and took to the streets to protest, arguably contributing to the failure of the motion to impeach.
5   The FTA agreement was in fact a legacy from the previous progressive administration.
6   The agreements allowed the import of beef that could come from animals 30 months old; bones and organs would also be imported to South Korea.
7   2MB originally stood for a computer's memory capacity but is now also used as president Lee Myung-bak's nickname. His family name (Lee) in Korean has same sound as 2 (ee) in Korean; MB are his initials. Agora is an Internet discussion café where anyone can register and express personal thoughts and opinions freely. Members of Agora are called as Agorians; this Internet café played a crucial role in organizing offline the candlelight vigils.
8   Abts & Rummens, "Populism versus Democracy," 417.
9   Mudde, "The Populist Zeitgeist."
10   Taggart, P. 2002. *Populism*. Buckingham: Palgrave.
11   Zaslove, "Here to Stay? Populism as a New Party Type."
12   Abts & Rummens, "Populism versus Democracy," 417.
13   Taggart, *Populism*, 2.
14   Taggart, *Populism*, 5.
15   Taggart, *Populism*, 5.
16   Taggart, *Populism*, 1.
17   Taggart, *Populism*, 8.
18   Abts & Rummens, "Populism versus Democracy," 408.
19   Canovan, "Talking Politics to the People"; Mudde, "The Populist Zeitgeist."
20   Mudde, "The Populist Zeitgeist."
21   Zaslove, "Here to Stay? Populism as a New Party Type," 321.
22   Canovan, M. 1999. "Trust the People! Populism and the Two Faces of Democracy." *Political Studies*. Volume 47, Number 1. Pp. 2-16. Taggart, *Populism*, cited in Abts & Rummens, "Populism versus Democracy," 408.
23   Zaslove, "Here to Stay? Populism as a New Party Type," 322.
24   Mudde, "The Populist Zeitgeist," 553.
25   Mudde, "The Populist Zeitgeist," 553.
26   Korea National Strategy Institute, http://knsi.org/~knsiorg/knsi/kor/center/view.php?no=5596&k=2&c=6.
27   Donga Ilbo, 5 September 2008.
28   Sports Hankook, 30 April 2008.
29   Sisa Journal, 15 July 2008.
30   This street blockade gained the popular nickname, "Myung-bak sanseong [walls]" or "Castle MB" (Hankyoreh, 22 June 2008).
31   Young-mi, Kim. 2008. "Intra-Party Politics and Minority Coalition Government in South Korea." *Japanese Journal of Political Science*. Volume 9, Number 3. Pp. 367-89.
32   Mudde, "The Populist Zeitgeist," 543.
33   Bobbio, N. 1987. *The Future of Democracy*. Cambridge: Polity. Hayward, J. 1996. "The Populist Challenge to Elitist Democracy in Europe." In J. Hayward (Ed.) *Elitism, Populism and European Politics*. Oxford: Clarendon Press. Pp. 10-32. Taggart, P. 2002. "Populism and the Pathology of Representative Politics." In Y. Mény & Y. Surel (Eds) *Democracies and the Populist Challenge*. New York: Palgrave. Pp. 62–80. Taggart, P. 2004. "Populism and Representative Politics in Contemporary Europe." *Journal of Political Ideologies*. Volume 9, Number 3. Pp. 269-88. Cited in Abts & Rummens 2007, 405.
34   Arditi, B. 2003. "Populism, or Politics at the Edges of Democracy." *Contemporary Politics*, Volume 9, Number 1. P. 26. Cited in Abts & Rummens 2007, 405-406.
35   Mudde (Quoting Taguieff P. 1995. "Political Science Confronts Populism: From a Conceptual Mirage to a Real Problem." *Telos*, Volume 103. P. 43), "The Populist Zeitgeist," 541.
36   Abts & Rummens, "Populism versus Democracy," 407.

Annotation

Sumandro Chattapadhyay

"The penetration of the Internet in Korean society is usually seen as a positive development..."

It is absolutely exciting to discuss the cultures of the Internet in the Republic of Korea, or South Korea, for two reasons at the very least—it is the country with the highest global average Internet connection speed (at 22.2 Megabytes per Second), and it is a country of legal and technological censorship of digital content (especially of the political kind) and violation of network neutrality to provide preferential treatment to domestic websites. The use of the word 'usually' must be read in this context.

The exploration of 'digital populism' in online political discourse in South Korea that we are about to read is situated in the aftermath of the signing of the Free Trade Agreement between the United States of America and South Korea in 2008. The signing of the Agreement led to physical protests on the streets as well as widespread political uproar and mobilisations through social media networks. These online political acts deserve to be read in reference to the then-prevailing system of regulation of freedom of expression across media channels in the country. Article 21 of the Korean constitution lays down the guarantee of freedom of speech and press of the citizens, while also clarifying that such speech acts may not undermine 'public morals or social ethics.' These constraints on the freedom of expression are further emphasised in the Telecommunications Business Act of 1991, which got revised by the Supreme Court in 2002 so as to expand the meaning of 'harmful content' and the government's ability to redefine the same. Various other laws addressing particular topics, like national security, or population groups, like the youth, also add to the legal instruments available for regulation of online discourse.

In February 2008, after the Presidential election that brought Lee Myung-bak into power, a new body named the Korea Communications Standards Commission (KCSC) was created as part of the media censorship reform. KCSC was given the task to receive complaints regarding the political, moral, and ethical standards of web-based content, and if found unsuitable, to stop access to the content either by ensuring that the content provider deletes the content concerned, or to suspend access to the same for a month at the least. The same government also made it mandatory for websites with greater than ten thousand visitors in a day to ensure that all visitors use their real names and social security numbers to create user accounts with the website. By July 2008, 'cyber-defamation' was approved by the Ministry of Justice as a category of crime for which creators of web-based content that may insult any person or organisation can be imprisoned or fined.

"After netizens identify a target, a true online war against the enemy can be waged... Moreover, the fact that at present Internet users can hide behind nicknames and hidden identities leaves these attacks mostly unsanctioned."

The topic of 'anonymity' has a complex relationship with democratic politics, and it is also one of the central problematics of our essay. On one hand, anonymity protects a citizen from being identified with particular views or actions (that may be critical of the authorities that be) and then getting ostracised for the same. So anonymity may allow citizens to truly express their opinions. On the other hand, being anonymous means that the person concerned will not have to face any consequences for her/his views or actions. This may lead to easy abuse of the *freedom* (from consequences) that anonymity offers. Further, anonymity may make it impossible to understand from which population or social group a view or action is coming. In other words, anonymity may allow for masquerading – maybe the already-empowered and already-articulate classes will capture the instruments of expression at the cost of those who are less able to use the same. Gabriella Coleman introduces the idea of the 'weapons of the geek' to talk about such usages of anonymity, when actors from the literate and privileged classes use computational skills to undertake politically transgressive acts, hidden under digital masks, so as to test out the "new possibilities and legal limits for digital civil disobedience."

"The problem here is that the candlelight vigils showed strong elements of what can be termed digital populism, namely a new type of political behavior marked by the use of the Internet as both a form of direct political participation and an instrument of social mobilization."

Let us sidestep the anatomy of 'digital populism' or 'populism' in general that the essay delineates, and ask if this is really a 'new type of political behaviour'? If so, what exactly is the 'new' thing here? And why is it a matter of concern? In recent public memory in India, a key encounter between populism and the Internet took place during the India Against Corruption movement in 2011-2012. The movement began with a demand that central and state governments institute overseeing ombudsman authorities (called 'Lokpal' in Hindi) that will be able to autonomously investigate and arrest government officials for charges of corruption and abuse of official powers. The movement touched a raw nerve of Indians, gathered a wide cross section of the society in sites and websites of protests, and used Internet-based communication very effectively to organise on-ground activities as well as to dominate cyber-conversations. At times, both the supporters and the critics of the movement agreed that it is 'populist': the former used the word to appreciate how it directly channels a political demand coming across the population and social groups of the country, and the latter used the word to undermine the same demand as an impractical or unrealisable one, or worse, as a demand of specific social groups that masquerade as a general demand of the whole population. Both these readings of 'populism' also agreed that the movement is anti-institutional; it is interested in political articulations outside institutional frameworks available in the country.

It is on this quality of the Internet, as simultaneously institutionalised and making possible extra- and anti-institutional articulations and exchanges, that one should perhaps focus to think about the 'new' possibilities of anti-institutional politics that it has created. We remember that on one hand, the Internet is a highly technologically-determined space of mediation under surveillance-by-design; but on the other, it is a space of endless possibilities of anonymous activities, connectivity failures, leakages, break-ins, data loss, disc corruption, and administrative and physical limitations of storage of information.

References and Further Readings

2012. "Country Profiles – South Korea." OpenNet Initiative. Accessed May 27, 2015. https://opennet.net/research/profiles/south-korea.
2014. "Countries with the Highest Average Internet Connection Speed as of 4th Quarter 2014 (in Mbps)." Statista. Accessed May 27, 2015. http://www.statista.com/statistics/204952/average-internet-connection-speed-by-country/.
2015. "Internet in South Korea." Wikipedia. June 12. Accessed June 16, 2015. https://en.wikipedia.org/wiki/Internet_in_South_Korea.
2015. "Internet Censorship in South Korea." Wikipedia. May 10. Accessed May 27, 2015. https://en.wikipedia.org/wiki/Internet_censorship_in_South_Korea.
Coleman, Gabriella. 2013. *Anonymous in Context: The Politics and Power behind the Mask*. The Centre for International Governance Innovation. Accessed May 27, 2015. https://www.cigionline.org/sites/default/files/no3_8.pdf.
Maass, Dave. 2013. "Online Anonymity Is Not Only for Trolls and Political Dissidents." Electronic Frontier Foundation. October 29. Accessed May 27, 2015. https://www.eff.org/deeplinks/2013/10/online-anonymity-not-only-trolls-and-political-dissidents.
Obsolete Capitalism (ed). 2015. *The Birth of Digital Populism. Crowd, Power and Postdemocracy in the 21st Century*. Obsolete Capitalism Free Press. Accessed May 27, 2015. http://obsoletecapitalism.blogspot.no/2015/01/obsolete-capitalism-out-now-birth-of.html.
Prakash, Gyan. 2011. "On Populism—A Response to Partha and Aditya." Kafila. September 1. Accessed on May 27, 2015. http://kafila.org/2011/09/01/on-populism-%E2%80%93-a-response-to-partha-and-aditya-gyan-prakash/

Many Clicks but Little Sticks: Social Media Activism in Indonesia

Merlyna Lim

In November 2010, a CNN Tech report designated Indonesia – a country mostly known for "sandy beaches, palm trees, and smiling inhabitants" – a "Twitter Nation" in reference to a ComScore report (2010) where Indonesia was dubbed the most Twitter-addicted nation on the planet. CNN reporter Sara Sidner (2010) enthusiastically pointed out: "Indonesia is crazy about online social networking ... but all the Tweeting, texting, and typing is not just for fun. It is also being used as a tool for change." CNN is not alone in highlighting the importance of social media in generating an unprecedented social movement within Indonesia's "online social networking-addict" society (Shubert 2009). Two successful social media activisms in Indonesia are most often mentioned in making this point: the so-called gecko vs. crocodile case (or the KPK case) and the Prita Mulyasari libel case (the Prita case). In the first, Facebook was used to support anti-corruption deputies, symbolised by a gecko, in their fight against Indonesia's senior police detective, symbolised by a crocodile. Beyond the online realm, Facebook supporters brought their activism to the streets in a show of support for the gecko and successfully forced the government to act in accordance with public demands and drop the anti-corruption charges.

The second case refers to the Facebook movement to support Prita Mulyasari, a 32-year-old mother of two who fought for justice after being prosecuted for libel when she complained about service at a private hospital in an email to friends and relatives. Tens of thousands of Indonesians joined a support page for Mulyasari on Facebook, shared their outrage on Twitter, and donated money to pay her court-imposed fine.

Echoing CNN, some observers say that social media is furthering democracy and freedom of speech, calling it democratising content (Sutadi 2011), "the fifth estate in Indonesian's democracy" (Enda Nasution cited in Lutfia 2010), and a civil society's tool for social change (Nugroho 2011). Does social media merit these accolades? If social media is really a tool for social change and democracy, why are there not many other successful cases of social activism from Indonesia? Why were these cases successful and others not? Social media activism has a tendency for being fast, thin and many. In other words, online campaigns emerge each minute and often quickly disappear without any trace. The result can be many clicks, not equally distributed for each and every cause, but little sticks in the sense that very few causes make for mass activism in an online environment.

Public discussion of the political implications of social media in some ways reinforces earlier debates on the supposed democratising nature of the internet. At the heart of the debate about whether social media is furthering democracy is the concept of participation. Two streams dominate the discourse. The first focuses on the ongoing and growing concerns about public participation (or lack thereof) in modern democracies where online activism is often perceived as banal, superficial and failing to transform or renew democratic institutions (see, for example, Morozov 2009; Shulman 2009; Gladwell 2010). Along with this sceptical view, terms such as slacktivism (lazy activism), clicktivism (click activism), armchair activism and keyboard activism emerged to question the worthiness of digital activism, often deeming it subordinate to "real" (physical) activism. The second stream focuses on the rise of new forms of participation in public life, enabled by emerging new technologies, particularly the internet and social media, which promote a more enlightened exchange of ideas, transform political debates, increase levels of citizen engagement, enable societal change and reform political systems (see, for example, Kamarck and Nye 1999; Rheingold 2002; Kahn and Kellner 2004; Shirky 2011). These dichotomised views are partial at best. They simplify the complexity and dynamics of the relationship between social media and its users. Our understanding of both the democratic potentials and the impacts of the internet and social media requires going beyond the binary oppositions of utopian versus dystopian. The social impacts of the internet and media, or "change" in society, should be understood as a result of the organic interaction between technology and social, political, and cultural structures and relationships (Lim 2012a).

So, what is social media capable of facilitating in the context of participatory politics? How do we locate social media in the discourse of democracy?

Unquestionably, social media possesses the conviviality of its predecessor, the internet. Characterised by convergence, low cost, broad availability and reasonable resistance to and censorship, the internet is a "convivial medium" (Lim 2003, 274). As such, it provides "a greater scope for freedom, autonomy, creativity, and collaboration than previous media" (Lim and Kann 2008, 82).

Social media inherits these characteristics and pushes for even greater collaboration and social interactivity. Beyond the old internet, social media facilitates "organic content, distributed processing and interaction, and converging media format" (Andreas 2007, 2). This "new" internet has broken the usual pattern of media production and consumption. It is no longer a media by which dispersed individual consumers retrieve content from centralised media producers. Instead, social media "operates as an interdependent grassroots community of individuals, organisations, and sites whose relevance and authority are established through interaction and participation" (Andreas 2007, 2). However, social media should not be perceived as a causal agent having a pivotal role in promoting social change or advancing democracy. There is nothing intrinsic in social media that automatically achieves this potential. Societal contexts and arrangements around the technology are key to its impact on politics (Lim 2012a).

Using both successful and unsuccessful cases of social media activism in Indonesia as an empirical framework, I call for a much more critical approach to the promise of social media. Rather than dismissing social media activism as mere "slacktivism" (some repertoires of online activisms, such as online petition, are meant to generate clicks; they do not necessarily need to translate into the streets to be meaningful) or applauding it as the forerunner of social change in the contemporary society, I provide a more nuanced argument by revealing the complexity of social media activism and identifying the conditions under which participation in social media might lead to successful political activism. I argue that social media does not inadvertently generate an ideal public sphere in which effective and robust public participation takes place. Social media enables multiple and diverse networked spheres to emerge. While not aiming to advance and deepen democracy, these contested spheres allow individuals to have a greater participation, culturally and socially. Under certain conditions, social and cultural participation in social media spheres may translate into civic or political engagement. As we will see throughout the article, such translation, however, is neither automatic nor unproblematic.

The cases presented in this article seek to provide a new framework to elucidate the linkage between participation in social media and populist political activism (online, offline, or a combination of the two), namely that for the former to translate into the latter it needs to embrace the principles of contemporary culture of consumption: light package (content that can be enjoyed without spending too much time, can be understood without deep reflection, and usually has a hype-based component), headline appetite (a condition where information is condensed to accommodate a short attention span and one liner conversations) and trailer vision (an oversimplified, hyped and sensationalised story rather than a substantial one or the oversimplified representation of actual information). In other words, only simple or simplified narratives can usually go viral. At the same time, simple or simplified narratives are associated with low risk activism and are congruent with ideological meta-narratives, such as nationalism and religiosity, have a much higher chance to go viral and generate massive activism. Success is less likely when the narrative is contested by dominant competing narratives generated in mainstream media.

Social Media in Indonesia

Before investigating the dynamic relationship between social media and politics in Indonesia, it is important to delve into the background knowledge on the social media in the country. While the internet serves only 55 million out of a total population of 240 million (in 2012), Indonesia has witnessed a tremendous growth in social media usage, with 90% of online activities devoted to browsing social networking sites (Galih and Ngazis 2012). Indonesia had become the third largest nation on Facebook (SocialBakers 2012) with 43 million users and fifth on Twitter with 29.4 million users (Semiocast 2012). The blogosphere has grown rapidly from only 15,000 bloggers in 2007 to 5 million as of 2011.

With such expansion, some might expect social media to be utilised greatly for political and social events. Previous studies, indeed, demonstrate that the internet has had some major political roles in Indonesian society. Under Suharto's regime, the internet and its physical nodes – the warnet (cyber café) – had become a free space of resistance for middle-class Indonesians (Lim 2003). During the reformation struggle against Suharto, warnet was the major source of "forbidden" information (Lim 2003) and, consequently, the internet appeared as a medium for civil society to challenge the state (Hill and Sen 2005; Lim 2006). In the political history of Indonesia, the internet had acted as a "cyber-civic space" in which individuals and groups generate collective activism online and translate it into real-world movements in an offline setting (Lim 2006). By being convivial, the internet is also friendly to uncivil activism as exemplified in the ethno-religious conflict in Maluku, where the internet functioned as a site for the revival of primordial, ethno-religious and communal identities (Brauechler 2005).

With the recent expansion of the Indonesian blogosphere, the internet continued to retain its socio-political importance. The blogosphere, as exemplified in the cases of the anti-pornography law and the movie Fitna, has opened a novel path for participation in political discourse and a space for assimilating experiences and voicing opinions (Lim 2009; 2012b). Does social media retain the internet's trajectory in politics?

Social media is about social relations and social networking. Accordingly, networks created in social media resemble those existing offline. Individuals are clustered based on age, interests and other social and cultural commonalities. Most Indonesians under 25 naturally do not occupy the same networks as their elders. They are drawn to different groups, interests, issues and conversations. They blog about their music idols, fashion trends, their favourite sinetron (soap operas) or romance. On Facebook and Twitter they post links of global teenage pop sensations and Indonesian stars.

While occupying a set of different networks, the previous generation is not necessarily political. Indonesians over 30 also use social media mostly to interact with each other and to maintain relationship with past friends from high school and college. Parents mostly blog about about their children and use Facebook to broadcast their children's activities, share parenting tips, post photos of their children, the places they go, and the food they eat or make. Adult males use Facebook and Twitter to broadcast their "important" activities and achievements. They are also interested in popular culture, although their favourites are not those of the teenagers.

While political content exists, it is located on the fringe of social activities. In the blogosphere, some of the top Indonesian bloggers are political bloggers who are largely disconnected from other types of bloggers. The growth of social media, Facebook in particular, introduces a new dynamic. Generally, individuals are still socially clustered within groups. In Facebook, however, users usually belong to multiple overlapping networks.

This multiplicity is much more transparent than in offline settings. The infrastructure of Facebook can connect disparate social groups by breaking the walls separating them. Two questions arise: Can this collapse of networks create a new type of issue diffusion? Does it create a possible path of convergence between participatory popular culture and civic engagement?

Participatory Culture to Civic Engagement?

Social media provides a space for individuals, especially the youth, to participate in the act of consumption as well as in the production and distribution of ideas, knowledge and culture. This very act of participation is called participatory culture and it is manifested in affiliation, expression, collaboration, distribution and circulation (Jenkins et al. 2009). According to Jenkins and colleagues (2009), this participatory culture can serve as an infrastructure that may readily be borrowed and used by socio-political activities and transformed into civic engagement. While I agree that such transformation is possible, using Indonesian cases I argue that it is neither straightforward nor easy. The cases illustrate that social media is biased towards a certain type of movement/cause. As will be explained in the later sections, those that may translate into civic engagement are of simple or simplified narratives that impersonate popular culture, associated with low risk activism, not incongruent with dominant ideological narratives, and uncontested by powerful alternative framing in mainstream media.

Two Successful Movements: KPK and Prita Cases

The first case is the Facebook movement to support the Corruption Eradication Committee – the "Gecko vs. Crocodile" case, and the second is the successful mass movement to support Prita – the Prita case. These two cases exemplify the convergence of participatory culture and civic engagement that resulted in two of the most successful online collective movements in the last decade in Indonesia.

Gecko vs. Crocodile

The Gecko vs. Crocodile case (or KPK case) started in April 2009 when Susno Duadji, the National Police chief of detectives, found that the Corruption Eradication Commission (Komite Pengentasan Korupsi, or KPK) had tapped his phone while they were investigating a corruption case. Indeed, KPK had armed itself with tools, such as warrantless wiretaps, to confront the endemic corruption among high rank public officials. In a press conference, Duadji expressed his anger and compared the KPK to cicak, a common house gecko, fighting buaya, a crocodile, which symbolises the police. In September 2009 two KPK deputy chairmen Chandra Hamzah and Bibit Samad Rianto, who had been suspended in July, were arrested on charges of extortion and bribery. The two men denied the charges, saying they were being framed to weaken the KPK. Most Indonesians perceived these charges as fabricated ones; some showed their support through an online campaign.

In July 2009 immediately after the case against KPK appeared in the mainstream media, especially television, Gerakan 1,000,000 Facebookers Dukung Chandra Hamzah & Bibit Samad Riyanto (Movement of 1,000,000 Facebookers Supporting Chandra Hamzah & Bibit Samad Riyanto)[1] was launched. By August 2009, the group has surpassed its goal of one million members in support of Bibit and Chandra. That particular Facebook support page was not the only one. Various other pages supporting KPK also emerged.[2] The slogan of CICAK – meaning gecko but also an abbreviation of Cinta Indonesian CintA Kpk (Love Indonesia Love KPK) – symbolising the support for KPK, appeared everywhere online. The first line of a KPK jingle says "KPK di dadaku, KPK kebanggaanku," meaning KPK is in my chest, KPK is my pride, was catchy for broad online dissemination.[3] YouTube videos about the case quickly emerged, including one with a Javanese rap song that was also distributed as a downloadable ring-tone. Online cartoons, comics and posters with depictions of "gecko vs.

crocodile" soon proliferated online. When the Indonesian Corruption Watch organised a street rally online, 5,000 Facebookers showed up on the streets of Jakarta showing support for "the gecko." This was followed by demonstrations in several other cities in support of the two men. On December 3, 2009, this public pressure saw charges against Bibit and Chandra dropped.

Case 2: Coins for Prita

Prita Mulyasari was ordered by Tangerang High Court to pay a Rp 204 million (around US$22,000) fine for defaming the Omni International Hospital in Jakarta. The defamation suit was a reaction to an email complaint sent by Prita to her friends and relatives about bad service at the hospital. Hospital lawyers accused Prita of violating the Information and Electronic Transaction Law (Indonesia's "cyber law"). The accusation led to Prita's arrest in May 2009 when she was detained for three weeks. Her case was reported in the media and was quickly disseminated online. Bloggers were outraged to learn that a nursing mother was jailed for sending an email complaint and they started publicly protesting in the blogosphere. Due to public pressure, Prita was released from prison. In July 2009 the court reopened the case as Prita's doctors at the Omni Hospital succeeded in convincing the prosecutors to challenge her release. The Tangerang High Court found Prita guilty of defaming her doctors. The court ordered her to pay a fine and sentenced her to six months in prison.

While bloggers who write on political and social issues are mostly from an older generation and had tapped into this case from May 2009, the case did not get the attention of the younger population until it was diffused through social networking sites, especially Facebook. Once the Facebook support page was setup with the idea of contributing 500 rupiahs (~ US5 cents) to the fine – the "Coins for Prita"[4] – the movement took off and many more Facebook pages emerged. Posters were created and disseminated online and many Facebookers made the poster their profile picture. Some YouTube videos showcasing sentimental ballads for Prita also emerged.

It is important to note that while the movement began online, mainstream media channels, especially commercial television stations, played an important role in popularising the case. After being broadcast on television, the number of fans of the "Coins for Prita" Facebook pages saw exponential growth. The mainstream media coverage amplified the Prita case and expanded the "Coins for Prita" movement. The "Coins for Prita" campaign launched in Jakarta soon spread to other cities, such as Bandung, Surabaya, Yogyakarta, and even to other islands. Indonesian communities abroad, such as students in the Netherlands, also contributed to the campaign. Some coins were donated through electronic bank transfer in the form of "electronic" coins, some coins were sent delivered directly in person and sent by mail. The collection of coins that took place from December 5 to 14 in 2009 gathered around US$90,000, far exceeding the fine. When the court decided that Prita was not guilty on December 29, 2009, the money was donated to a charity organisation to help other "Pritas."

Leveraging Infrastructure

How can Facebook create a pathway for participatory culture to transform into civic engagement? From the infrastructure point of view, this pathway is made possible with Facebook's propensity to promote radical transparency and to diffuse issues in multiple weak-tie networks. As opposed to strong social ties, corresponding to family and close friendship, weak ties are less binding, involving acquaintance and loose/distant friendship that, as argued by Granovetter (1973, 1366), provide platforms and structures for better access to information and opportunities.

Involuntary, Radical Transparency

Unlike older platforms, such as mailing lists, forums, or even blogs, on Facebook consuming information is not always a voluntary act. In the blogosphere, for example, an interaction between bloggers and their readers requires a voluntary act of reading and commenting. On Facebook, such an act of reading or "glancing" is not always voluntary. When everything is thrown at you on your Facebook wall the possibility of cross-reading, cross-listening and cross-watching, which might lead to cross communication between strangers (you and your second-degree network), is high.

The communication between a user and her/his "friends" has become transparent in the sense that everybody can also read the communication. Of course, technically one has a choice to filter which contents are available to which groups. But such a choice is neither explicit nor easy to recognise. The core of the Facebook infrastructure, in Kirkpatrick's (2010, 210) term, is "radical transparency" which revolves around the Facebook founder Mark Zuckerberg's conviction that people, and even society, will be better off if they make themselves transparent. Ironically, while Facebook forces its users to be transparent, the company itself lacks of transparency, especially in its treatment of individual data and users' privacy.

Such "radical transparency" is almost unavoidable. Unlike the old internet where individuals could be anonymous and liberated from conformity, as reflected in the old adage "on the internet nobody knows you are a dog," on Facebook "everybody knows you are a dog." It brings back users to the "small town" dynamics where everybody knows your business. However, this forced transparency easily leads to forced conformity as it generates peer pressure among interconnected users. Bak and Kessler's (2012) research on Facebook users shows that conformity is highest among frequent Facebook users. Likewise, Egebark and Ekstrom (2011) found that even though people do not communicate face to face, conforming behaviour exists among Facebook users and it stems from the fact that a large number of users can observe each other's actions.

In the cases of Prita and KPK, some online participants admitted that their participation in the movements began after they saw many of their Facebook friends joined the causes announced in their walls. Teen users were particularly driven to accept such an invitation to join the cause. One middle school student confessed, "I kept getting invitation to join the [KPK] movement, like a dozen times. I also saw that most of my friends had joined, so I joined" (interview with Lala, Jakarta, January 6, 2010). Another student commented, "I quickly joined the Prita cause because one of the boys I know, the cool one, had joined," implying that he, too, would look as cool as he showed his participation in his Facebook wall (interview with Andi, Jakarta, January 6, 2010). Certainly not everybody joined these causes because of peer pressure or the pressure to conform. Some joined for different reasons, as will be explained shortly later.

Issue Diffusion in Multiple Networks of Weak Ties

With Facebook, the act of writing creating and reading-watching-listening is changed to joining and sharing. It needs only one click of the "like" button to gain a membership to a Facebook page. The act of sharing can be done without any self-production, by sharing content on others' walls by simply clicking the "share" button. The infrastructure of Facebook also expands conversations from one-to-one to the combination of one-to-one, one-to-many and many-to-many all of which happens simultaneously in public. Interactivity easily shifts from two-way to multiple ways. For example, from writing and commenting to multiple steps of commenting: commenting on the comments about a comment (status), creating the "I know that you know that I know you know" network.

The effortlessness of sharing, joining and interacting makes it easy to diffuse information in multiple and overlapping networks. In fact, one cannot isolate an issue to a certain social group, as it would always travel in multiple directions penetrating several and various networks and groups. In both cases under study, some participants mentioned that an invitation from random Facebook friends had made them aware of the issue. They also stated that they received more than one invitation on the same cause from different types of "friends" thus seemingly increasing the cause's importance.

Unlike friends in offline settings, which are based on strong ties, a Facebook "friending" can often based on weak ties. Facebook encourages the rise and expansion of weak-tie networks. Granovetter's (1973) theory of "the strength of weak ties" provides an explanation of the process by which micro-level interactions on Facebook affect macro level phenomena, such as in the online mobilisation of the Prita and KPK cases. Granovetter (1973, 1376) argues that "weak ties are more likely to link members of different small groups than are strong ones, which tend to be concentrated within particular groups." Even though on the individual level weak ties have weaker absolute impact, they can potentially "unlock and expose interpersonal networks to external influences [from] individuals in distant networks" (Goldenberg, Libai, and Muller 2001, 213) to provide a trajectory for the spread of information to the masses.

Framing the Movement

As mentioned previously, the infrastructure of Facebook makes it easier to spread information and diffuse a cause. However, this does not provide any assurance that an issue would travel far and wide or that any Facebook-based mobilisation would be successful. What else should be done to ensure the successful convergence of popular participatory culture and civic engagement? One key element contributing to the success is how the movements are framed.

For social movement scholars, the concept of "frame" is significant in explaining how meaning is constructed to legitimise collective activities and actions (Gamson 1992). Originating in the work of Goffman (1974, 21), frames indicate "schemata of interpretation" that allow individuals "to locate, perceive, identify, and label" events and experiences in their life space and the world. By rendering events meaningful, frames function to organise and guide actions (Snow et al. 1986). Frames for collective action perform this function by simplifying the reasons for and rationales of participation. Beyond usual social movement framing, to be successful in social media, movements need to frame themselves to impersonate successful viral stories in mainstream popular culture.

Simplification of the Narrative

Not every issue is widely diffused. In the social media environment, networks are vast, the content is over-abundant, attention spans short and conversations are parsed into short incomplete sentences instead of complete paragraphs. This circumstance is evident in Indonesia, where a majority of social media users access the networking platform from mobile phones. In such an environment, those that go "viral" are of a light package, they tap into headline appetites and they embrace a trailer vision. In other words, only simple or simplified narratives can usually go viral.

While the two cases represented complex problems, news producers, journalists and social media users framed them as simpler narratives. The case of KPK was framed as a simple story of hero versus villain, where Duadji was the bad guy who victimised the heroes, Bibit and Chandra. A similar narrative was presented in the case of Prita as well, which was framed as a non-ideological story of a good, innocent small person being victimised by a big and powerful bad guy. In terms of their media identities, Bibit, Chandra and Prita became "victims." Victimisation framing identifies specific villains or perpetrators – usually powerful actors such as political leaders and big corporations – whose actions purportedly threaten weaker individuals or groups. Such framing is not dissimilar to other "Cinderella" or "David vs. Goliath" stories present in popular culture. Victimisation framing is commonly used in contemporary television shows, especially in reality shows, as a way to capture audiences' enthusiasm and participation. This framing can be presented in a light package with a short, catchy, sensationalised caption and a simple tale to satisfy headline appetites. To fit the light package, such framing does not incite any dissonance, morally and ideologically.

Icons and Symbolic Representation

In addition to their simplified narratives and victimisation framing, both the KPK and Prita cases have strong symbolic representations that are non-ideological, compelling and resonate within multiple social clusters and successfully grab the attention of social media users and their trailer vision. In the KPK case, the icons used to symbolise the movements were extremely vivid and visual. A small cicak or house gecko can easily be associated with small, innocent, ordinary people, the majority; after all, geckos are literally harmless. In Indonesia, they live among humans and can be commonly found in most living rooms. A house gecko symbolises the common, the ordinary, the "us." On the other hand, a crocodile crudely symbolises a beastly characteristic of the powerful man. The juxtaposition of gecko and crocodile symbolises a battle between "them" and "us," unifying "us" against "them" as a common enemy. Discussing and defining "who we are," – the "us" – establishes "the profound ontological shift from a collection of individuals to a single unit" that provides a basis for members of a movement to act as a collective (Harquail 2006, 8).

The Prita case took a different route in its symbolisation. Prita Mulyasari had been portrayed textually and visually as an ordinary young mother of two. The most circulated image related to the case showed Prita wearing a head scarf with two infants on her lap. Symbolising religious piety, the scarf also demonstrates the moral character of the subject in determining her status as an icon. The mother of two was a perfect icon to portray a "feminine movement," which is a movement "... that mobilises on the basis of women's traditional roles in the domestic sphere, usually as mothers and wives" (Baldez 2002, 14). As such, the movement appealed to both women and men who subscribe to traditional family values and gender roles. Just like cicak in the KPK case, for them, Prita symbolised the common, the normal and the women they knew. One participant who identified herself as a housewife stated: "She is just like us. If this could happen to her, it could happen to me, to any one of us" (interview with Gita, January 8, 2011).

At the same time, the very act of Prita in challenging the power of the big players – an international hospital and the government – can also be interpreted as a symbol of a feminist movement that explicitly challenges conventional gender roles in patriarchal society (Alvarez 1990). While lending itself to diverse interpretations, for Indonesian women, the Prita movement is a women's movement; a women's protest. What unites women – feminine, feminist and those in between – is their systematic "exclusion from the political protest and their collective status as political outsiders" (Baldez 2002, 15).

Easy Symbolisation, Amateur Production and Low-risk Activism

The rise of social media has developed a participatory culture characterised by "amateur and non-market production, networked collectivities for producing and sharing culture, niche and special interest groups, and aesthetics of parody, remix, and appropriation" (Russell et al. 2008, 45). These are reflected in both the Prita and KPK cases; the amount of amateurish artwork devoted to an issue is astounding, especially if we calculate how much individual time, energy and creativity spent to make digital posters, cartoons, animations, songs or video compilations. Easy symbolisation enables the amateur production of culture, in the visual and audio forms, to rise. The artwork in both cases helped the movements to embrace trailer vision even further and contributed to the movement's success in reaching various networks and groups.

In the KPK case, most of the artwork, including YouTube animations and videos, make use of a gecko and crocodile as central themes. There are also some different approaches to the artwork. One of the most attractive online posters is one that resembles a movie poster. Entitled Ketika Cicak Bersaksi (When a Gecko Testifies), the poster looks slick and professional. It showcases all "actors" in the case, including Susno Duadji, Bibit and Chandra, and some other politicians, and points out that they are part of the sinetron (soap opera) of Indonesian politics.

In the Prita case, much of its artwork doubled as campaign tools in the forms of logos and campaign posters. In this case, most of the artwork revolves around the central icon, with a headshot of Prita adapted and transformed in all manner of forms. While there were not as many YouTube videos in this case, one music video is particularly interesting, created by an elderly man who had never posted any YouTube videos before, showing himself playing a keyboard in music dedicated to Prita and juxtaposed with flashing images of her.

In all of this it is noticeable that the outcome is easy or low-risk activism. Such activism can function to reinforce a narrative and thus help translate online actions, such as clicking, typing and sharing, into offline collective movements. Certainly, low-risk, accessible and affordable action, such as giving one coin via a click, is easier to mobilise than getting protesters on to the streets. For example, in the KPK case, while there were more than one million clicks supporting the case, there were only 5,000 individuals who engaged in related street activism. By propagating the message that "your coins can solve the problem," the Coin campaign effortlessly transformed participants (coin givers) to be part of the solution, providing an instant gratification, and simplifying the actual problem embedded in the Prita case.

The Limits of Social Media Activism

The two cases discussed in the previous section have shown that social media activism can translate into populist political activism. Successful cases, such as Prita and the KPK, however, are not the rule. As mentioned previously, social media activism generates many clicks, but little sticks. Many others have failed to achieve critical mobilisation. The social media environment is not neutral, being bound to disparity and subject to domination. Conversations and information that dominate social media reflect the interests, choices and preferences of its users. Issues propagated by mainstream media that engage urban middle-class interest receive the most coverage. As illustrated in Figure 1, even bloggers who are concerned about social and political issues tend to discuss issues that were popularised by mainstream media. In Figure 1, we see that the Prita case was intensely discussed only in June 2009 and a pornography scandal involving artists Ariel and Luna Maya engaged ongoing discussions from July 2009 to March 2011. Meanwhile, the Lapindo and Ahmadiyah issues, which involved the poor and a religious minority, received minimal coverage (details on both cases will be provided in a later section).

While not generating massive participation like Prita, the Sri Mulyani Indrawati/ Century (SMI) case in Figure 1 did attract significant public attention and was discussed among top bloggers especially in July and December 2009 following widespread television coverage. The SMI case refers to the controversy around the bailout of Century Bank in 2008 by the Minister of Finance Sri Mulyani Indrawati who has a reputation as a reformer and a clean politician. In 2009, the legislature, spearheaded by Golkar Party, accused her of crimes, pointing out that the bailout was done without legal authority and without proving a capital injection was needed (see Barta 2010). Sri Mulyani Indrawati defended the bailout as necessary given the global economic uncertainties at the time. In all of the investigation of the Century Bank bailout there was no evidence that she profited from her decision. Like the KPK and Prita cases, the SMI case was often portrayed in the media as a conflict between a symbolic figure in Sri Mulyani Indrawati and predatory interests identified with Aburizal Bakrie of the Golkar Party. The largest Facebook SMI group had more than 50,000 followers. In its later development, the SMI case became more complex and, hence, did not translate into massive activism.

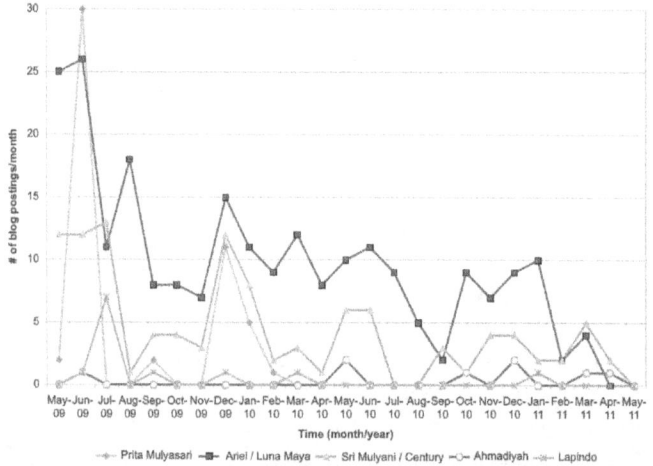

[Figure 1] Popularity of issues in top 80 Indonesian socio-political blogs. Source: author's calculation based on the occurences of blog postings that contain keywords associated with five selected issues. The figure is generated from 4.065 postings recorded in 80 blogs.

The first two cases, Prita and KPK, show that social media activism can be successful in mobilising mass support by embracing simplified narratives, popular symbols, and low risk activities. In the next section, I will look at unsuccessful cases – those that failed to gain mass support – to provide a more rounded understanding of the dynamics of social media activism in Indonesia. In order to demonstrate that the above-mentioned features are crucial to turn social media into successful mobilisation, I will present an analysis of how the absence of these features has prevented the mobilisation of the masses in other cases.

Lapindo and Ahmadiyah Cases

The Lapindo case refers to a mudflow disaster in a sub-district of Porong in Sidoarjo, East Java, where the blowout of a natural gas well drilled by Indonesian oil and gas exploration company Lapindo Brantas Inc., created the biggest mud volcano in the world. The main shareholder in Lapindo Brantas was the Bakrie family, one of the country's wealthiest. The disaster began on May 29, 2006, when hot mud starting erupting from the ground. The flow rates quickly increased and the volcanic mud covered over 7,000 hectares of lands, impacting eight villages and displacing more than 17,000 people. Some scientific evidence claimed the disaster was caused by Lapindo Brantas drilling, yet the company argued the cause was an earthquake in Yogyakarta, 250 km away. The company asserted that the incident had natural causes, meaning responsibility for the damage lay with the government. The company's argument was often repeated by Aburizal Bakrie, a Lapindo Brantas owner, who also was the Minister of Welfare at that time. Currently, Bakrie is the chairman of the Golkar Party, one of the most influential political parties, and is running to become the party's nominee for the 2014 presidential election. Lawsuits against Lapindo Brantas had been filed since 2006, but the current legal status of the incident is still pending with no foreseen certainty. In the meantime, the residents affected by the mudflow have not been properly compensated.

With frequent mass media coverage, including national television, discussions of the Lapindo case extended into the online sphere from May 2006 to 2009. These discussions, however, did not trigger mass reactions. Activists attempted to mobilise Indonesians to seek justice for the victims by setting up support pages on Facebook[5] and, yet, only received modest participation. Nearly every year on the anniversary of the incident, including in May 2012, activists and the victims held small street protests and online activisms. In 2010, activists held the competition of Lapindo-related Facebook status and in 2011 a similar competition was held for blog posts. After years of undertaking, activism is slowly growing, and thus far still has not generated substantial public participation.

Ahmadiyah is a religious movement founded by Mirza Ghulam Ahmad in India in 1889. There are about 200,000 Ahmadis in Indonesia. Like mainstream Islam, its teachings are based on the Quran and the Hadith. The difference is whether there can be other prophets after Muhammad. Ahmad claimed that he had fulfilled the Quranic prophecy of the second coming of the Mahdi, the Messiah, awaited by Muslims. Because of this claim, Islamist conservatives and many mainstream Muslims perceive Ahmadiyah as a heresy and it was suppressed under a 2008 Presidential decree requiring Ahmadis to "stop spreading interpretations and activities that deviate from the principal teachings of Islam" (The Jakarta Globe, February 25, 2011). Violations of the decree can result in jail sentences up to five-years.

The Ahmadiyah case refers to the February 2011 brutal attack on the Ahmadiyah community in Cikeusik where three were killed by a small group of radical Islamists who considered the Ahmadis as heretics. Following the attack, disturbing footage of the victims' bodies being repeatedly stoned and beaten, while police watched, were circulated on YouTube. Such videos took the incident global and triggered condemnation from international organisations, such as the Human Rights Watch. Despite the videos, the incident generated very little social media activism. As seen in Figure 1, the incident was hardly discussed among top socio-political bloggers. Following the attack, groups condemning the attack appeared on Facebook. Other groups, supporting Ahmadiyah to be a recognised religion, also emerged.[6] While these groups attracted only a handful of members, by June 2012 there were 104 anti-Ahmadiyah Facebook groups advocating the repression of the group and even supporting the killing of members of the group.[7]

While the Lapindo and Ahmadiyah cases represent important challenges for Indonesia and involved far more victims than the Prita case, attempts to use social media to mobilise public opinion resulted in very limited participation. Despite the propensity of social media to promote radical transparency and to diffuse issues in multiple networks, activism around these cases failed to reach critical mass. Unlike KPK or Prita, both Lapindo and Ahmadiyah did not lend themselves to easy simplification. While both can be framed as David vs. Goliath stories, these cases are complex and do not easily fit mainstream popular culture.

Voice, the Poor and Ambiguity

In the Lapindo case, the victims are the rural poor. The poor lack the voice and recognition necessary to engage in civic action (Appadurai 2004, 63). Framing the struggle of the rural poor so that it resonates with the interests of the urban middle class is a particular challenge. Often without strong symbolic representation and no iconic figures thrusting themselves into the fore-front of the issue, the plight of the poor often does not generate headlines. Remarkably, given the scale of the disaster, Lapindo activists failed to gain popular support. Part of the reason for this is that the legal process provides no clear-cut picture of whom to blame for the disaster. While sympathising with the victims and developing a sense of pity, the case's ambiguity makes it difficult for social media users to mark it as distinctive from other disasters. Unable to deliver a black-and-white story of victimisation, the case does not fall into a light package category.

Additionally, mainstream media, especially national television, has been successful in shifting the framing of the case as a special incident – where there are perpetrators and victims – to a "usual" natural disaster. Bakrie's own television channel, TV One, has been very active in endorsing this frame (on ownership, see Sudibyo and Patria 2013). TV One has re-named the incident Lusi, abbreviated from Lumpur Sidoarjo (Sidoarjo mud), instead of Lapindo mud, distancing Lapindo Brantas from the disaster. As a result of the prevailing intervention of TV One, the term Lusi is now widely used by the mainstream national media (Novenanto 2009). The Lapindo case indicates that social media is influenced by the larger media system where control through ownership can be extended online and determines the course of social media activism by the mainstream framing of events. Hence, we see that a movement would be less likely to succeed if it is contested by more powerful competing narratives.

The Ahmadiyah case is even more problematic. Its complexity sets it far away from a light package principle. While the Ahmadis are victims, many apparently see the attack as somehow justifiable. For those who are anti-Ahmadiyah, the attack is perceived as a defence of Islam and a reaction to the Ahmadiyah's claimed blasphemy. Here, the narrative does not fit the simple framing of David vs. Goliath and Ahmadiyah is transformed into the perpetrator. The belief that Muhammad is the last prophet is one of the core teachings of Islam, making it a meta-narrative for most Indonesian Muslims – a grand narrative that gives a totalising account based upon the appeal to universal truth (Lyotard 1984, 29) – and, thus, it is considered taboo to challenge it.

What was missing was a considerable body of users who were prepared to voice theiropinion and join pro-Ahmadiyah groups, leading to a supremacy of anti-Ahmadiyah accounts in social media. There are two explanations for this loss of voice. First, some Indonesians are not for Ahmadiyah. While they are against the killing, they are in a great doubt that Ahmadiyah's teachings are acceptable in Islam. Hence, they did not belong to any Ahmadiyah-related groups and were silent. Second, some Indonesians believe that the attack was inhumane and that Ahmadiyah's rights should be protected. They, however, felt they were in minority and avoided expressing an opinion publicly. The latter situation reflects the "spiral of silence" where people tend to keep their opinions or thoughts to themselves when they think they are in minority, fearing separation or isolation from those around them (Noelle-Neumann 1974). The Ahmadiyah case demonstrates that any sub-narrative that complicates the story can make the case unqualified for light package activism. The case also indicates the supremacy of religious meta-narrative and how it influences how people express themselves in social media.

At the same time, lacking iconic value, the Lapindo and Ahmadiyah cases did not generate the production of amateurish arts. While visual and artistic symbolisation serves as a tool to communicate a narrative in a more salient way, it becomes difficult where narratives cannot be transformed into simplified problem definitions and causal interpretations. Additionally, in a religious society, such as Indonesia, moral assessment is significant in symbolising narratives. Easy identification of right and wrong, good and bad, moral and immoral, is important in the production of symbols. The Lapindo and Ahmadiyah cases present a challenge to such binary moral judgements. In the absence of easy moral identification, neither cases generated visual symbolic representations needed in embracing a trailer vision.

As noted above, low-risk activism tends to encourage more participation. However, the risk is not always associated with action. Low-risk actions, such as clicking, can also be perceived as high risk if the movement represents or involves non-mainstream ideologies. In the "I know that you know that I know you know" network where conformity is desirable, such a click can incite undesirable social consequences. Further, the presence of ideology can complicate the narrative that is, otherwise, relatively simple. Nationalist and religious narratives are the strongest ideological narratives in Indonesia. Naturally, to be associated with any issue that is incongruent with these ideological narratives is perceived as risky. This risk was particularly apparent in the Ahmadiyah case. To sympathise with this non-mainstream religion was and is a risky choice where such an action can be interpreted as anti-Islam.

Beyond the case studies, it is useful to look at other issues that help us to understand the role of ideology. Human rights abuse in West Papua is one such example. The Papua case is ideological by its association with the story of separatist Papuans where their struggles for self-determination are perceived as endangering the integrity of the Unitary State of the Republic of Indonesia (NKRI). NKRI harga mati (NKRI is final, absolutely nonnegotiable) is a nationalist mantra often used to suppress ideologies and movements deemed not a part of "Indonesia." With the absoluteness of nationalist meta-narratives such as this, it is difficult to mobilise any issues likely to be associated with an anti-NKRI stance. While violating human rights can be morally framed as "bad" and "wrong," the West Papuans cannot be simply classified as "victims" because many non-Papuan Indonesians associate them with anti-NKRI actions. In addition to separatism, in the nationalist meta-narrative, communism, socialism and atheism, too, are associated with anti-nationalism (see Anderson 2001; McGregor 2007). Social media activisms associated with these "isms" would find it difficult to gain popular support.

To provide a subtler example of the role of ideology, it is worth briefly revisiting the SMI case, as depicted in Figure 1. Despite its early popularity, unlike the KPK and Prita cases where their supporters reached millions, the SMI case never yielded immense activism. While the SMI story easily generated an icon, activism around the SMI case was deeply polarised. SMI supporters perceived Sri Mulyani as a victim as well as an idol.[8] Some others questioned the real motive behind her decision to bailout the Century Bank. Further, Sri Mulyani's friendly relationship with the West, especially with some in the USA, led to her association with neo-liberalism (antek neolib), deemed as a "foreign" ideology that would corrupt Indonesia and nationalism. When, ultimately, Sri Mulyani left the ministerial post for the World Bank position in Washington DC, some saw this as evidence of her neo-liberalist agenda.

The Simplified Narrative

The cases presented suggest that participation in social media leads to populist political activism when it embraces the principles of contemporary culture of consumption: light package, headline appetite and trailer vision. Simple or simplified narratives that are associated with low-risk activism and are congruent with ideological meta-narratives have a much higher chance of going viral and generate significant activism. Success is less likely when the narrative is contested by dominant competing narratives generated in mainstream media. Why does political activism in social media need to be couched in simplified terms that resonate with terms of popular culture? The answer can be drawn from the following underlying explanations.

Social Media Ecology: Network is Vast, Content is Overabundant

A first explanation originates from the ecology of social media itself. Social media epitomises the most extreme example of an overall acceleration of production and circulation of information. In social media, a user is part of multiple, hyper-connected "communities" which constantly produce and consume. How to appeal to the mass in such an environment? Moreover, social media platforms, such as Facebook and Twitter, do not encourage long "conversations." Their features direct users to nurture short quick interactions and encourage multi-tasking. The escalation of velocity and size of information combined with the rapidity and briefness of interaction make social media more hospitable to simple and/or simplified narratives than complex/complicated ones. Obviously an image of a small gecko fighting against a huge crocodile in the KPK case is more likely to stand out in the information abundant environment of social media than a seemingly generic image of poor mud-flood victims in the Lapindo case. Similarly, a familiar story of Hollywood-style victimization, such as the story of Prita, can easily be told and retold in a casual online chat by exchanging just a few quick lines whereas a sensitive and complex story of Ahmadiyah cannot be discussed in the same manner.

Social Media as Part of a Larger Media System

The second explanation comes from the dependency of social media on the larger media system. While bloggers and social media users produce their own information, when it comes to news and events, most of them tend to become the echo chamber of traditional mainstream media, especially television channels. The more convivial environment of social media does encourage the rise of citizen journalists who produce alternative news. However, the alternative production is still too miniscule to challenge the dominance of mainstream content.

As we can see in the case studies, commercial national television channels played significant roles in amplifying, curtailing and intervening issues in social media activism. The successes of the KPK and Prita cases were reliant on a boost coming from national television channels. On the other hand, the Lapindo case saw TV One intervene with a more powerful competing narrative, reducing social media-generated participation. Because social media is embedded in systems of control, power and domination in the larger media system, issues and interests that dominate mainstream media also influence social media activism.

The success of social media activism is dependent on its congruency with the mainstream media culture. A sound bite is characterised by a short, quotable, and memorable remark that captures the essence of the larger message or conversation (Burke 2010).Using the case of weekday evening network newscasts in the USA, Adatto (1990) reveals that the average sound bite fell from 42.3 seconds in 1968 to only 9.8 seconds in 1988. Today, the average sound bite is even shorter. For social media activism to permeate the media network, its message size needs to fit the shrinking sound bite.

Techno-materiality of Social Media Access

The third explanation falls under the logic of access. Social media is not free from the techno-materiality of access, which not only determines who has access, but also how they access and consume information, and what kind of information they prefer to consume. There are two aspects to techno-materiality. First, the distribution of access and, second, the device to access. Regarding the first, the internet infrastructure in Indonesia is not equally distributed throughout the country. Rural areas lack access to even the most basic telecom infrastructure. Of the 76,613 villages, 57% remain disconnected from the internet and 16.8 million rural households (27% of the population) still have no electricity service (Depdagri 2011; Suhendra 2012). Access to social media strongly reflects this pattern, with over 60% of traffic coming from big cities, such as Jakarta, Bandung, Medan, Yogyakarta, Surabaya and Semarang (SalingSilang 2011). Most of the users prefer entertainment to other online content (Galih and Ngazis 2012). To attract public attention, a political message needs to contend with the pervasiveness of entertainment content that predominantly serves urban middle-class consumers.

On the second aspect, from 2009 to 2012 online access through internet cafes declined from 64% to 42% and access on mobile phones increased from 48% to 62% (Miftachul 2012). The proliferation of mobile phones, with over 220 million users in 2012 (MobileMonday 2012, 6), growing exponentially from only 32,792 in 1993 (Lim 2002), has become a driving force of the growth of the mobile internet. This is supported by cheaper internet rates and the increased availability of the wireless network in urban areas. One-third of 55 million internet users access the internet from mobile phones (MobileMonday, 2012, 6). The prevalence of mobile internet usage not only makes social media more portable and accessible, it also influences the way people consume content. The shift from the rich features found in laptops and desktops to mobile devices inevitably comes with a loss of some of its richness with a smaller screen, smaller text, fewer options and lower fidelity. Mobile has enabled people, in a disruptive sense, to produce and consume content more frequently, yet, mainly in "bite-size chunks." In Indonesia, where the speed and bandwidth are generally low, it is neither easy or nor cheap to download heavy rich information. For example, Indonesians I interviewed spoke about how they had to get YouTube videos completely retrieved before watching them as real-time streaming was not possible. Mobile device suits social networking tools that are tailored for consumption based on light package, headline appetite and trailer-vision principles.

Conclusions and Implications

Using the Indonesian context as an illustrative case, in this article I offer a critical perspective to the existing literature of social media activism. There, some specificities of the argument, such as the dominance of certain meta-narratives and the state of internet infrastructure, may not always be applicable to other contexts. The overarching argument, however, can be applied more generally. Similar explanations derived from cases presented here can help us to understand social media activism in countries such as Tunisia, Egypt and the USA. In Tunisia, the story of Mohammed Bouazizi's self-immolation saw a poor street vendor who never finished high school become an unemployed university graduate slapped by a female official even though nobody knew whether the slap really happened. This framing and its strong symbolisation through Bouazizi's burning body images enabled a working class movement to culturally and politically resonate with the rest of the population, especially the educated urban middle-class youth (Lim 2013).

Similarly, in Egypt, Khaled Saeed, a young man who died under disputed circumstances after being arrested by Egyptian police, was mythologised as "a powerful figure who can encapsulate the young generation: young, social media savvy, anti-authoritarian, and was martyred at an internet café ... By elevating him into a figure with saint-like qualities, minimises and simplifies the dynamics of his life" (Ali 2012), Egyptian activists conveniently used Khaled Saeed as a symbol of resistance that resonated with the entire population (Lim 2012a).

The successful Invisible Campaign in mobilising people to support the Kony 2012 cause, a video about the Lord's Resistance Army that went viral, is another example (see Drumbl 2012). As argued by Zuckerman (2012), the campaign:

> is so compelling because it offers extremely simple narrative: Kony is a uniquely bad actor, a horrific human being, whose capture will end suffering for the people of Northern Uganda. If each of us does our part, influences powerful people, [the United States] military force will take action and Kony will be captured.

Using an overly simplified narrative and calling for a low-risk activism that easily transforms individuals to be part of the solution, the Kony campaign is the quintessence of the light package activism that fully gratifies headline appetites and skilfully embraces trailer vision.

Such instances suggest that the Indonesian experience is not unique. At the same time, social media activism cannot be viewed in a dichotomous perspective. Rather than viewing it as a harbinger of progressive social change or dismissing it as "slacktivism," the article provides a more nuanced argument, identifying the conditions under which participation in social media may lead to successful political activism.

By studying social media activism in Indonesia, we learn that the participatory nature of social media certainly is most suitable to disseminate popular culture-related content. While this participatory culture can be borrowed for civic engagement and political mobilisation, it is limited in its capacity to mobilise complex political issues. The limitations are derived from, at least, three circumstances. First, in social media, the network is vast and the production and circulation of information is constantly accelerated.

This environment is more genial to simple and/or simplified narratives than complex/ complicated ones. Second, social media is not independent from the large media system. Social media activism, thus, needs to attune with "the incredible shrinking sound bite" culture of mainstream media. Third, social media is not detached from its technomaterial aspect, namely the distribution and device of its access. With a high concentration of social media access in urban areas, the narrative of activism always competes with entertainment content tailored for urban middle-class consumers. Furthermore, a high proportion of users access social media from mobile devices that are tailored for the quick bite experience.

Social media activisms, thus, are most successful when their narratives, icons and symbolic representations mimic those that dominate the contemporary popular culture. In other words, they have to embrace the principles of contemporary culture of consumption: light package, headline appetite and trailer vision. Beyond that, the activism must neither be associated with high-risk actions nor ideologies that challenge the dominant meta-narratives (such as nationalism and religiosity in Indonesia). Further, it also needs to be uncontested by powerful competing narratives endorsed in mainstream media. As such, social media activisms are always in danger of being *too fast*, *too thin* and *too many*. While online activism may see *many clicks*, these are *little sticks* – while we may witness many clicks, there are very few causes that make for widespread activism in the vast online social media environment.

Social media activism marks a period of innovation and experimentation in the use of new media technologies and participatory culture. Online expression, popular culture, combined with sociality, create multiple spheres where millions of Indonesians come together. On Facebook, Twitter and the like, these Indonesians find each other, organise, collaborate and act. Social media, however, does not lend itself to facilitate deliberative discourses on complex, difficult issues. It does not lend itself to the deliberation needed in a deepening democracy. As noted elsewhere, "[r]ule-bound deliberation is slow and ponderous, emphasises the acquisition of knowledge and expertise, focuses on government laws and policies, and succeeds when citizens partners with government in the service of good decisions, political legitimacy and social stability" (Lim and Kann 2008, 100).

These characteristics are unmatched by the features of social media, which is, first and foremost, social. Social media activities for urban middle classes mostly revolve around fun, self-expression and social gain. None of these is readily categorised as part of civic engagement that contributes to democratic processes. Social media does not inherently promote civic engagement and should not be perceived as a causal agent for social change and democratisation. At its best, it facilitates and amplifies a culture that helps establish a foundation, a training ground, and a learning space for individuals to express their opinions, to exercise their rights and to collaborate with others. By understanding the nature and limitations of social media activism and its conditions for success, activists may utilise, employ and transform it into meaningful civic engagement and political participation.

Acknowledgements: This article is based on the research that was partially supported by the Ford Foundation under the Advancing Public Media Interest in Indonesia project and the National Science Foundation's Social-Computational Systems (SoCS) Program (Award#: IIS-1110868 and IIS-1110649). Figure 1 resulted from the Blogtrackers project funded by the US Office of Naval Research (Award#: N00014101010091). Part of this article was completed while the author was a fellow-in-residence at the Royal Netherlands Institute for Southeast and Caribbean Studies (KITLV) in Leiden, the Netherlands. The author gratefully acknowledges all support. Especial thanks go to Jason Abbott, Kevin Hewison, Pamela Sari, James O'Halloran, and anonymous reviewers, for their valuable input.

Notes

1. Available at http://www.facebook.com/pages/Gerakan-1000000-Facebookers-Dukung-Chandra-Hamzah-Bibit-Samad-Riyanto/192945806132 (accessed January 25, 2013).
2. Examples include http://www.facebook.com/SelamatkanIndonesia and http://www.facebook.com/pages/Saya-Cicak-Berani-Melawan-Buaya/167520472821 (both accessed January 25, 2013).
3. The jingle can be found at http://www.youtube.com/watch?v=bSHwQDhDvF0 (accessed January 25, 2013).
4. The original page was at http://apps.facebook.com/causes/290597?m=7c7df20b. It is no longer available.
5. An example is http://www.facebook.com/groups/26083340518 (accessed January 25, 2013).
6. Examples of pages supporting Ahmadiyah are http://www.facebook.com/antikekerasan.ahmadiyah (accessed January 25, 2013), http://www.facebook.com/pages/Dukung-Ahmadiyah-Menjadi-Agama-Baru-di-Indonesia/190168814338999 (the link no longer works as the page has been closed) and http://www.facebook.com/groups/197293916964081/ (accessed January 25, 2013).
7. Examples include http://www.facebook.com/pages/Gerakkan-FACEBOOKers-bubarkan-AHMADIYAH/102692336450372?ref=ts and http://www.facebook.com/groups/188601241161606/ (both accessed January 25, 2013).
8. Loyal supporters of Sri Mulyani continue to use social media for further, more ambitious, agenda by campaigning for her nomination as a 2014 Presidential candidate. Some SMI social media activists became part of the newly-formed Independent People's Union Party (Partai SRI), whose main goal is to support Sri Mulyani's campaign in the 2014 Presidential election.

References

Adatto, K. 1990. "The Incredible Shrinking Sound Bite." The New Republic, May 28: 20–23.

Ali, A. 2012. "Saeeds of revolution: De-mythologizing Khaled Saeed." Jadaliyya, June 5. http://www.jadaliyya.com/pages/index/5845/saeeds-of-revolution_de-mythologizing-khaled-saeed.

Alvarez, S. 1990. Engendering Democracy in Brazil: Women's Movements in Transition Politics. Princeton: Princeton University Press.

Anderson, B. 2001. Violence and the state in Suharto's Indonesia. Ithaca: Cornell Southeast Asia Program Publications.

Andreas, S. 2007. Web 2.0 and the Culture Producing Public. Accessed March 13, 2012. http://www.scribd.com/doc/40127/Web-20-and-the-CultureProducing-Public.

Appadurai, A. 2004. "The Capacity to Aspire: Culture and the Terms of Recognition." In Culture and Public Action, edited by V. Rao and M. Walton, 59–84. Palo Alto: Stanford University Press.

Bak, P., and T. Kessler. 2012. "If You Like It, I Like It! Conformity on Facebook." Journal of Business and Media Psychology 3 (2): 23–30.

Baldez, L. 2002. Why Women Protest: Women's Movements in Chile. Cambridge: Cambridge University Press.

Barta, P. 2010. "Reformer Resigns, Rattling Indonesia." Wall Street Journal, May 6. Accessed January 15, 2013. http://online.wsj.com/article/SB10001424052748703866704575225262408521190.html.

Brauechler, B. 2005. Cyberidentities at War: Der Molukkenkonflikt im Internet. Bielefeld: Transcript.

Burke, S. 2010. "Three Keys to Laying a Strong PR Foundation." CBS News, October 5. http://www.cbsnews.com/8301-505143_162-46340159/three-keys-to-laying-a-strong-pr-foundation/.

ComScore. 2010. "Indonesia, Brazil and Venezuela Lead Global Surge in Twitter Usage." Accessed May 23, 2012. http//www.comscore.com/Insights/Press_Releases/2010/8/Indonesia_Brazil_and_Venezula_Lead_Global_Surge_in_Twitter_Usage.

Depdagri. 2011. "Menkominfo: Seluruh kecamatan tersambung internet Juni 2011." May 23. http://www.kemendagri.go.id/news/2011/05/23/menkominfo-seluruh-kecamatan-tersambung-internet-juni-2011.

Drumbl, M. 2011. "Child Soldiers and Clicktivism: Justice, Myths, and Prevention." Journal of Human Rights Practice 4 (3): 481–485.

Egebark, J., and M. Ekstrom. 2011. "Like What You Like or Like What Others Like? Conformity and Peer Effects on Facebook." Stockholm: Research Institute of Industrial Economics IFN Working Paper No. 866.

Galih, B., and A. Ngazis. 2012. "Entertainment Contents Get More Clicks." VivaNews.com, June 27. http://us.en.vivanews.com/news/read/330214-entertainment-contents-get-more-clicks.

Gamson, W. 1992. "The Social Psychology of Collective Action." In Frontiers in Social Movement Theory, edited by A. Morris and C. Mueller, 53–76. New Haven: Yale University Press.

Gladwell, M. 2010. "Small Change: Why the Revolution Will Not Be Tweeted." The New Yorker, October 4. http://www.newyorker.com/reporting/2010/10/04/101004fa_fact_gladwell.

Goffman, E. 1974. Frame Analysis. New York: Free Press.

Goldenberg, J., B. Libai, and E. Muller. 2001. "Talk of the Network: A Complex Systems Look at the Underlying Process of Word-of-Mouth." Marketing Letters 12 (3): 211–223.

Granovetter, M. 1973. "The Strength of Weak Ties." American Journal of Sociology 78 (6): 1360–1380.

Harquail, C. 2006. "Making Use of Organizational Identity: Icons as Symbolic Identity Proxies." Stockholm: Institute for International Business, Stockholm School of Economics, working paper.

Hill, D., and K. Sen. 2005. The Internet in Indonesia's New Democracy. London: Routledge.

Jenkins, H., R. Purushotma, M. Weigel, K. Clinton, and A. Robison. 2009. Confronting the Challenges of Participatory Culture: Media Education for the 21st Century. Cambridge The MIT Press.

Kahn, R., and D. Kellner. 2004. "New Media and Internet Activism: From the 'Battle of Seattle' to Blogging." New Media & Society 6 (1): 87–95.

Kamarck, E., and J. Nye. 1999. Democracy.com? Governance in a Networked World. Hollis: Hollis Publishing.

Kirkpatrick, D. 2010. The Facebook Effect: The Inside Story of the Company. New York: Simon & Schuster.

Lim, M. 2002. "From Walking City to Telematic Metropolis: Changing Urban Form in Bandung, Indonesia." In Critical Reflections on Cities in Southeast Asia, edited by T. Bunnell, L. Drummond, and K. Ho, 75–100. Singapore: Times Academic Press.

Lim, M. 2003. "The Internet, Social Network, and Reform in Indonesia." In Contesting Media Power: Towards a Global Comparative Perspective, edited by N. Couldry, and D. Miller, 273–288. Lanham: Rowan and Littlefield.

Lim, M. 2006. "Cyber-urban Activism and Political Change in Indonesia." Eastbound 1 (1): 1–19.

Lim, M. 2009. Global Muslim Blogosphere: Mosaics of Global-Local Discourses. In Internationalizing Internet Studies: Beyond Anglophone Paradigms, edited by M. McLelland, and G. Goggin, 178–195. London:Routledge.

Lim, M. 2012a. "Clicks, Cabs, Coffee Houses: Social Media and Oppositional Movements in Egypt (2004–2011)." Journal of Communication 62 (2): 231–248.

Lim, M. 2012b. "Life is Local in the Imagined Global Community: Islam and Politics in the Indonesian Blogosphere." Journal of Media and Religion 11 (3): 127–140.

Lim, M. 2013. "Framing Bouazizi: Social Media, Intermodality, and Participatory Journalism in the Tunisian Uprising." In Journalism: Theory, Practice and Criticism. Forthcoming.

Lim, M., and M. Kann. 2008. "Networked Politics: Deliberation, Mobilization and Networked Practices of Agitation." In Networked Publics, 77–107. Cambridge: MIT Press.

Lutfia, I. 2010. "Journalist, Bloggers Weigh in on Role of New Media." Jakarta Globe, August 6. http://www.thejakartaglobe.com/home/journalists-bloggers-weigh-in-on-role-of-new-media/389727.

Lyotard, J. 1984. The Postmodern Condition: A Report on Knowledge. Minneapolis: University of Minnesota Press.

McGregor, K. E. 2007. History in Uniform: Military Ideology and the Construction of Indonesia's Past. Singapore: NUS Press.

Miftachul, A. 2012. "Yahoo! TNS Net Index: Advertiser Needs to Strengthen their Mobile Strategy." DailySocial, June 28. http://dailysocial.net/en/2012/06/28/yahoo-tns-net-index-advertiser-needs-to-strengthenmobile-in-their-strategy/#more-9251.

MobileMonday. 2012. "Mobile Southeast Asia Report 2012: Crossroads of Innovation." Accessed May 23, 2012. http://www.mobilemonday.net/reports/SEA_Report_2012.pdf.

Morozov, M. 2009. "The Brave New World of Slacktivism." Foreign Policy May 19. http://neteffect.foreignpolicy.com/posts/2009/05/19/the_brave_new_world_of_slacktivism

Noelle-Neumann, E. 1974. "The Spiral of Silence: A Theory of Public Opinion." Journal of Communication 24(2): 43–51.

Novenanto, A. 2009. "The Lapindo Case by Mainstream Media." Indonesian Journal of Social Sciences 1 (3):125–138.

Nugroho, Y. 2011. Citizens in @ction. Manchester: Institute of Innovation Research, Manchester Business School, University of Manchester.

Rheingold, H. 2002. Smart Mobs: The Next Social Revolution. Cambridge: Perseus Publishing.

Russell, A., M. Ito, T. Richmond, and M. Tuters. 2008. "Culture: Media Convergence and Networked Participation." In Networked Publics, edited by K. Varnelis, 77–107. Cambridge: MIT Press.

SalingSilang. 2011. "Indonesia Social Media Landscape Q1 2011." Accessed May 23, 2012. http://www.slideshare.net/salingsilang/indonesia-social-media-landscape-q1-2011-2nd-salingsilangcom-report.

Semiocast. 2012. "Twitter Reaches Half a Billion Accounts, More Than 140 Millions in the US." July 30. http://semiocast.com/publications/2012_07_30_Twitter_reaches_half_a_billion_accounts_140m_in_the_US.

Shirky, C. 2011. "The Political Power of Social Media." Foreign Affairs January/February. Accessed March 13,2012. http://www.foreignaffairs.com/articles/67038/clay-shirky/the-political-power-of-social-media.

Shubert, A. 2009. "Indonesian Court Case Spawns Social Movement." CNN, December 22. http://articles.cnn.com/2009-12-22/world/indonesia.prita_1_indonesians-legal-system-social-media?_s=PM:WORLD.

Shulman, S. 2009. "The Case Against Mass E-mails: Perverse Incentives and Low Quality Public Participation in U.S. Federal Rulemaking." Policy & Internet 1 (1). Accessed March 13, 2012. http://faculty.washington.edu/jwilker/tft/Shulman.pdf.

Sidner, S. 2010. "Indonesia: Twitter Nation." CNNTech, November 23. Accessed March 13, 2012. http://articles.cnn.com/2010-11-23/tech/indonesia.twitter_1_twitter-nation-social-media-social-networking?_s=PM:TECH.

Snow, D., E. Rochford Jr, S. Worden, and R. Benford. 1986. "Frame Alignment Processes, Micromobilization,and Movement Participation." American Sociological Review 51 (4): 464–481.
SocialBakers. 2012. Indonesia Facebook statistics. Accessed March 13, 2012. http://www.socialbakers.com/facebook-statistics/indonesia.
Sudibyo, A., and N. Patria. 2013. "The Television Industry in Post-Authoritarian Indonesia." Journal of Contemporary Asia. http://dx.doi.org/10.1080/00472336.2012.757434.
Suhendra, Z. 2012. "16, 8 juta keluarga di Indonesia belum bias nikmati listrik." Detik Finance, November 26. http://finance.detik.com/read/2012/11/26/115709/2101258/1034/168-juta-keluarga-di-indonesia-belum-bisanikmati-listrik.
Sutadi, H. 2011. "Sosial media dan demokrasi 2.0 di Indonesia." Kompasiana, February 12. http://politik.kompasiana.com/2011/02/12/social-media-dan-demokrasi-20-di-indonesia.
Zuckerman, E. 2012. "Unpacking Kony 2012." my heart's in accra, March 8. http://www.ethanzuckerman.com/blog/2012/03/08/unpacking-kony-2012/.

Annotation

Nishant Shah

Merlyna Lim's essay is perhaps demonstrative of all the concerns that this Reader espouses. It helps us understand that the digital cannot be taken too literally. It requires qualifications and contextualisation. Digital is not just about the access to technologies and cannot be reduced to questions of penetration and adoption. She shows clearly that there is a gentrifying effect that the digital has, as only certain communities and class-clustered individuals get access to digital playing fields, thus producing skewed representations of reality. Within Indonesia, she shows the need to look at the population that is getting wired, to understand why certain political positions are being taken and how the impulses of transformation are shaped by the contexts of these users who can easily stand in for the larger population that has limited or no access to these spaces of intervention and discourse. At the same time, the essay, in its analysis of how the digital gets operationalised in mobilising social and cultural movements and protests, shows that the digital is not as universal as we would have imagined. While there might be structural similarities that emerge from the form and aesthetics of the digital platforms and apps as they traverse around the world, the movements cannot be merely labelled as the same, under labels like "Facebook protests" and "Twitter Revolutions". Even as the number of tools and spaces of expression get reduced under the massive monopolies of digital social web, it is important to remember that these tools get hugely shaped by the contexts where they are put into practice. Decoding them as micro processes and understanding them as specifically used to address particular questions of the region is important so that we do not privilege the digital in the formulation of 'Digital Activism'.

Her take on activism also mimics this need to qualify and substantiate what we mean by activism. Drawing upon the dual nature of responsibility and entitlement, of safety and openness, of privacy and trust, she shows how we need to think of activism, not only as a goal based solution to a problem but the beginning of a series of processes that have different material and experiential practices. Particularly in her critique of clicktivism, Lim helps to understand how we might need to reconsider the traditional indicators like impact and spread, which have been the measures of the efficacy of activism. New faces of digital activism, which are more tactics than strategies, require a new vocabulary and new imaginations of what it means to act, when that act is a click. Her conception of activism demands that we see action in different registers, and look at a value-chain of actions, where we see the chain reactions which are not necessarily aimed at a pre-defined goal but reveal the possibilities of digital engagement.

The formulation of 'Digital Activism', for Lim, is still not free of the geographies of operation and intention. She shows how taking the geographical locations – national, regional, global – is not only important but necessary in understanding what it means to be active and the subjectivity of this actor based on the place of the body. Ensuring that her critique is embedded in the specificity of Indonesia, and the diversity of the social, cultural, and political terrain of the region, Lim argues for a need to find the materiality and the geography of the digital, when it becomes a space for activism and intervention.

References and Further Readings

Shah, N (Ed.) 2010. *Digital Natives with a Cause? Thinkathon Position Papers*. Den Haag: Hivos Publications.

Cortesi, S. & Gasser, U. (Eds.) 2015. *Digitally Connected: Global Perspectives on Youth and Digital Media*. Cambridge: Berkman Centre for Internet and Society.

Joyce, M. C. (Ed.) 2010. *Digital Activism Decoded: The New Mechanics of Change*. New York: Idebate Press.

Rising Voices: Indigenous Language Digital Activism

Subhashish Panigrahi

This narrative is based on a talk by Subhashish Panigrahi at the Global Voices Citizen Media Summit 2015, Cebu City, Philippines on January 25, 2015.

My name is Subhashish Panigrahi and I work at the Centre for Internet and Society (CIS) in Bangalore, India. I have been working with the Wikimedia Foundation since 2012 and then the program got shifted to Access To Knowledge at CIS. It is focused to support all the Indic languages, and the communities contributing to Wikipedia and its sister projects. I have been working with 63 different tribes from the Indian state of Odisha speaking various diverse languages. These communities speak about 15 unique languages as their native languages out of which only 10 have scripts. And they don't have a common language to communicate among themselves. And the state's language is kind of dominating their native languages. None of the languages have an application in their mobile phone or computer to type in their languages. And because of various such reasons these languages are slowly vanishing from the native speakers' tongues. Similar instances might happening in the rest of the world as well. I will be talking about the setbacks that are stopping these languages to grow (technical challenges, linguistic challenges, and consensus), strategies and opportunities.

A language is a gateway to the linguistic and cultural heritage of a society and is a medium to communicate. Languages die out because of the dominance of the official languages in a state or country. Because of the predominant use of official languages for governance, languages spoken by indigenous people are often repressed and die out slowly. This language "Bo" (of the great

Andamanese language family) died with the last living person of the community.[1] That is sad! Hundreds and thousands of languages are dying every year because of the dominance of other languages. Language is also a tool to express any native practice of a community in its best way. When knowledge is transferred via translation there is always a "loss in translation". Languages have historically been used to document and archive religious, cultural and other text for the future generation to enable them to learn about their ancestors.

[Image 1] Subhashish Panigrahi speaking at the Global Voices Citizen Media Summit 2015, Cebu City, The Philippines. Credit: Jeremy Clarke, shared under Creative Commons BY-SA 4.0 license.

The challenges that the indigenous communities face are mostly the reach of modern technology. Many languages don't have their writing systems in the computer, their scripts have not been standardized, many languages do not have Unicode support (Unicode is a script encoding standard by the Unicode Consortium that defines the character or glyph standards for a script). A lot of non-Latin script based languages have the problem of the script not being rendered in a computer. Many of the scripts have conjuncts where more than one character is joined with another and when you type them in a computer they look like gibberish. A lot of languages do not have native input methods built in the computer or mobile phone to type. Fonts that are used in a script do not exist for many languages. I have been working on a project for getting a font designed for this script Ol - chiki for the language Santhali . This language is spoken in at least seven Indian states by about 6 million people. It is one of the official languages of India and has its own unique script. But it probably did not have a Unicode font until 2013. And then Google came up with a font Noto Ol-chiki which at the moment is the only available Santali Unicode font.[2]

We are working with a designer to design a font that could be used for print, mobile, web and everywhere else.

There comes the strategies around digital activism for languages. Many languages need external intervention by promoting its use in mainstream media. The web as a platform could be used to popularize a language. [Drawing an example,] may be sending text messages to farmers with the weather forecast could help common people to use their language more for knowledge sharing. Many languages and scripts need standardization and this work has to [involve] academics, linguists and researchers. A consensus has to be made for communities that are dispersed to have a single stand while creating standards. If a language is not feeding someone then there is no way it could be used by more people. Many communities today are pro-English because it is easier to get a job with English proficiency. Lack of jobs with native language competence has led to many people moving away from their languages. So there is a strong need to raise the languages in a societal system to a level that it enables people to earn equally with competence in their own languages. There is a need for adopting a multiple official language policy so that the enforcement of many languages being used in many places will make smaller languages get life that are otherwise dying out. Collaborating with other communities, leveraging the strength of local hacker or developer communities to build language input and other language related tools, designing good quality fonts, getting advertising media to promote regional languages will be very useful for enhancing usability of the languages. There is always a need for capacity building. Indigenous communities would not care for the preservation of their language using modern technology which requires some kind of external intervention from the academic, linguistic and researcher community. All of these will contribute to build an ecosystem to collaborate with native language speakers and empower them with advanced tools and technology to use their native language in every possible way. This has a parallel to how the missionaries started preaching in colonies. They learned the local languages, published books in people's languages and that is how the Bible has been the first ever published book for many languages. A similar strategy is possible to design without of course a religious intent.

Endnotes

1   2015. "Aka-Bo Language." Wikipedia. March 12. https://en.wikipedia.org/wiki/Aka-Bo_language.
2   "Noto Fonts." Google. http://www.google.com/get/noto/#/.

Annotation

Padmini Ray Murray

Designations such as "millennials" and "digital natives" implicitly connote a techno-utopian vision, underpinned by an assumption that all young people have equal digital access. However, it is safe to assume that the language of the digital native will almost inevitably be hegemonic in its scope, not only because of the foundational role the American military-industrial complex played in the creation of seminal operating systems such as UNIX, but also, as Tara McPherson persuasively argues, the philosophical principles that underlie the very structure of the digital tools we use. As McPherson goes on to demonstrate, the rules of modularity that underpinned UNIX computing, for example, "underscore a worldview in which a troublesome part might be discarded without disrupting the whole." In this article, Subhashish Panigrahi writes on how to challenge these hegemonies by crowdsourcing efforts to help preserve endangered indigenous languages. Panigrahi's observations regarding the efficacy of languages to articulate native practices provides an object lesson regarding how local epistemological legacies can provide different ways of seeing and knowing; a learning that is crucial for those of us working on digital cultures and dissemination in South Asia, in order to create our own theoretical frameworks in response to technological change.

Consistency and standardization for Indic languages input is still a significant challenge for major living languages, let alone endangered ones, and it is imperative that consolidated efforts are made to amend this to ensure representation and survival. There are debates as to whether the Unicode Consortium, who are responsible for building and maintaining the scaffolding for a universal character set, are doing enough to ensure the interoperability of languages spoken by large swathes of the world's population, or whether the responsibility rests with governments and native speakers. However, what Panigrahi manages to persuasively illustrate in his piece is that such endeavours are only effective when carried out with the relevant communities, as it endows agency and authority to those to whom it rightfully belongs.

References and Further Readings

McPherson, Tara. 2012. "Why Are the Digital Humanities So White? Or Thinking the Histories of Race and Computation." In *Debates in the Digital Humanities* [Digital Edition]. Minnesota: University of Minnesota.

Mukerjee, Aditya. 2015. "I Can Text You A Pile of Poo, But I Can't Write My Name." *Model View Culture*. Accessed March 19, 2015. https://modelviewculture.com/pieces/i-can-text-you-a-pile-of-poo-but-i-cant-write-my-name.

Towards 2 Way Participation

Prabhas Pokharel

Formal actors are increasingly using technology in order to push youth participation forward. Incredible stories of grassroots youth engagement efforts that use technology have given and continue to give inspiration to many of these efforts. In this essay, I use this inspiration as a premise to argue that the power of story-making and narrative formation is important to consider when designing participation efforts. Using examples from UNICEF Kosovo Innovations Lab, I urge practitioners in this area to loosen their narrative constraints on efforts encouraging youth participation through technology, and to re-interpret youth participation as a two-way dynamic.

Story and narrative

In order to make my argument coherently, I will first try to describe two objects, the narrative and the story.

A story is simple; roughly, it has a beginning and an end, a plot and a flow that guides one from the beginning to the end, some characters, and some action. It is a tale, a set of events glued together one after the other, a set of characters moving through time or space in one form or another. The narrative, on the other hand, is the framework within which these events and actions happen. It sets the rules that stories must follow: The types of characters that are allowed, and the kinds of interactions they can have with each other. The fairy tale narrative, for example, includes magic, wizards and witches, princes and princesses, gingerbread men, and happy endings. The western rational narrative of the world, on the other hand, insists on causality according to the laws of physics, biology and various other sciences. Stories simply exist (are told) within these narrative frameworks. In a fairy tale, Cinderella finds her prince in a ballroom, uses pumpkins that turn magically into chariots, and has a fairy godmother. In the western rational world, Darwin rides a boat through the Caribbean, observes many different kind of animal life as they progress through generations, and deduces the existence of evolution.

Simply put, the story is the flow of events, a motivation that prod some actions which are followed by consequences. The narrative is the framework, the rules and constraints that dictate what kinds of interventions are appropriate given certain motivations and what consequences actions can have.

And now that I have described these two objects, I will move on to the subject of this paper: the contemporary practice of youth participation through technology.

Youth participation through technology

In this paper, I will talk to and about formal actors involved in the practice of youth participation[1] through technology. But before getting to technology, the practice of youth participation that formal actors engage in is worth breaking down, as participation is a broad term. In the paper, formal actors mean government organisations, aid organisations, non-profits, and even private sector participants—entities with budgets, employed staff, rules of operation and so on. And youth participation refers to the practice of involving young people in the kinds of processes the aforementioned formal actors perform.[2] To give an example, I am referring to something like UNICEF Kosovo's effort to engage young people in its anti-smoking program, by hosting debates to bring out issues important to youth, and by asking young people to design media campaigns that would appeal to their peers. Another example would be the program through which Plan Benin has been getting young people to contribute reports about child-related abuse and violence, in order to help the organisation get a better understanding of the child protection needs in Beninoise communities.[3] Youth participation efforts like these can be thought of as participatory planning[4] extended to action — involving young people directly into work formal actors are engaging in. Planning is one type of work in which people can be engaged, but also included are activities such as designing new campaigns (for example against smoking), developing better maps of communities, or creating better pictures of on the-ground situations (for example of child-related violence). And formal actors like UNICEF, Plan, and governments around the world have been interested in such efforts for a long time, for reasons that range from enabling youth participation itself, to electoral considerations, promotion of volunteerism, and many other reasons.

Such kind of youth participation both exists and is desired by many formal actors.

It is here then, that technology and recent history enter. For in the recent years, what has arisen is that the very "audience" of these participation efforts has been organising themselves using technology in highly notable ways.

I will use an example that I am intimately familiar with, that of the NepalUnites protests organised in Kathmandu in demand for Nepal's new constitution to be written in May of 2011. By then, Nepal's constituent assembly was running short on its second deadline for writing the constitution (the first was a year before, in May 2010), and phenomenally little progress had been made.[5] So young people got together using Facebook as a primary organisational tool, to protest against the inaction of the constituent assembly members. Starting with the slogan of:

ज्याला पुरै लियौ, अब संबिधान देऊ

("You have taken your full salaries, now give us the constitution"), the group organised protests ahead of the constitutional deadline, gathering crowds of thousands of people repeatedly.[6] The protests were interesting in that (1) their declared interests were simply those of tax-paying citizens, and (2) they were organised and led by youth not affiliated with any political party, union, or organisation — both rare enough in Nepal for people to take notice.

And notice people did: the protests received media coverage for many weeks of their existence. It started with simple reports of the protests that people had organised, but moved quickly on to the discussions of the pure "citizen" stance of the effort, criticism of the classed nature of technology-based organisation in a country with 58 percent literacy,[7] and rebuttals cautioning against sticking only with supposedly tried and true but ineffective methods of influence. All in all, the protests stayed on national newspapers for at least two weeks around the constitutional deadline. The protests didn't receive any concrete goals in terms of achieving constitutional progress, but media coverage extended even to international media. The story of how young people in Nepal organised themselves using technology, and articulated their demand loudly, was indelibly entered into the annals of national and international media,[8] and the minds of the public consciousness.

What this means is that any designer of a program for youth participation in Nepal's future will now be forced to confront, discuss, and address this set of protests of May 2011. Formal actors can no longer frame youth participation efforts inspiring apathetic youth to action; they will instead have to frame their audience in terms of one that was able to use technology to organise themselves and articulate themselves loud and clear in May of 2011. As the access to and usage of technology increases (as it has been), more and more youth participation efforts in fact will be using technology directly. And more than any other participation efforts, these will have to speak to movements such as NepalUnites.

And they have. While the example I have used is so recent that it forces me to foretell consequences, many events of the past lend credibility to what I have argued. The 2011 revolutions in North Africa and the Middle East, the Pink Chaddhi campaign in India, the Ushahidi Haiti crowdsourcing effort, the Map Kibera project, and the uprisings in Iran and Moldova are just a handful of youth efforts with a heavy technology component that the world knows about. Efforts like these are notable, widely discussed, and already play a crucial part in the design of new youth participation efforts by formal actors. I myself have seen these very examples repeatedly appear in opening paragraphs and motivating slides talking about formal participation efforts that deal even tangentially with technology. Often, these grassroots efforts act as the very catalysts for technology usage within youth participation projects. And even when not, they are bound to act as inspiration, or at the very least as examples who can provide lessons learned.

To me, this is a very welcome way of doing things. Formal efforts for youth participation should learn from how young people themselves organise and have their own say using technology. What I want to do in the rest of this essay is break down two particular attributes of participation efforts: story-making and narrative power, and argue for their inclusion (and if not inclusion, at least consideration) in new participation methods that use technology.

Crowdsourcing and competitions: Storymaking and narrative power

In this section, I want to describe two methods of youth participation through technology: crowdsourcing and competitions. In the process, I will tease out two properties of youth participation efforts: storymaking and narrative power.

One increasingly popular method of technology-based participation uses the technique of crowdsourcing. The idea of crowdsourcing is to get large numbers of people (the 'crowd') to contribute information or an action of some sort. The goal is to obtain (source) something from the crowd; the something varies from some information individuals already have to small tasks they have to complete. Popularised by the Ushahidi initiatives to solicit information from large numbers of people during crises in Kenya and Haiti, the method has been used for soliciting reports of child violence in Benin as well as to collect information during disasters by UN-OCHA.[9]

Crowdsourcing depends on a crowd, i.e., a large number of people. The tools that enable crowdsourcing, because of its very nature, try to enable as many people to contribute to an effort as possible. The reliability of aggregate results is improved by the number of contributions; 'number of contributions' to a crowdsourcing effort are in fact one of the measures of its success. In order to enable large-scale participation in such a way, however, the barrier to action has be reduced as much as possible—the action each person performs has to be made atomised and simple. But when contributions, or 'participation' if you will, are (is) so atomised, the crowd is left with control of neither story nor narrative. By the time a young person is invited to participate, the task that should be done is already defined, the story of the why and the how are already told. In what ways the crowd is supposed to contribute, how the need for the effort translates to the specific pieces of data or action that the crowd has to be performed, all of that is determined pre-'participation'.

Simply put, crowdsourcing efforts give participants very little control of either the story or the narrative. There will be a story produced by the information that the crowd contributes. But the story of why the effort was started (i.e., the need that motivated the effort), how that translated into the specific actions the crowd is now performing, and decisions to change these actions based on new information: all of that is out of participants' hands. This is especially true in formal efforts, where there tends to be a large separation between the 'crowd' (the participants) and the 'crowdsourcers' (the formal actors). The language of crowdsourcing itself carries with it the notion of a disempowered 'crowd' which can be 'sourced' for effort and information. But the crowd cannot define the 'why' (the story) or the 'how' (the narrative) of what they contribute.

In contrast is yet another popular method for youth participation through technology: Competitions. The World Bank's apps4dev competition, state department-sponsored Apps4Africa, and challenges sponsored by private sector companies such as GSMA (2011 Mobile App Challenge) and Nokia (Calling All Innovators program) work by developing a broad problem definition, and then accepting a wide range of submissions to solve the problem. The problem statements reflect the needs and priorities that the formal institutions seek to be addressed, but there is usually plenty of freedom to define why and what to do. Apps4Dev, for example, asked technologists young and old to create apps (applications) using World Bank data. Creators of apps could tell their own stories about what kinds of data they wanted to use, how they wanted to use the data, why, who the audience would be, and so on. The basic constraint was only that the application had to use WorldBank data. This of course restricted approaches to be datacentric and analytic. But besides that, there was a lot of freedom in choosing what kind of story to tell and what narrative to use. The MigrantsMovingMoney app,[10] for example, told a story about migration around the world, while DevelopmentTimelines tried to tell the stories of development of individual places through time. And the narrative constraints by which their motivations manifested to interventions were their own. Participants defined 'app' in their own way (MigrantsMoving-Money was a simple web-based visualisation of data; Get a Life! presented intuitions in the form of a game; Bebema was a mobile app directed towards mothers), thereby defining what interventions were appropriate for the kind of story they were trying to tell.

I have on purpose not yet argued which of these is the better approach as no technique of enabling youth participation is a panacea. However, I find this property of story-making and narrative to be an important one to consider when designing youth participation efforts. In the next section, I will bring out examples from my experience at the UNICEF Innovations Lab Kosovo, which has suggested to me that allowing for these freedoms in fact enables more powerful mechanisms of youth participation.

Some real life examples

Here, I would like to share my experience from UNICEF Innovations Lab Kosovo, which was founded in November 2010, and which I led for the initial six months of its existence. The Lab has a mandate of increasing youth participation through technology among other things, and experience with young people's projects there has me convinced that narrative and story-making powers are of great value in youth participation efforts.[11]

An early challenge that the Lab was given was to make better digital maps of Kosovo for UNICEF's use—existing public maps had little information about points of interest such as health facilities, youth centres, schools, and other public service resources. Young people, including those from the organisation Free Libre Open Source Software Kosova (FLOSSK) wanted to make better maps of Kosovo and were already working on this issue. Given that part of our mandate was to increase youth participation through technology, then, our task was to craft a methodology to involve these (and other) young people in processes of making maps that would be useful for UNICEF (and ultimately the Kosovo government and the Kosovo public). Two basic methods were obvious: (1) to start with a certain set of interesting points to map from UNICEF's perspective, define the correct way to map each point, and ask young people to contribute individual pieces of data; (2) to simply tell young people what we were doing, and ask them how they wanted to contribute to our effort. The first method is the method of atomisation: to define the process and break the task into small chunks. The second is a non-atomised method that leaves all of the 'how questions' (and some of the 'why') to be defined by young people themselves.

We tried both methods. Kosovo Youth Map (http://kosovoinnovations. org/youthmap) was a project to map youth resources in Kosovo using the atomised/crowdsourced approach. We defined exactly the kind of data we wanted ("youth resources": youth NGOs, youth centres, student councils and peer clubs), atomised the data collection process (give us information for one of these resources; here is a form to fill), and invited young people to contribute points of interest onto the map (after starting with a base layer of data we obtained through other means). Two projects were born out of the latter method, of just putting our request to young people of Kosovo. One of the projects was to map polling stations throughout Kosovo (http://kumevotu. info), and another wanted to map public facilities (schools, municipality offices, health centres, etc.) throughout the country. The methods for mapping were similar in both these youth-defined projects: they included getting as much public data as possible, and then using GPS units to locate specific facilities and putting them on the Wikipedia-like mapping platform OpenStreetMap.

I worked with all three projects. While I have no rigorous evaluation method to stand behind me, and more confounding variables that anyone could count, young people's engagement in projects they defined themselves, and told their own stories for, were much higher than the project where participation was more atomised. I can particularly differentiate between the KuMeVotu project and the Kosovo Youth Map, two projects that were more or less completed during my tenure at the Lab. Judging by number of contributions received, number of person-hours contributing to a given project, and the amount of material contributed, the participatory output was simply higher for the youth-defined project.

One of the reasons why I think the engagement was higher in this case points directly to narrative power; a lot of it came down to simply the somewhat technical choice of a mapping platform. For a UNICEF that wanted good maps most of all, the slight preference of open source tools was no match to the much greater quality and quantity of data available from proprietary vendors like Google. So the Kosovo Youth Map used proprietary map information from Google as the default base layer, and Ushahidi, the popular crowdsourcing software for collecting information about youth resources. The polling station and public institution projects, on the other hand, were working with OpenStreetMap, which is a community-based mapping platform that places very few restrictions on public consumption and re-use of mapping data. The young people we engaged with had already been working on OpenStreetMap, and had a very high preference for continuing to work on that platform for ideological reasons (the license that OpenStreetMap uses is a Creative Commons license that puts only two basic restrictions on usage of data: that credit be given, and that any new work based on that work must also have a similar license and therefore also allow re-use). The group of youngsters wanted to contribute to a global knowledge base that would be expounded on by others after them, and was simply more excited to work using these tools.

So ultimately, engagement was driven by the how of the project (ie, how it was implemented), with the hidden politics of choice of tools. It was a narrative choice, a choice of how motivation (need for mapped polling stations) translated to intervention (create points mapped on OpenStreetMap). The Lab could have done interviews with the young people to bring out this preference and accounted for it in designing our atomised participation tools. But allowing narrative flexibility was another, easier way to deal with the same issue. And there might be subtler issues that our assessment tools might miss, issues that can only be captured by putting young people in the driving seat of the narrative.

There was also something behind the story-making power that the youth-defined projects offered the participants. Motivations for all three projects were built with somewhat of a collaborative approach, but the main responsibility and ownership of storytelling fell on the young people for the project they themselves defined. There was simply a greater feeling of ownership and therefore responsibility that led to higher engagement. Moreover, this is not an uncommon phenomenon—it has been documented repeatedly by those working in issues of community and sustainable development.[12]

The drawbacks

There are drawbacks to such approaches. I see three big drawbacks: potential cost, loss of outcome control, and loss of process control. The first one is simple: some ways of providing young people their own storymaking and narrative facilities can be costly, precisely because there is a greater domain to explore. The WorldBank Apps4Dev competition needed to put forth substantial resources in the form of competition prizes as incentives for people to participate, because it wanted to draw in and incentivise a wide audience. Most atomised participation methods, where participation is made as effortless as possible, have no need for such incentives. The second drawback is that there isn't always full control of what the outcome will be. UNICEF was interested in better maps of Kosovo, but its first priority for mapping wasn't necessarily polling centres — health facilities would have been preferred without doubt. The Lab was lucky that youth participation was part of its mandate, and it could afford a narrative-rich approach to participation that didn't yield preferred outcomes. Other formal actors may be more constrained. And finally, there is the possibility of the loss of process control. When formal actors let young people control the narrative of progress (i.e. the how), it will likely not fit exactly with the processes already being employed by the former. There will be differences in the kinds of communications protocols, archiving, decision-making, and evaluation processes that communities of young people and formal institutions employ, and this will simply be something extra to deal with.

Towards 2 way participation

Despite the drawbacks, however, I think many institutions can commit to youth participation through technology efforts that let young people make up their own stories and narratives of progress. And those who can, should, for story-making and narrative power are building bridges towards real 2 Way Participation.

I believe many institutions are beginning to focus increasingly on such approaches. I will share here my knowledge of UNICEF Innovations Lab Kosovo, which certainly has. The Lab has tried to design programs that meet young people halfway in participation platforms—where formal processes (such as the use and development of digital maps) and young people's inclination (such as of using digital tools that ensured public contribution) are both respected. One way it has done so is by creating a project framework where young people are asked to "submit innovative projects for social good". Young people define social good themselves (their motivational story) and "innovative" themselves (their narrative of change), and the project framework is innately flexible enough to let people define their own motivations and methods.

I think one of the most interesting things that comes out of this is that the notion of "youth participation" itself is re-interpreted. Usually, when formal institutions talk about "youth participation", it is framed in terms of some decision-making or formal process that young people are encouraged and invited to participate in. There is no thought of formal institutions themselves participating in the processes of youth, despite the motivation I provided in the beginning of this essay, of the need and responsibility for formal actors to learn from grassroots efforts of young people using technology. This has to change—formal institutions need to think about how they can tap into the realities of communities like NepalUnites.[13]

The release of story-making and narrative power in youth participation efforts through technology is one way to start working on this issue immediately. By allowing young people to define the why and the how of projects, institutions can tap into ecologies of existing practices that people are already a part of. When the Innovations Lab asks young people to submit "innovative ideas for social good", young people submit ideas that they are already working on, whether they be about developing open maps, tackling environmental issues using photography, or developing new methods for inter-ethnic cooperation through the arts.[14] When the ideas are new, they build on existing communities, existing sensibilities and values. When participation includes the ability to define the story of why, and the narrative of how, participation begins to become two-way.

Endnotes

1. Actually, what I really want to talk about is participation efforts geared towards a digitally active public: perhaps best represented with a term such as "digital participation". However, such a term delinks the efforts I want to talk about from very similar efforts which do not use technology, which to me have much more similarity than differences. Therefore, I will use the cumbersome phrase "youth participation through technology". For then, the base idea is "youth participation", a universe in which technological and non-technological interventions lie close together. Many of the efforts I talk about do include non-youth actors, but the audiences of technologically-capable audiences are largely young people, and the language about digitally-capable publics and youth correspond closely. Therefore, despite the impreciseness, I find "youth participation" to be the best established term I can pick up and talk about.
2. To make this even clearer, it might be worth breaking down the relationship between youth and formal process. Four basic relationships between youth and formal process are obvious: formal process for youth, youth for formal process, youth in formal process, and formal process with youth. I am talking about the latter two — formal process (or action) with youth, and youth in formal process. I am not talking about the formal processes that are designed for young people, or the process of mobilising young people in support for formal process. I am talking about incorporating young people directly into the processes themselves: formal institutions enacting these processes with young people as involved participants.
3. More about UNICEF Kosovo's anti-smoking efforts: http://kosovoinnovations.org/w/?s=smoking&search=Search. More about Plan Benin's work on child-violence reporting: http://www.globalhealthhub.org/2011/01/13/revisiting-the-smsviolence-reporting-project-in-benin/.
4. Wikipedia: Participatory planning is an urban planning paradigm that emphasises involving the entire community in the strategic and management processes of urban planning or community/.
5. Before the last month, in the entire one-year extension period, the constituent assembly met for a total of 95 minutes and even then on procedural issues rather than those of content (http://www.ekantipur.com/the-kathmandu-post/2011/05/17/top-story/atale-of-idleness-in-365-days-constituent-assemblysweated-for-95-minutes/221797.html). By the time the one-year extension was again renewed, only two major issues were decided, one of which was the name of the constitution (http://www7.economist.com/node/18775293).
6. http://nepaliblogger.com/news/nepal-unites-viafacebook-and-speaks-up-at-khula-manch/2062/attachment/nepali-singers-at-nepal-uniteskhulamanch-event/
7. UNICEF Nepal Statistics http://www.unicef.org/infobycountry/nepal/nepal_nepal_statistics.html
8. Even the Economist began an article on Nepal's political climate with "A gaggle of protesters want to turn the Arab Spring into a Himalayan Summer". (http://www7.economist.com/node/18775293)
9. See Plan International's SMS violence reporting networking in Benin (ref. http://www.globalhealthhub.org/2011/01/13/revisiting-the-sms-violence-reportingproject-in-benin/) and UN-OCHA's crisis map for Libya at http://libyacrisismap.net/.
10. This, and the rest of the apps mentioned in this paragraph can be found at http://apps-fordevelopment.challengepost.com.

11   And here I do have to add the disclaimer that the Lab is only less than eight months old at the time of writing, and therefore has not "proven" its success or the robustness of its approach yet (however that will be defined).

12   For instance, a quick Google search finds a product sheet from the Sustainable Development Group International which includes the following sentence as motivation: "SDGI believes that the best governed projects are those in which communities are encouraged to take an active part in identifying needs and formulating solutions". http://www.sdg-int.org/view/english/ensuring-local-participation-andownership.

13   One possible method is the Innovations Cafe hosted at UNICEF Innovations Lab Kosovo. The Lab is essentially hosting a community of young people working for social change using technology. These include people working on projects supported by the Lab, but include an open and welcome invitation for anyone working on similar projects. The Lab brings this community together every two weeks in an informal event where everyone gets together. The discussions involve Lab staff and sometimes revolve around the work that young people are doing in various ways, or ideas and problems posed by either UNICEF or the various government ministries UNICEF partners with.

14   See http://kosovoinnovations.com/w/byfy/projects for a list of projects that young people are working on at the Innovations Lab.

Annotation

Padmini Ray Murray

Prabhas Pokharel's article focuses on a specific shift in Nepalese protest culture that saw the country's youth mobilise themselves with tools traditionally used as an instrument of intervention by 'formal actors.' Pokharel defines formal actors as government and aid organisations, not-for-profit and private sector operations that work with and for young people to achieve social change.

This shift was occasioned by the NepalUnites protests, which urged the constituent assembly to frame the country's constitution, a process that had already been considerably delayed. A cursory search for the campaign throws up evidence of sustained organized endeavor, with a Twitter, Facebook, and blog presence, as well as diasporic groups united under the same banner. However, while these fora represented spaces where the youth could seize agency, it is worth considering some offline features that may have contributed to the success of the project. Nepal's inhabitants had already rallied behind the Citizen's Movement for Democracy and Peace in 2005, thus creating a blueprint for activism that was keen to distance itself from any rhetoric of being a "formal" or "political" organization. This lack of party bias presented a refreshing alternative to past struggles, and this characteristic may have also helped to contribute to the success of the NepalUnites campaign. While its online nature attracted criticism, as lack of access and literacy obviously prevented large swathes of the population from participating, and the protest itself did not accomplish its stated goals, it created a template for youth protest using the Internet as a mobilizing force. However, this brings up the question of how we quantify the success of such projects.

Looking back on this admirable initiative through the thicket of social network activity that now exists, in contrast to 2011, one can imagine a far more undiluted and immediate response than what might be fostered today by the constant attention deficit economy that currently prevails in online spaces. Added to this, the kneejerk activism encouraged by Facebook's 'liking' and 'sharing' mechanisms seem counter-productive to actual sustained protest.

While the protest itself did not yield political change, it can be argued that it succeeded on a level of affective spectacle. The increased ubiquity of media-producing gadgets and platforms for sharing such media almost demands the photogenic spectacle, in order to go viral and thus increase the visibility of the cause at hand. Paulo Gerbaudo describes this sort of decentralized, social-media-mobilized protest as "emotional choreographies," and images of the silent NepalUnites protest bear out the truth of this—the theatrical pervades and elevates the protest with an aura of the iconic, which then immediately fulfils its purpose as eminently shareable media.

What differentiates these hyper-documented protests from their predecessors is their dissemination through a citizen-powered, alternative media outlet, congregating under hashtags and @ characters but also that of a slogan: NepalUnites. Eric Kluitenberg designates the affective slogan as a "resonance object" which is "semantically void." It is instructive to observe that in this case, the slogan says nothing about what the campaign hopes to achieve; rather the emphasis is on mobilization, the more achievable goal. The slogan also marks the shift in status of the citizen from 'audience' to 'public' by virtue of the collapse of the private and public caused by the personal networked device—as Sonia Livingstone points out: "teenagers communicate privately in space that is conventionally public (texting in the cinema) and communicate publicly in space which is conventionally private"—and these behaviours are no longer restricted to the youth.

The most significant difference between the NepalUnites moment and the digital media landscape four years on, is how this public/private collapse has been negotiated and navigated by more traditional news organizations. The turn towards long form, multimedia narrative journalism (see The Guardian's seminal 'Firestorm' news story) has been spurred on by the decline of the print newspaper, and the struggle for such entities to remain relevant. These journalistic formats, along with disruptors such as clickbait sites and listicles, are most successful when deploying an empathetic human interest approach, replicating and reproducing affect. The algorithmic preferences of social sites can sometimes work counter to the demands of users, but I would argue that the force of the affective spectacle counteracts such logic by persuading readers to share such content, thus mobilizing themselves as actors working in favour of the cause.

References and Further Readings

Fuchs, Christian. 2014. *OccupyMedia! The Occupy Movement and Social Media in Crisis Capitalism*. Winchester: Zero Books.

Gerbaudo, Paolo. 2012. *Tweets and the Streets: Social Media and Contemporary Activism*. Pluto Press.

Henley, Jon, & Laurence Topham et al. 2013. "Firestorm: The Story of the Bushfire at Dunalley." The Guardian. May 23. http://www.theguardian.com/world/interactive/2013/may/26/firestorm-bushfire-dunalley-holmes-family.

Kuitenberg, Eric. 2015. "Affect Space: Witnessing the Movement(s) of the Squares." Online Open. March 10. http://www.onlineopen.org/article.php?id=298.

Livingstone, Sonia. 2012. *Audiences and Publics*. Intellect Ltd.

Papacharissi, Zizi. 2015. *Affective Publics: Sentiment, Technology, and Politics*. Oxford; New York, NY: Oxford University Press, USA.

Wikipedia, Bhanwari Devi and the Need for an Alert Feminist Public

Urvashi Sarkar

Until June 20th 2014, if you visited the Wikipedia entry on Bhanwari Devi—a women's rights Dalit activist who was raped for taking on child marriage in an upper caste community in her Rajasthan village—you would have been in for a nasty surprise.

The following lines from the biography section of the article would have stood out starkly:

> Bhanwari, the young, illiterate potter woman...strutting about the village giving gratuitous, unctuous advice to her social superiors made attempts to persuade the family against carrying out their wedding plans. Standing unveiled in the street outside the house of the brides-to-be she loudly berated the elderly patriarch... flaunted her government appointment... and threatening them that she would stop at nothing to ensure their public disgrace by stopping the planned marriage.

The citation for this paragraph was provided as 'Bhateri Rape Case: Backlash and Protest' by Kanchan Mathur published in the Economic and Political Weekly (EPW).

Not a single sentence from that paragraph features in the EPW article; but a preceding paragraph in the Wikipedia entry, which describes Bhanwari Devi's work as a *sathin* or grassroots worker with the Women's Development Project of the Rajasthan Government, is correctly attributed to the EPW piece.

Another paragraph titled 'The alleged gang rape' stated that after the Deputy Superintendent of Police (DSP) who examined Bhanwari for signs of injury "found only two extremely minor bruises" and doubted her story—Bhanwari is alleged to have claimed that she was a minor, "and therefore any intercourse with her, even if she had been a willing participant… was a criminal offense." It further notes that the DSP sent her to the Primary Health Centre (PHC) for a test "confirming the age of the victim". The citation for this is provided as a chapter titled 'The Politics of Patriarchy and Sathin Bhanwari's Rape' by Taisha Abraham from the book *Women and the Politics of Violence*.

While the chapter in question notes that the DSP, with whom Bhanwari tried to lodge an FIR, doubted her story — there is no reference to Bhanwari's claims of being a minor. Instead, it questions how a medical examination confirming the age of the victim — standard procedure for determining child marriage — could be relevant for a woman over 40 years old.

The entry also has parts highlighting Bhanwari's trials and triumphs – such as her being forced to deposit her skirt at the police station as evidence; mentioning her national and international recognition and awards, as well as the Vishaka guidelines relating to sexual harassment at the workplace, which were a direct outcome of her struggles.

Thus, the Wikipedia piece revealed a distinct pattern – of factually accurate information from sources such as The Indian Express, Tehelka, People's Union of Civil Liberties, The Hindu and Rediff, interspersed with large chunks of anonymous points of view, often wrongly attributed to these sources.

The 'Summary of evidence' section, which lacks citation, is described as confirming the claim of Bhateri villagers that Bhanwari was a "village slut", "a professional prostitute who felt cheated by life and exploited by men", it being "easiest for her to claim that she was raped."

The entry included the claim that Bhanwari refused compensation offered by her rapists because she was "enjoying unprecedented fame and publicity from the media and money from various organizations…" Some of the court observations are mentioned, which state that Bhanwari's husband couldn't have passively watched his wife being gang-raped and that since the accused included an uncle-nephew pair, it was implausible that a middle-aged man from an Indian village would participate in a gang rape in the presence of his own nephew. These court observations, sourced from Shivam Vij's 'A Mighty Heart', published by Tehelka, are twisted out of context and distort the intent of the attributed article which is to highlight Bhanwari's struggles and tenacity. This information is instead used to justify how her upper caste Gurjar rapists won the court case "because of the sheer strength of Truth."

Interestingly, the article steered clear of the most crucial and infamous part of the verdict: "Since the offenders were upper-caste men and included a brahmin, the rape could not have taken place because Bhanwari was from a lower caste." But the interpolating author's leanings are evident in the sympathetic language used for the accused Gurjar men who are described as being poor; illiterate and knowing nothing about court procedures or media management. "Unlike Bhanwari, they received no help from any social organization, activist, agenda-pusher or busybody." No citation is provided for this information.

It was claimed that a speedy verdict was given despite media scrutiny and pressure from women's groups, and that several judges felt coerced, "and unable to deliver the obvious, adverse judgment."

It appears that a standard piece with two citations originally, has been added to by several editors over the course of time.1 While some have made responsible additions, others have distorted the basic structure of the entry in misogynist and casteist ways.

Violation of Wikipedia's Content Policy

The problems with the Wikipedia article as I read it before June 20th are several—wrongly citing information is only one of them. Even more troubling is that such insertions are deliberately aimed at discrediting Bhanwari Devi herself. Further, the article in the form in which I read it violated Wikipedia's 'biographies of living people' policy according to which contentious material which is unsourced or poorly sourced must be immediately removed, especially if potentially libellous. Further such articles must adhere to a neutral point of view, verifiability, and contain no original research—comprising the website's core content policy. Wikipedia clarifies on its website that it is not a tabloid, but an encyclopaedia, and its job is not to be sensationalist or titillating. The article violated all these norms; in being poorly sourced, defamatory, lacking neutrality or verifiability, containing new unattributed information; and being both sensationalist and titillating.

Editing Wikipedia – The Perils of Democracy on the Internet

The fact that anyone can edit Wikipedia entries is its biggest plus and also a drawback. For instance, changes made by one editor can be repeatedly reversed by others. How easy is it to edit Wikipedia? Says Bishakha Datta, who is on the Wikimedia Foundation Board of Trustees:

> Wikipedia can be relatively hard to understand because it is a certain model of open knowledge. Most users are not knowledge producers, rather they are knowledge seekers. But they can be both and there can be barriers that people experience such as the technical barrier. There are editing options such as 'edit source' and 'editbeta' and the latter is easier.

But how does one know beforehand? Another barrier relates to policy and rules, wherein you are unsure of the rules and policies that govern editing and writing for Wikipedia. The time barrier is also a deterrent – properly editing a Wikipedia is time consuming and requires high motivation.

Editing or writing a Wikipedia entry is akin to writing a research paper, complete with citations and references, requiring a lot of work. In cases such as the Bhanwari Devi page, one can flag concerns by visiting the 'Talk' tab on page. There are also ways of protecting articles, so that they cannot be edited by one and all.

Need for an Alert Feminist Public

"Wikipedia is the world's fifth largest website and managed entirely by unpaid volunteers. There are 80,000 active editors who try to improve Wikipedia's content which is always a work in progress," says Bishakha. This is not an easy task given that most people have jobs, and work on Wikipedia on an unpaid volunteer basis. Frequent Wikipedia workshops [2] could be held for familiarisation with editing.[2] More importantly, there is need for an 'alert feminist public', both online and offline, which can remain vigilant and combat misogynist tendencies in all kinds of spaces – whether cultural, lingual, political, economic, or academic. Finally, we must not forget that Bhanwari Devi who was raped in the line of duty in 1992—and to whose struggle and courage we owe the Sexual Harassment of Women at Workplace (Prevention, Prohibition and Redressal) Act, 2013—has still not received justice 22 years after she was raped. After a sessions court verdict found the accused not guilty in 1995, the Rajasthan state government filed an appeal against the verdict in the Rajasthan High Court where it continues to languish.

The Wikipedia page on Bhanwari Devi is currently undergoing extensive edits by concerned editors.

Endnotes

1   2010. "Bhanwari Devi." Wikipedia. April 07. Accessed June 15, 2015. https://en.wikipedia.org/w/index.php?title=Bhanwari_Devi&oldid=354489880.
2   2014. "Wikipedia:Workshop." Wikipedia. November 19. Accessed June 15, 2015. https://en.wikipedia.org/wiki/Wikipedia:Workshop.

Annotation

Shobha S.V.

Today, Wikipedia is the largest open source encyclopaedia in the world. Before the advent of Wikipedia, knowledge creation, was always restricted to few people. Wikipedia brought with it the era of decentralisation and democratisation of knowledge creation. The intrinsic appeal of Wikipedia is that absolutely anyone can edit it. But is it that easy?

While it is true in principle, access to Wikipedia is also restricted by various factors. Who can edit Wikipedia is not a simple question. It is also a reflection of existing power dynamics within our society. Knowledge creation and dissemination do not exist in isolation. The varied levels of schism that exist in a society are reflected in the so-called democratised space of knowledge as well. Just as an electoral democracy sees fewer members of marginalised groups in power, the Wikipedian community reflects similar dynamics. Factors including lack of access to infrastructure in the form of computers, lack of proficiency in a language, lack of access to economic resources, and gender bias, among many others, end up having a profound impact on the way knowledge gets produced and used in the world. In India, a combination of factors of caste, class, and religion, among others, also ends up playing an important role in restricting people's access. Lack of access by certain communities results in homogeneity in terms of the contributors.

For instance, it is a well-documented fact that Wikipedia has been facing a shortage of women editors on a global scale. One of the consequences of the shortage of women editors on Wikipedia is that articles about women tend to be short or absent completely. There are multiple reasons why there aren't many women editing Wikipedia. Studies have shown that the so-called collaborative space within Wikipedia often turns out to be a space that is conflict-driven, and women have experienced bullying from fellow male contributors driving them away from the space. Few numbers of women attract even fewer women to the space, and the vicious cycle continues. The editing of the Wikipedia article on Bhanwari Devi is a classic example of how a dominant caste narrative tries to censor subaltern narratives. Add sexism to the dynamic and we get a deadly mix!

There are many efforts underway in different parts of the world to address the gender imbalance. For instance, Wikipedia edit-a-thons are being conducted by many groups all over the world. FemTechNet is a group of feminist academics, scholars and students that tries different ways of using Wikipedia to address the gender gap within Wikipedia and also in technology. Their edit-a-thons - where they come together and edit articles on Wikipedia - and other pedagogical methods that involve students using Wikipedia are some of the innovative ways by which they try to address the problem of the gender gap. In India as well, there is a small community that conducts Wikipedia edit-a-thons all over the country to encourage more women from diverse backgrounds to participate in editing the open source encyclopaedia.

Wikipedia is a product of knowledge activism. Encyclopaedic knowledge, which was hitherto accessible to only a few, is now free. However, it doesn't end there. What gets passed off as knowledge, and who gets to write it, are critical questions that one needs to ask. The Internet is like a street. Having your voice heard on the street can only happen when you have access to the street. Having your voice heard when you barely have access to the street is an act of activism. And ensuring that marginalised voices also have similar access to a democratic space is the only way one can truly live up to the spirit of Wikipedia.

References and Further Readings

Gardner, Sue. 2011. "Nine Reasons Women Don't Edit Wikipedia (in their Own Words)." Sue Gardner's Blog. February 19. Accessed April 26, 2015. http://suegardner.org/2011/02/19/nine-reasons-why-women-dont-edit-wikipedia-in-their-own-words/.

Hussein, Netha. 2013. "Indian WikiWomen Celebrate Women's History Month." Wikimedia Blog, April 24. Accessed April 26, 2015. https://blog.wikimedia.org/2013/04/24/indian-wikiwomen-celebrate-womens-history-month.

Liss-Schultz, Nina. 2013. "Can These Students Fix Wikipedia's Lady Problem?" Mother Jones. August 23. Accessed April 26, 2015. http://www.motherjones.com/mixed-media/2013/08/storming-wikipedia-women-problem-internet.

Meyer, Robinson. 2013. "90% of Wikipedia's Editors Are Male—Here's What They're Doing About It." *The Atlantic*, October 25. Accessed April 26, 2015. http://www.theatlantic.com/technology/archive/2013/10/90-of-wikipedias-editors-are-male-heres-what-theyre-doing-about-it/280882.

Mirk, Sarah. 2014. "An Epic Feminist Edit-a-Thon Takes Aim at Wikipedia's Gender Gap." Bitch Magazine. January 24. Accessed April 26, 2015. http://bitchmagazine.org/post/an-epic-edit-a-thon-takes-aim-at-wikipedias-gender-gap.

Phadnis, Renuka. 2014. "Pushing Women Scientists." The Hindu. October 20. Accessed April 26, 2015. http://www.thehindu.com/news/cities/bangalore/wikipedia-editathon-attempts-to-raise-awareness-of-the-contribution-of-indian-women-to-science/article6517035.ece.

Roth, Matthew. 2012."Fem-Tech Edit-a-Thon Sparks Discussions about Wikipedia Gender Gap." Wikimedia Blog. November 26. Accessed April 26, 2015. https://blog.wikimedia.org/2012/11/26/fem-tech-edit-a-thon-sparks-discussions-about-wikipedia-gender-gap/.

Rogers, Kaleigh. 2015. "Wikipedia's Gender Problem Has Finally Been Quantified." Motherboard. February 4. Accessed April 26, 2015. http://motherboard.vice.com/read/wikipedias-gender-problem-has-finally-been-quantified.

"Teaching with Wikipedia." FemTechNet Commons. http://femtechnet.newschool.edu/teaching-learning-resources/teaching-with-wikipedia/.

Digital Natives in the Name of a Cause: From "Flash Mob" to "Human Flesh Search"

YiPing (Zona) Tsou

The emergence of newly imagined communities

The dominant discourse around use of digital and internet technologies has been either mired in celebration or pathologisation. On one hand are the people who bask in the participatory power of Web 2.0 technologies, announcing the emergence of new public spheres and democratic spaces of engagement and expression. On the other hand are the detractors who remain sceptical of the 'newness' that digital technologies bring, often repeating the axiom of how, more the things change, the more they remain the same. In this discourse, even though the warring lines are clearly drawn and the dialogue is often fraught and tense, there is something that remains unexamined and unquestioned – In the imagination of either of the warring factions the users who remain at the centre of the discourse are identical.

Scholars and practitioners alike, whether they are hopeful all the way, waiting to witness the bright, promising future that the information and communication technology (ICT) is going to bestow upon us, liberating all the oppressed from the tyranny of the authoritarian regimes and repressive censorship, or skeptics who stay alert of "the dark side of internet freedom"and are addressing the issue with sentiment of disillusionment, mourning for the failed (or not yet fulfilled) promise of a digital utopia, presume that the beneficiaries and architects of this new public spheres are still well intentioned, progressive, liberal and tolerant users. Sure, there might be occasional exclamations at questions of piracy, pornography, bullying, etc. but it is always believed that there is something intrinsic in the nature of the internet that 'cures' the existing evils of our times. Even in the discourse around these subversive activities, there is a resilient hope that the 'user' of cyberspaces would necessarily be a civic-minded person.

However, as blogger and commentator Evgeny Morozov perceptively points out, no matter how wistful we are, social media and Web 2.0 do not always foster civic engagement and democratic reform. In effect, the very tools the revolutionaries use to undermine the authoritarian governments are just as likely to grant dictators with more powerful weapons to crush a popular uprising or any budding rebellious force.[1] This essay tries to look at the 'other' side of cyberspaces to show that digital natives and the causes they espouse are not automatically desirable. These new generations of prosumers, who consume, produce, share and disseminate information in participatory and collaborative ways, can also mobilise their resources for regressive and authoritarian ambitions. This essay shows, how, in this age of ubiquitous computing, hitherto contained violences find greater supporters and audiences than ever before. The very platforms and techniques of user-generated content archives, collaborative production of information, peer-2--peer loose affiliations and an unregulated space for germination of ideas can also lead to the production of a digital native identity that can be dangerous and destructive.

It is not the intention of the essay to be steeped in paranoia and call for a censorship or regulation of the internet spaces. Rather it seeks to make us aware of the biases we hold when talking about digital natives by locating them only in progressive liberal contexts.

In the process, it also develops a new way of understanding contexts, which are not only about the geo-politics but also about the imagined histories and legacies, ambitions and aspirations that we attribute to digital natives.

In order to make this argument, I look at two significant processes which have emerged with participatory technologies, use the same technological impulses and yet achieve very opposite results. The first is the phenomenon of flash-mob – a viral networking mobilisation that calls for people who do not know each other but are connected with each other through the technologies and digital platforms that they consume, to come together in public spaces and perform a series of unexplained, often bizarre actions that subvert the logic and intended design of the spaces. Flash mobs have been used successfully as political statements, cultural innovation, social rejuvenation and a tool for mobilising large numbers of people to engage in civic and leisure activities collectively. The second is the phenomenon of "Human Flesh Search" (人肉搜索renrousousuo) that has lately gained currency in the People's Republic of China (PRC) and Taiwan – The Human Flesh Search is a peer-2-peer network that harnesses the 'wisdom of crowds' to search for people who might have offended a community or a collective but escaped the ire of the mobs by remaining anonymous online. Human Flesh Searches mobilise masses of people online or offline to identify certain violators of 'morality' that the community seeks to punish because the 'crimes' might not be punishable by the law. In looking at both these, I'd like to lay bare the grey area between the bright side of a cyber-utopia that would be attained through the egalitarian progressive valuesinbuilt in the prevailing discourse of ICT and the other side that we tend to overlook where the risk of alternative use, or purely abuse of the internet, lies in the name of a cause.

Digital natives with a thousand voices

With the advance of technology, the world seems to have become widely wired, operating on the common language of digital literacy. In this wired world emerged what the scholars called 'Digital Natives', which is still a highly contested term.[2]

The *Digital Natives with a Cause?* Knowledge Programme began with each of us seeking to define and identify with the term Digital Native; however, the real journey started after all participants from different regions and cultures agreed to disagree that we do not wear the term Digital Native uniformly. Some of us proudly claimed the title of 'geek' and declared "geek is the new sexy" while others exclaimed "we are not all techies!"[3] Some members felt "staying offline" sounded worse than "committing suicide" and some believed in "the right to unplug" or "to lurk online".[4] Probably the only thing everyone agreed on was the fact that, apart from a very (un)privileged few, no matter what we do, most of people today can hardly operate outside the parameters of digital technologies.

"When in doubt, Google" is a motto virtually shared by all of us. Turning to social networking websites and mobile devices has become an everyday activity so embedded in our routine that we do not even feel we are "utilising" the digital technology. Surrounded by all pervasive digital devices as we are today, even though we do not claim or avow to be digital activists who aim for a radical, social reform, our concept of activity/activism is being so radically reformatted that we are constantly inventing new modes of engagement with public events, the much condemned "slacktivism" or "clicktivism" included.[5] Criticism aside, the dominant discourse tends to have a positive outlook on the emergent imagined communities shaped by digital technologies, attributing the recent progressive and democratic development to digital natives who speak the new-fangled language of this information age and hence are supposed to act upon a greater cause for the betterment of the world.

In fact, such discourse is quite powerful as shown by the comments after successive revolutions in the Middle East and North Africa which are taking place in 2011. The world seems to have witnessed the glory that is the "smart mob", a gathering of those who know how to utilise the communication technologies, and are able to connect and mobilise themselves, and successfully congregate in a physical space so as to make social impact in person.[6] The mass media and a vast array of commentators along with popular bloggers sing in unison, eulogising over these "smart mobs" who symbolise a new face of revolutionaries armed with their smartphones and other high-tech gadgets, and predict a latest wave of revolution employing tactics unseen before the advent of digital technologies.[7] Such success stories have set many other authoritarian regimes on high alert, including the People's Republic of China[8] that took quick steps to ensure that such mobilisations of masses questioning the authority of the government do not mushroom in the country.[9]

The dark force of digital natives

The PRC government has been known for its strict control over the "internet freedom" (or more precisely, speech freedom both online and offline) while ironically, everyday civilian Chinese are among the most destructive and intrusive hackers that pose a serious threat to cyber-security all over the world (aside from China itself). However, these Chinese hackers, though not in direct association with the central government, are more in line with the Communist party politics than against it.[10] Their cyber-attacks are often instigated by nationalistic prompts and mainly targeted at the so-called offending countries instead of challenging the overriding ideology of the Communist Party, and rarely focus on the domestic public affairs within China.[11] In effect, some Chinese patriotic hackers even call themselves "red hackers" and are highly esteemed among the general public as they appear to set a model for the nation.[12] The acclamation for these hackers is akin to the accolade for the brave smart mobs, who purportedly aspired to "activate" a revolution via social networking sites and digital communication tools in an attempt to achieve democracy in the Middle East and North Africa (MENA) discourse. Of course, hackers are not equivalent of smart mobs in that they simply manipulate the systems so as to make a virtual announcement of their existence without making a physical presence in public. Simply put, even though they may make an impact socially, in reality their faces remain hidden behind the screen.

Locating digital natives in China helps us unpack the different presumptions that build the idea of a Hacker. They are not necessarily hackers, but there are undeniably some overlaps, and if the aforementioned mentality is any indicator, it would not seem so surprising when there is no serious attempt at a Chinese version of a "Jasmine Revolution" initiated by the smart mob in the PRC.[13] Moreover, if we know the socio-historical context of China, then there is no surprise at all why a smart mob has never become a driving force in the

PRC that compels any political or social change so far. In effect, ever since the Tiananmen Square protests of 1989 (a series of students' non-violent demonstrations for economic reform and liberalisation) were met by a militant massacre (which was claimed to never have taken place by the PRC press and media),[14] the authorities concerned have been successfully suppressing any potential revolt with the aid of their 'Law of the People's Republic of China on Assemblies, Processions and Demonstrations' enacted right after the Tiananmen crackdown.[15] Hence the political gathering in public could cause the participants a great risk of ending up in prison. Accordingly, any open gathering even just purely for fun, such as flash mob activity, is still few and far in between.[16] While the smart/flesh mob is somehow kept in check in the PRC, there is a curious collaborative cyber activity called "人肉搜 索引 renrousousuo yingqing," or simply ren'rousou'suo, literally and graphically translated as "Human Flesh Search Engine".

This Human Flesh Search Engine, according to James K. Yuann and Jason Inch, the authors of *Supertrends of Future China*, seems to share many of the characteristics of Clay Shirky's networked social collaboration: "Enabled and made cost-effective by technology, channeling an existing motivation that was not possible to act upon as a group before".[17] But while the types of group-forming that Clay Shirky, in his book *Here Comes Everybody* describes as "flash mobs" have been staging certain anti-authoritarian demonstrations (such as the flash mob gathering in Belarus where people came to a public square in the capital Minsk to do nothing but eat ice cream together while the government agents still treated this as an illegal assembly and arrested some of the young participants),[18] such flash mobs are hard to spot in China. Even in the few successful mobilisations that attracted media attention, flash mobs in the PRC seem yet to have evinced any element of confrontation and have been often described as a whim of fashion to the public.[19] On the other hand, the Human Flesh Search, which basically deploys similar tactics and mechanics, and draws on the wisdom of the crowds, crowd sourcing, Friend-of-a-Friend structure, and may well be deemed an alternative form of flash mobs, has virtually turned into a nation-wide operation that engages and mobilises a great and growing number of Chinese internet users (often referred to by the Chinese media as *'netizenwang min'* or 網民" who would stay online virtually all the time). Although similar occurrence of crowd-sourced virtual detective work has been seen in other countries, quite a few commentators claim Human Flesh Search is a culture-specific phenomenon that had started as early as the year 2001 in China and quickly spread to other parts of East Asia (Taiwan in particular).[20]

Witch Hunt 2.0: Digital natives with a chase

The allegedly first case of Human Flesh Search took place in 2001 when a netizen posted the Hong Kong actress Ziyao Chen's photo online and claimed her to be his girlfriend. This instigated the other unbelieving netizens to start a crowd-sourced detective network through Chinese forums and bulletin boards and discover her true identity - stripped off the vested interest and exposed the naked truth, the pure "flesh". But it was not until 2006 with the "kitten-killer" incident in which a video of a girl crushing a kitten to death with her stilettos was posted online, that *Renrou Sousuo* became a widely known and fast spreading phenomenon in the PRC.

Within hours of the posting of the said video, indignant Chinese netizens scrutinised the footage and traced back the unknown 'faceless' perpetrator in the video to her exact locale by mobilising human and digital resources aided by their smart gadgets. They initiated a project on Mop forum[21] calling for "hunting down the lady and the cameraman" which went viral on many popular forums and soon formed a nationwide network of "human flesh search" powered by a combination of computer networking skills as well as human connection. An anonymous netizen traced the original video link and revealed the video was posted by someone registered as Ganimas. Then the crowd followed up to conduct keyword search in Baidu (China's equivalent of Google) and quickly discovered many purchases of high heels (the above stilettos included) under the same user ID, and since online transactions need certain verification of personal information, Ganimas was quickly nailed. Meanwhile, another netizen identified the locale of the incident as his/her hometown in Heilongjiang province and provided similar photos featured on local government's tourist information website, which further prompted a Google Earth search confirming the locale. With this crucial information, a man who had done transactions with Ganimas and worked in a local TV station followed up on the leads. Four days after the search began, the traditional media picked up the story, and people all across China saw the kitten killer's photo all over the TV and newspapers. And the lady, Wang Jiao, was soon identified by a netizen who lived in the same town and had seen her working as a nurse in the local hospital.[22]

In less than a week, the cyberposse exposed every single detail of this woman's life—including her real name, age, marital status, whereabouts (address of domicile as well as office), which resulted in constant bombardment of thousands of malicious phone calls and even death threats, and eventually led to her forced suspension from her position and eventually she had to leave her hometown.[23] If there were a theme song for this incident, it would probably be "Ding-Dong! The witch is dead! Now let's go searching for other witches among us!" As we can sense from internet comments, media coverage and even official response, the majority seems to have taken this case as a "just" execution, which has probably spurred more netizens to take on a self-appointed mission to go on more of such "witch hunt" in ensuing years.

In fact, by the year of 2008, it had become so popular that Google even made a mock webpage of *Renrou Sousuo* for the April Fool's Day prank in simplified Chinese, recruiting experts with "a spirit of Gossipism and preferably a casual and cavalier style" along with volunteers as long as the applicant "owns a computer, a telephone, some chalks, a box of napkins, a whole set of 40 volumes The Charts of Popular Gossip Figures, sixteenth edition (large print)".

The descriptions of this manpowered, all-powerful search engine are hilarious, especially when they proudly declare their mission statement, and no one can render it better and more poetic than the Google Translator itself. *Renrou Sousuo* does not have an inherent or consistent cause: "the truth behind a certain door", "public recognition of a moral position", "the most beautiful jungle girl", "the most touching Alpine herdsmen", "the most mysterious desert cave", "the most romantic encounter".... An infinite possibility seems to lies in such endless search for truth and justice, beauty and romance, and everything that touches a heart and strikes a chord with the audience. Poetic, isn't it? It seems to start out as such an innocuous and effective way of searching and sharing the information.

However, Human Flesh Search has gradually turned into a double-edged sword, cutting through the line between good and bad.[24] Tom Downey, *The New York Times* journalist, elucidates such a conceptual turn in his article entitled "China's Cyberposse," pointing out that "[t]he popular meaning is now not just a search *by* humans but also a search for humans, initially performed online but intended to cause real-world consequences."[25]

As the name suggests, the Human Flesh Search graphically depicts this kind of search that is conducted by human connections rather than machine-based algorithms to locate the sources of information as well as calculate the relevance of the data for the sake of ferreting out and hunting down the human target who has committed all sorts of wrongdoings, ranging from telling a lie (as in the allegedly first case), blocking the ambulance and flashing the middle finger,[26] refusing to yield the seat to the elderly,[27] abusing a cat,[28] sexually harassing a girl,[29] having an affair,[30] hit-and-run[31] to anything that is considered "immoral" or "improper" by the wide wired world which could virtually go wild in the name of justice and vengeance.[32]

As aptly put by Downey, "[t]hey [Human Flesh Searches] are a form of online vigilante justice in which Internet users hunt down and punish people who have attracted their wrath. The goal is to get the targets of a search fired from their jobs, shamed in front of their neighbors, run out of town." Kevin Bloom, a writer and critic based in South Africa, further points out that after the "kitten-killer" incident, what used to be "a form of harmless crowd-sourcing, suddenly became a network for fed-up social activists with a taste for non-conceptual blood".[33]

In a sense, the prevailing Human Flesh Search Engine feeds on flesh and blood of those who are accused of committing misdemeanours, moral vices or simply dissidence; in other words, it has somehow transformed into a man-powered censorship machine spontaneously run by the civilian netizens, operating "search and punish" mechanism.

Not only is the Big Brother watching you, but now that the little brothers and sisters join force to monitor all the aberrant and deviant who do not act in conformity with the societal norms, social mores as well as political ideology, a more effective surveillance has come in force from the bottom-up.

Hence, any case of aberrant behaviour, once spotted, recorded and uploaded online, could trigger moral panic as well as mass hysteria and can lead to public shaming and lynching of the target by the angry mob.[34]

Human Flesh Search, in this sense, is just like an updated, modern and perhaps more "civilised" form of medieval witch-hunt, with the same self-righteous mentality, the modern cyberposse equipped with the new technology would sniff out "the witch" in no time. Once the human target has been singled out from a myriad of "open calls for human flesh search" [人肉搜索令], without so much as a trial but a persecution, the net vigilantes would go into great lengths to expose every single detail of the targeted individual's personal life, flaying the flesh and blood alive, and condemning the privacy of the sought to a virtual death. In a grim case, such Human Flesh Search has even caused an actual death.[35] Despite grave admonitions some commentators put forward, warning us of the consequences of misuse of technology and privacy violation, the term "人肉搜索引擎 *renrou sousuo yingqing*" has become so trendy that the youth have started to use "Human Flesh *ren'rou*人肉" as a verb. Discussion forums are always inundated with "calls for human flesh search人肉搜索令"to the point that the expression "人肉他！*ren'rou ta*", literally translated as "human flesh him/her", has taken on an uncanny nuance of cannibalism.

One signature picture posted on Mop.com, from which the term "Human Flesh Search" originated, in which two girls are waving knives with blood on them, and the slogan at the right bottom reads "We are the chopper gang".[36]

Mob 2.0: Digital natives with/out a cause

Some scholars have taken positive positions and made optimistic predictions about the Human Flesh Search Engine, thinking it could remedy deficiencies of the legal systems and redress the failing moral values in the Chinese society, such a mechanism of "search and punish" has a serious flaw when the issues it readdresses are not so clear-cut black and white. This is aptly pointed out by Bloom.

Nestling somewhere between the related concepts of "tyranny of the majority" and "the irrationality of crowds," said flaw was illustrated in June 2008 by the story of a young woman named Gao Qianhui, who just wanted to watch her favourite programme on television.[37]

Gao became a target since she recorded a video to give full vent to her frustration about the three-day national mourning period for Sichuan quake that disrupted regular TV schedules. The video was clearly for her to rant and rave, but her remarks such as "Come on, how many of you died? Just a few, right? There are so many people in China anyway," triggered a Human Flesh Search to, again, hound down the "witch/bitch". Within hours, her identity was exposed, and the next day local police came to arrest her, albeit without any legitimate reason to detain her.[38]

However, the "tyranny of the majority" and "the irrationality of crowds" are even more palpable in the case of Grace Wang (王千源), who was a freshman at Duke University when she tried to mediate the two camps between the pro-Tibet independence and pro-Chinese protesters in April 2008.[39] The netizens again reacted as one, mobilising the wired world to dig out her personal information in an attempt to punish her "treason" in siding with Tibetan independence. The Human Flesh Search instigated by the nationalist sentiment was so powerful that once her parents' home address was posted online, they had to flee from their house and go in hiding for the sake of safety.

It is not unheard of that "the wisdom of the crowd" could verge on "the noise of the mob," which is probably best manifested by the innumerable edit wars on Wikipedia talk pages where people engage in heated discussion about certain edited page yet end up in fierce verbal swordplay and personal attack. In most parts of the world, fierce and brutal though such warfare of ideologies is, none has ever gone "physical" and actually attacked people beyond the virtual domain, which is not the case with a lot of "virtual wars" on discussion forums and bulletin boards that have gone "real", or rather, real dirty in the Human Flesh Search phenomenon in China.

Both cases demonstrate the ease and speed with which people can be mobilised for a cause, whether it is just or not, it would be justified by the mob mentality when "all becomes one". Just as the saying goes, "the mob has many heads, but no brains". In carrying out a shared cause, the individual netizens coalesce to form a vigilante group of some sorts, often bordering on a lynch-mob mentality. Thus, once the mob is formed by any sensationalised call for Human Flesh Search, the authenticity of the piece of information shared might not be of primary concern, and no one would actually go into length to first examine whether the poster is telling a lie. There has been a weird sentiment "we are in this together", so no one can really question whether the original poster has the right to initiate such search, and even if the mob got the wrong target, the cause is still right.[40] In fact, whenever such a cyber mob is formed, "right is determined by a kind of process of consensus-building where the strongest, earnest, motivated voices may dominate," as Yuann and Inch perceptively point out.[41] Those who believe that internet and communication technology can serve as a power equalizer and has greater democratic potential may feel disappointed since the Human Flesh Search in China has proven quite the opposite.[42] ICT does not help equalise distribution of resources, and by extension, power in the digital age. In some sense, it empowers people with tools and skills to begin with, and as the optimists expect, there have been indeed some successful cases of Human Flesh Search that exercise citizen surveillance. Yet most of the time, they have nothing to do with governmental officials but merely an ordinary someone who used to be able to hide among the crowd. But now, as we can see from the miserable outcome of those who have become the target of the Human Flesh Search, they are forced to face a multitude of netizens, anonymous, gregarious and ubiquitous, executing many-to-one surveillance in perfect unison.

There is no way to hide from the public gaze when everybody is watching everybody, but don't panic, we have nothing to worry about as long as we "stay in line" both online and offline, we will live together in perfect harmony, happily ever after... Or at least, so says the Communist Party, stressing a utopian vision of a "harmonious society".[43] Under such a big banner, all the surveillance and censorship seems to be justified, and in some sense, these internet vigilantes, cyberposse or "norm polices" are in line with the "red hackers," working hand in hand with the dominant ideology, fighting against the enemy abroad while hunting down the enemy within who disrupts the "harmony". Freedom of speech? Personal privacy? Democracy? That's heresy of the West! When Mob 2.0 is mobilised, "the many" has become ONE (and this ONE cannot be challenged) even in the so-called democratic society such as Taiwan.

Out of many, comes ONE

As soon as the controversial ruling of disqualification during the mid-bout of a Taekwondo contestant Yang Shu-chun from Taiwan when she was leading 9-0 at the Asian Games on 17 November 2010 was announced, the whole wired world in Taiwan was immediately flooded with indignant posts and many started to investigate the "truth" by gathering information from different sources, uploading live recording of the match online.[44] Their coverage of the story appeared online almost instantaneously, if not faster, than all the main-stream media reports in Taiwan and overseas.[45] When our official association and government was slow in reaction, many digital natives initiated campaigns on Facebook and some even went to lengths to translate the incident into English to spread the word out.[46]

While all voices chanted in unison, targeting the Korean judge and Chinese officials, the dissidence stood out: A student posted remarks on his Facebook, declaring that he was "totally supportive of the Korean's ruling" and that he "felt great since Korean judge's hard-line dealing would give Team Chinese Taipei a good lesson". The reaction was immediate and sensationalised. The online community soon proved the old saying still goes: "Unity is strength" by executing Human Flesh Search to dig out every bits and pieces of his personal information and share it with the whole world. In no time, his blog was inundated by furious posts accusing him of being a "traitor", his cellphone kept receiving foul text and voice messages, and he claimed to be stalked when he walked home. Eventually he shut off his Facebook account, agreed to be interviewed and warned those who had harassed him that he had the freedom of speech and would file a lawsuit if they did not stop harassing him.

It seems that the Human Flesh Search, though done in different regions and by different people, manifests exactly the same pattern and exercises a routine that hunts the heretic all the way from online to offline life. Of course, digital natives in the PRC and Taiwan claim they are doing this for a cause, and a noble one in their sense, to find and stop/punish the immoral, but exactly who lays down those rules and standards to judge and evaluate the 'morality', 'integrity' or 'patriotism' of someone whom we may never even know in person and meet in life? Who has the right to decide who ought to be searched or punished? How do we know whether the cause is justified and wouldn't turn into an excuse? When the multitude of voices becomes ONE, it could be a dangerous sign. Even though most of us start from the "right" side (or so we believe), it is hard to say we would never end up on the other side.

The name of the cause

Clearly, there is no returning of this digital revolution, and the newly imagined communities that we call Digital Natives are of a thousand voices, fighting for a variety of causes, may not be all progressive, liberal and striving to make a change for the better. The ICT grant us a new set of powerful tools, but a social tool is only as good or as bad as the people who are using it.

No matter how "liberating" and "empowering" we imagine the tools to be, *a tool is a tool is a tool*... Meanwhile, it does not matter what certain flash mobs or smart mobs have done in the past, digital natives all over the world are not of one face, there is an undeniably dark force breeding among us. On occasion, the changes could be violent and the causes could verge on or end up as excuses to exploit the ICT so as to hunt down any dissident or "peacebreaker" that disrupts "harmony".

The Causes that we espouse and the ambitions that we enable with the use of digital technologies and the tools that they provide, hence, need to be questioned. Merely the use of digital technologies do not make us digital natives – the impulses, the aspirations, the desires, the contexts, the impetus and the motivation, all add to understanding our relationships with digital and internet technologies. It might be true that one becomes digital and is not born so, but before one becomes digital one wears many different identities. Not all of these identities necessarily endorse individual freedom and rights. The technologies that allow us to create processes of change for a just and equitable world are also technologies that enable massively regressive and vigilante acts that exercise a mob-based notion of justice. Maybe we need to add qualifications to our understanding of who a digital native is. Maybe we need to define not only the users, but also the politics behind their actions; And we definitely need new frameworks and vocabularies to account for a section of the population who might be equally skilled and fluent with these digital technologies but produce another kind of change, using the same tools and processes that we rejoice in.

Endnotes

1. See the introduction of the The Net Delusion — The Dark Side of Internet Freedom. http://www.publicaffairsbooks.com/publicaffairsbooks-cgi-bin/display?book=9781586488741.
2. Marc Prensky coined the term digital native in his work Digital Natives, Digital Immigrants published in 2001. In his seminal article, he assigns it to a new group of students enrolling in educational establishments. The term draws an analogy to a country's natives, for whom the local religion, language, and folkways are natural and indigenous, compared with immigrants to a country who often are expected to adapt and begin to adopt the region's customs. (http://en.wikipedia.org/wiki/Digital_Natives).
3. Maesy Angelina's comment left on the art installation at the Thinkathon.
4. The Digital Natives With a Cause? blog. http://www.digitalnatives.in.
5. Slacktivism (sometimes slactivism or clicktivism) is a portmanteau formed out of the words slacker and activism. The word is usually considered a pejorative term that describes "feel-good" measures, in support of an issue or social cause, that have little or no practical effect other than to make the person doing it feel satisfaction.
6. Howard Rheingold's definition from Smart Mobs: The Next Social Revolution.
7. http://tribune.com.pk/story/122242/a-new-wave-of-revolution/; http://www.miller-mccune.com/politics/the-cascading-effects-of-the-arab-spring-28575/.
8. http://www.jamestown.org/programs/chinabrief/single/?-tx_ttnews[tt_news]=37487&tx_ttnews[backPid]=25&cHash=91247-dc039a331a186c9182ccd7317b2; http://www.insideriowa.com/index.cfm?nodeID=17818&audienceID=1&action=display&newsID=11615.#.VZuLhaaFbSc
9. http://chinadigitaltimes.net/2011/04/jasmine-in-the-middle-kingdom-autopsy-of-chinas-failed-revolution/; http://www.miller-mccune.com/media/media-and-revolution-2-0--tiananmen-to-tahrir-28595/; http://www.theglobeandmail.com/news/world/asia-pacific/uprooting-the-chinese-jasmine-revolution/article1987779/page2/.
10. In a 2005 Hong Kong Sunday Morning Post article, a man identified as "the Godfather of hackers" explains, "Unlike our Western [hacker] counterparts, most of whom are individualists or anarchists, Chinese hackers tend to get more involved with politics because most of them are young, passionate, and patriotic. [...] Jack LinchuanQiu, a

communications professor at the Chinese University of Hong Kong who spent the 2001 hacker war logged into mainland forums, agrees. "Chinese hackerism is not the American 'hacktivism' that wants social change," he says. "It's actually very close to the state. The Chinese distinction between the private and public domains is very small."

11 http://www.popsci.com/scitech/article/2009-04/hackers-china-syndrome?page=2.
12 "This culture thrives on a viral, Internet-driven nationalism. The post-Tiananmen generation has known little hardship, so rather than pushing for democracy, many young people define themselves in opposition to the West. China's Internet patriots, who call themselves "red hackers," may not be acting on direct behalf of their government, but the effect is much the same."http://www.popsci.com/scitech/article/2009-04/hackers-china-syndrome#. "A 2005 Shanghai Academy of Social Sciences survey equates hackers and rock stars, with nearly 43 percent of elementary-school students saying they "adore" China's hackers. One third say they want to be one." http://www.popsci.com/scitech/article/2009-04/hackers-china-syndrome#.
13 http://chinadigitaltimes.net/2011/04/jasmine-in-the-middle-kingdom-autopsy-of-chinas-failed-revolution/; http://www.miller-mccune.com/media/media-and-revolution-2-0--tiananmen-to-tahrir-28595/; http://www.theglobeandmail.com/news/world/asia-pacific/uprooting-the-chinese-jasmine-revolution/article1987779/page2/.
14 http://globalspin.blogs.time.com/2011/06/04/22-years-after-tiananmen-shadow-of-crackdown-looms-large-over-china/.
15 See http://www.ahga.gov.cn/falv/GAZHFLFG/FL/1083.htm; http://reason.com/archives/2009/06/04/china-after-tiananmen.
16 There are indeed some fun incidents of youth dancing or playing a prank in public. Nonetheless, occurrences of a smart or flash mob that have taken place in the PRC are, demographically speaking, relatively insignificant and sporadic compared to the prevalent and vigourous happenings elsewhere. But they do have websites set up for flash mob gathering such as http://www.hlo.cc/, http://www.artmy.cn/ but there are few successful mobilisation drives known to the public. In effect, the coverage is few and far in between at its best.
17 In their blog article "China's Human Flesh Search Engine - Not what you might think it is...", James K. Yuann and Jason Inch share a lot of insights on this phenomenon which they argue is unique in China. http://www.chinasupertrends.com/chinas-human-flesh-search-engine-not-what-you-might-think-it-is/.
18 See "Ice cream politics: flash mob in Belarus" posted by Howard Rheingold on October 3rd, 2006 http://www.smartmobs.com/2006/10/03/ice-cream-politics-flash-mob-in-belarus/.
19 Almost all of the flash mob activities that have successfully took place in the PRC so far have been staged like a performance, most people either sing a song or dance, or perform a skit at best. Here are the rare news coverage in English: "'Flash Mob' Puzzles Bystanders" http://www.china.org.cn/english/entertainment/220084.htm; "'Flashmob' of 12 Proposed to One Girl in Beijing" http://english.cri.cn/3100/2006/09/03/202@134346.htm.
20 For an insightful overview of this argument in English, see "Human Flesh Search: Old Topic, New Story" posted on Friday, June 27, 2008 by Xujun Eberlein http://www.insideout-china.com/2008/06/human-flesh-search-old-topic-new-story.html; in Chinese, "Manpower Search: Cyber public space, Social Functions and Legal Regulations" [人肉搜索：網絡公共空間、社會功能與法律規制] http://cdn851.todayisp.net:7751/article.chinalawinfo.com/Article_Detail.asp?ArticleId=47680.
21 Mop Forum is one of the most popular social networking sites in China. You can read more about it at http://en.wikipedia.org/wiki/Mop.com.
22 See Dongxiao Liu's Human Flesh Search Engine: Is It a Next Generation Search Engine?
23 http://hplusmagazine.com/2009/06/02/search-and-destroy-engines/.
24 You can still access it at http://www.google.cn/intl/zh-CN/renrou/index.html. As the article "China's Human Flesh Search Engine - Not what you might think it is..." points out, "The fact that day was April 1st should tell readers it was meant as tongue-in-cheek (and may not entirely be a joke - a number of search engines have tried human-assisted search and

relevance checking), but it put a name to a movement that has been happening online in China for some time: Online collaboration by Netizens to search via the power of China's massive 225 million Internet users." (http://www.chinasupertrends.com/chinas-human-flesh-search-engine-not-what-you-might-think-it-is/ posted on May 25, 2008 3:56 pm). A famous online magazine in Hong Kong dedicated a feature on this phenomenon entitled "'Human Flesh Search'—Is it a Demon or an Angel?「人肉搜索」是 惡魔還是天使" which has provided a comprehensive overview of this controversial issue. (http://hot.wenweipo.com/2008035/).

25 http://www.nytimes.com/2010/03/07/magazine/07Human-t.html?_r=2&pagewanted=-all; See the list among the most notorious cases in China: http://xzczkt.gicp.net/show.asp?id=205; http://en.wikipedia.org/wiki/Human_flesh_search_engine#Notable_examples

26 "University student under fire for ambulance incident": This Human Flesh Search took place in Taiwan in December 2010 when a doctoral candidate at National Taiwan University allegedly blocked an ambulance that was rushing a gravely ill woman to the hospital and gave it the middle finger. The incident caused public outrage and the man was charged with causing bodily harm and obstruction of official business. (http://www.taipeitimes.net/News/taiwan/archives/2010/12/30/2003492244; http://www.taipeitimes.com/News/taiwan/archives/2011/02/02/2003495037). For the video footage and an English discussion on a Malaysian forum, see http://forum.lowyat.net/topic/1700216. For a detailed documentation http://zh.wikipedia.org/zh-tw/%E6%96%B0%E5%BA%97%E6%95%91%E8%AD%B7%E8%BB%8A%E9%98%BB%E6%93%8[B%E4%BA%8B%E4%BB%B6.

27 Take the most recent case in Taiwan for example: a young woman refused to yield the seat to the elderly and got into a fierce verbal fight, which was recorded and posted online. http://www.nownews.com/2011/06/15/91-2720382.htm.

28 Such cases of animal abuse and cruelty have instigated many cases of international internet vigilantism and calls for web hunt, as in the case with "vacuum kitten killer" who suffocated two kittens in a plastic bag after sucking the air out with a vacuum, which had infuriated many animal rights activists, animal lovers, and Facebook users across the world to unite to hunt down the man and revealed him to be a 25-year-old bisexual porn star based in France. http://news2.onlinenigeria.com/odd/64590-Vacuum-kitten-killer-hunted-after-making-snuff-movie-suffocation.rss by James White 24/12/2010; http://teddyhilton.com/2011-01-13-boy-who-killed-kittens-identified-as-gay-porn-star.

29 "Chinese official shamed by 'human flesh' search engine'": A government official accused of molesting a girl in a restaurant has been fired from his position. (04 Nov 2008) http://www.telegraph.co.uk/news/worldnews/asia/china/3377338/Chinese-official-shamed-by-human-flesh-search-engine.html.

30 See "Commit adultery in China, Web vigilantes will hunt you" by Greg Sandoval (posted on November 25, 2008. http://news.cnet.com/8301-1023_3-10107679-93.html) and "Human Flesh Search: Vigilantes of the Chinese Internet" (http://news.newamericamedia.org/news/view_article.html?article_id=964203448cbf700c9640912bf9012e05) New America Media, News feature, Xujun Eberlein, Posted: Apr 30, 2008. In December 2007, a 31-year-old Beijing woman named Jiang Yan jumped off the 24th floor balcony of her apartment. A post on her blog before her suicide blamed her death on her husband's extra-marital affair. News of this "death blog" spread on the Chinese internet and soon, a mass of outraged netizens launched a Human Flesh Search Engine to track down the guilty parties. Within days, every detail of her husband's personal life was all over the internet. For months, this man, his alleged mistress and their parents were bombarded with attack messages and even death threats. In March, the husband sued three websites for cyber violence and privacy violation.

31 The most infamous case took place in the PRC when Li Qiming, driving a black Volkswagen Magotan, hit two female students at Hebei University on October 16, 2010. Li continued to drive on after hitting the two students, one of whom later died. When Li was stopped by campus security guards, he yelled, "Li Gang is my father". (http://china.globaltimes.cn/

society/2010-10/585212.html). For a detailed documentation, see http://en.wikipedia.org/wiki/Li_Gang_incident.

32 Tom Downey has provided quite a comprehensive coverage of the infamous cases taking place in the PRC. (http://www.nytimes.com/2010/03/07/magazine/07Human-t.html?_r=2&pagewanted=all).

33 "Human-flesh search engines: China takes instant justice online" by Kevin Bloom. http://www.thedailymaverick.co.za/article/2010-03-16-human-flesh-search-engines-china-takes-instant-justice-online.

34 "A witch-hunt is a search for witches or evidence of witchcraft, often involving moral panic, mass hysteria and lynching, but in historical instances also legally sanctioned and involving official witchcraft trials." http://en.wikipedia.org/wiki/Witch-hunt.

35 "Human Flesh Search Ends in Bloody Case": It all began with an unexamined lie, the man claimed he was abandoned by his girlfriend after supporting her for four years, and that he had terminal leukemia and would like to see her again. After having successfully mobilised Human Flesh Search, he tracked her down and stabbed her to death in public. http://big5.xinhuanet.com/gate/big5/news.xinhuanet.com/video/2009-05/17/content_11388430.htm. For a detailed narrative of the incident in Chinese, see http://blog.sina.com.cn/s/blog_5ee0e8640100d74v.html~type=v5_one&label=rela_prevarticle; http://big5.eastday.com:82/gate/big5/news.eastday.com/s/20090225/u1a4200069.html.

36 Pan, Xiaoyan, "Hunt by the Crowd: An Exploratory Qualitative Analysis on Cyber Surveillance in China". Global Media Journal. FindArticles.com. 22 Jun, 2011. http://findarticles.com/p/articles/mi_7548/is_201004/ai_n53931440/.

37 "Human-flesh search engines: China takes instant justice online" by Kevin Bloom http://www.thedailymaverick.co.za/article/2010-03-16-human-flesh-search-engines-china-takes-instant-justice-online.

38 For the video, see "Online lynch mobs find second post-quake target; Liaoning girl detained by the police" http://shanghaiist.com/2008/05/22/online_lynch_mo.php. For a series of discussion and rebuttal, see "Internet Mob Rides Again – Liaoning Bitch-Girl"http://blog.foolsmountain.com/2008/05/21/internet-mob-strikes-again-liaoning-bitch-girl/.

39 "Chinese Student in U.S. Is Caught in Confrontation" http://www.nytimes.com/2008/04/17/us/17student.html?st=cse&sq=china+tibet+Duke&scp=1.

40 "人肉搜索" 若搜錯了, 誰才能" 平反?" "What if "Human flesh search" got it wrong, who should we find to "redress [a grievance]"? http://big5.home.news.cn/gate/big5/www.xj.xinhuanet.com/2009-01/22/content_15526532.htm.

41 http://www.chinasupertrends.com/chinas-human-flesh-search-engine-not-what-you-might-think-it-is/.

42 Pan, Xiaoyan, "Hunt by the Crowd: An Exploratory Qualitative Analysis on Cyber Surveillance in China." Global Media Journal. http://findarticles.com/p/articles/mi_7548/is_201004/ai_n53931440/.

43 The construction of a Harmonious Society (和諧 社會héxiéshèhuì) is a socio-economic vision that is said to be the ultimate end result of Chinese leader Hu Jintao's signature ideology...The idea has been described as resembling characteristics of New Confucianism in some aspects. In a country where political class struggle and socialist slogans were the normative political guidelines for decades, the idea of societal harmony attempts to bring about the fusion of socialism and democracy. http://en.wikipedia.org/wiki/Harmonious_society.

44 Just to list a few videos with English subtitles or commentary: http://www.youtube.com/watch?v=09Ht7l1Jdkg; http://www.youtube.com/watch?v=QgiAx-zDpIQ; http://www.youtube.com/watch?v=z9drPmoXTKE&feature=related; and http://www.youtube.com/watch?v=ydZh9It7Wds&feature=related.

45 Since most of the news is in Mandarin, I only include reports in English here: "Taiwan taekwondo athlete in Asian Games sock sensor row" (17 November 2010, Last updated at 15:30 GMT) http://www.bbc.co.uk/news/world-asia-pacific-11775465; "Taiwan fury after

athlete's Asian Games disqualification in China" (November 17, 2010 - Updated 20:50 GMT) http://edition.cnn.com/2010/SPORT/11/17/asian.games.china.taiwan/index.html; "Taiwan taekwondo storm casts cloud over Games" (Wed, Nov 17 2010) http://in.reuters.com/article/idINIndia-52974420101117.

46 Here is a partial list of Facebook pages for reference: http://www.facebook.com/AntiRogue#!/Justice.For.Taiwan.Yang.ShuChun; https://sites.google.com/site/dirtytaekwondo2010/; http://www.facebook.com/AntiRogue; http://www.facebook.com/event.php?eid=161214030582670; http://www.facebook.com/pages/zhi-chi-yang-shu-jun-wo-men-ting-nai-dao-di/140944652624862?ref=ts&v=wall; http://www.facebook.com/pages/yang-shu-jun-shi-ge-shi-jianqing-zong-tong-fu-li-ji-xiang-zhong-guo-biao-da-zui-zui-zui-qiang-lie-de-kang-yi/169393219756510. Screenshot of his Facebook page taken by a PTT user: http://img408.imageshack.us/img408/7568/facebookqs.jpg; "學生書PO挺韓網友人肉搜索" http://video.chinatimes.com/video-cate-cnt.aspx?cid=10&nid=42491; "po文失格大快人心挺韓 網友引公憤" http://www.ctitv.com.tw/news_video_c14v22957.html.

Annotation

Nandini Chami

YiPing Tsou, in her essay 'Digital Natives in the Name of a Cause,' explores how the very 'same technological impulse' of 'viral networking mobilisation' underpins two very different kinds of political actions: the radical *Flash Mob* protests that epitomise the resistance of pro-democracy interest groups against authoritarian and dictatorial regimes, and the digitally-enabled vigilante justice drives as exemplified by the *Human Flesh Search* phenomenon in China and Taiwan. The latter uses crowdsourcing as a witch-hunting technique to ferret out and punish individuals whose online conduct is perceived as being disrespectful of prevailing moral codes. Through a case study analysis of *Human Flesh Search*, Tsou seeks to demonstrate that there is nothing inherently democratic about the online public sphere, contrary to the assertions of techno-deterministic and Internet-centric political theorists (Shirky 2011; Johnson 2012). In her view, the positionalities of the actors in the online public sphere, as shaped by their specific socio-historical contexts, determine the kinds of political action that ensue – and she is primarily interested in challenging naive theorisations of digital activism that automatically ascribe progressive intentions to any effort that falls under the umbrella of Internet-enabled and Internet-mediated political action.

However, it is important to avoid extending Tsou's analysis to justify a social determinist theoretical standpoint on digital activism, that reduces everything to a function of pre-existing social and political forces without paying adequate heed to the new affordances that the ICT-enabled public sphere offers, for participatory communication and collaborative action. It may be more productive to adopt a median approach that unpacks the dialectics between the digital platforms of Web 2.0 and the field of political action (Fuchs

2012), recognising the co-constitutive relationship between technology and society. In particular, this approach, grounded in critical theory, requires us to examine the specific ways by which social media (and other participatory digital spaces) "stand in contradictions with influences by the state, ideology and capitalism" (Fuchs 2012), in specific historical moments.

Such structural analysis offers another pathway to explain the differential (and sometimes contradictory) political outcomes produced by the very same technological affordances of openness and collaboration – a useful counter-analysis to an agency-centric theory that locates these differences as stemming from variances in individual political motivations (which is the position that is implicit in Tsou's essay). This kind of analysis is also helpful in building on Tsou's critique of the inadequacy of 'openness' as a value, in pushing the progressive political agenda forward. For this analysis helps us identify the limitation of the mainstream imaginary of 'online openness' that over-valorises "purposeful individual actions rather than (challenging) systemic bias" (Reagle 2012) in realising an inclusionary vision of transformation (even in those web-based communities such as FOSS whose members profess a commitment to democratic ideals).

Pushing this analysis to its logical conclusion, we start to recognise that to realise the affordances of the Internet and ICTs for furthering a transformative political agenda, it is important to create participatory digital spaces whose organising principle is 'openness with equity' rather than *openness per se* (Gurumurthy & Singh 2013).

References and Further Readings

Fuchs, Christian. 2012. "Some Reflections on Manuel Castells' Book 'Networks of Outrage and Hope. Social Movements in the Internet Age.'" *TripleC*. Volume 10, Number 2. Pp. 775-797. http://www.triple-c.at/index.php/tripleC/article/view/459.
Gurumurthy, Anita & Parminder Jeet Singh. 2013. "Establishing Publicness in the Network: New Moorings for Development - A Critique of the Concepts of Openness and Open Development." In Matthew L. Smith & Katherine M. A. Reilly (Eds.) *Open Development: Networked Innovations in International Development*. Cambridge, MA: MIT Press.
Johnson, Steven. 2012. *Future Perfect: The Case for Progress in a Networked Age*. Riverhead Books.
Reagle, Joseph. 2012. "'Free as in Sexist?' Free Culture and the Gender Gap." *First Monday*. Volume 18, Number 1-7. January. http://journals.uic.edu/ojs/index.php/fm/article/view/4291/3381.
Shirky, Clay. 2011. "The Political Power of Social Media." *Foreign Affairs*. Volume 90, Number 1. Pp. 28-41.

Three Forces Acting behind the Development of the Internet

Hu Yong

This article is the transcript of the speech delivered by Prof. Hu Yong of Beijing University at the workshop "Consensus and Spring Luncheon" on March 29, 2014.

This year marks the 20th year of the advent of Internet in People's Republic of China; besides the annual commemoration day also falls in April. Many people might be wondering, after all, what has the Internet brought into China during the past two decades. And by extension, what all can we make out on the basis this nodal point?

As I look at the past history of the Internet, basically I can find that there are three forces acting behind it: the country, the market, and the masses. And as the Internet was forged by these three dissimilar forces, there emerged three dissimilar governance models, too. The first governance model is the model guided by the country. The second model is the one guided by the market. In the year 1995, two British scholars put forward a concept, called: "The Californian ideology." Thanks to [this ideology] the West coast of America witnessed a brand-new ideological trend and this very same brand-new ideological trend ultimately gave birth to today's free and open Silicon Valley; besides, it pushed the industry from semiconductors to computers and again from computers to the Internet, until it reached today's mobile Internet, all of which are the products of "the Californian ideology." The third model is the one led by the masses. And this model has a rather extreme variant and I would call this variant the radical libertarianism. And this radical libertarianism actually appeared in the year 1996; at that time there was a rock music writer called Barlow; and, Barlow in that year had an extremely famous thing called, "Declaration of independence by Cyberspace" and it was told through the article thus: You are a bunch of predator Giants, you are a bunch of past governments, don't get into our net and interfere with us; we are the future while you folks constitute the past, we enjoy sovereignty in the cyberspace." So, this is the typical third model.

What is curious about this third model is that, actually it has been built with efforts of each other and is intertwined with each other and therefore cannot be completely separated. While "the Californian ideology" and things like that do represent the independent market, however such things cannot exist without the government in the background. Conversely, to an extent we also know that "the Californian ideology" has also spawned acts of the State; such things are called the Information Superhighway. And things like the Information Superhighway are in fact the infrastructure built up with the power of the government, including in China. In reality, these three things act together. The information Superhighway has ultimately brought in thinking like this to everyone: that the technology utopia could be achieved through a certain technology. And with this technology utopia in backdrop, it may be said, for instance, that the designer may materialize some dreams for humankind with the help of certain institutional systems; and therefore in this sense the Internet could be viewed as a catalyst for democracy and liberation. In this sense, it is associated with the "Declaration of independence by Cyberspace" of Barlow, and they overlap each other.

However, let us see how the situation will change twenty years from now; for instance, as for the sovereignty issue of the Internet, the sovereignty mentioned by Barlow meant that we do not want any act of interference by the government or commerce in matters regarding the net and netizens. But, in the year 2010, China had for the first time issued to the world a white paper on "China's Internet Situation." In fact there was a background behind coming out with this white paper by China, in that China and Google had fought a battle as an outcome of which Google had to withdraw from China. The Chinese government had made it clear through the white paper that the infrastructure existing within the Chinese territory is part of China's internet sovereignty, and therefore you are required to abide by our internet sovereignty. To put it another way, so long as you carry out any activities within our territory, or your physical servers remain in our territory, you must then adhere to the rules and regulations of the Chinese government.

You may make out that there exists a whole galaxy of difference between the two accounts in terms of internet sovereignty. However, what is interesting is the West regards this Internet sovereignty as an extension into the Cyberspace of the already backward and bankrupt political sovereignty; actually the traditional national sovereignty is also encountering great challenges. The people of the West then thought that such a statement posed a problem; however, following the 'Snowden incident' that occurred the previous year,

China's justification totally disrupted the lessons learnt by the West in regard to this issue. To put it another way, the re-delineation of Internet space (re-nationalization) has now become a trend. To cite an example, following the occurrence of the 'Snowden incident', Brazil demanded that if Google wanted to operate in Brazil, the physical server of Google must be installed in Brazil and they shall not have it in California nor could they install it wherever they would find it convenient, because how can one know, from where they could or could not infringe upon the right to privacy of the citizens of Brazil, even the right to privacy of the President of Brazil.

This implies that we may not be having a world with only one Internet, we may have multiple Internets; in other words, it may be that the Chinese model might still have certain victory in the domain of Internet, because China has all along insisted that it should have its own Internet. This is the paradox with regard to the matter. In the whole process, the Internet companies have again played a certain role of castigating the people, and everybody knows that all major Internet companies have provided the information concerning them to the government, but where the government has carried out various kinds of analyses or various types of monitoring with respect to them, the Internet companies have gone on record saying they were helpless; therefore, the ethics with respect to the Internet companies themselves has also become a big challenge.

We have stated upfront that out of the three models, two have been called into question. Therefore, at the moment, all those who have felt that the Internet belongs to the masses have come up with an initiative, which is described as: "We want to reclaim the Internet." The reason being, the country and the enterprises have betrayed the Internet. With the result that the Internet we have today is not in the same shape as we dreamt of in the year in which it was put up. Among them there is a well-known representative [named Bruce] Schneier, an American cryptology expert, who has put forward three aspects as regards to how to reclaim the Internet.

First, we have to expose all monitoring by the governments because it is not something we can allow. Second, we have to redesign the Internet. This call is majorly to be granted to the engineers, and the engineers can carry out new designing with respect to the present framework of the Internet. Third, improve upon the governance of the Internet. The core issue with regard to the Internet is that one country cannot be allowed to decide on the trend of the Internet. For instance, a situation cannot be allowed to prevail where America has the Internet of America, Iran has the Internet of Iran, China has the Internet of China. Secondly, the Internet should not just remain an affair between the governments of countries; on the contrary it should be an affair to be discussed together by global civil societies.

I feel we have to carefully watch as to how the Internet will proceed in future and how a trade-off will come about among these three forces. But, let me sum up finally, one thing has become extremely plain during the past twenty years. When you proposed the idea of an Internet twenty years ago, you uttered some beautiful words; you talked about equality, democracy, and independence; whereas today as you talk about the Internet, it is control and review. Will such a shift in discourse be pulled over in future, I do not know, but it is also something we have to continue to watch. Thank you all!

Annotation

Puthiya Purayil Sneha

> When you proposed the idea of an Internet twenty years ago, you uttered some beautiful words; you talked about equality, democracy, and independence; whereas today as you talk about the Internet, it is control and review.

This telling statement from Prof. Yong's speech perhaps sums up for us the aporetic idea that is the Internet for most of us today. The Internet, like with most other new technology, has always been a bone of contention in most parts of the world; given its strange paradox of democracy and openness, and virtually unlimited possibilities in terms of access to people, knowledge and resources, but also multiple concerns of regulation and control of the flow of information. In the context of China, this paradox becomes even more significant due to the short but very chequered history of the Internet in a country which has the largest number of Internet users in the world, at a figure of 642 million in 2014. The speech lays out what have been some key events of this history in the recent past, and the conditions within which the political economy around the Internet has emerged in China, which also has significant implications for many years to come.

Chief among these are the issues of Internet sovereignty and governance, both of which have emerged as important problems for the rest of the world to contend with in the last couple of years. An important aspect of Internet development in China is that all online access is controlled by the government, with bandwidth being rented out to telecom service providers, and only a few private players in the market. With such a control over infrastructure and networks, the government also brought in very early a regime of censorship, in which citizens' access to the Internet is closely monitored by the 'Internet police,' a force numbering 2 billion in 2013. The infamous 'Golden Shield project' also known as the 'Great Firewall of China,' has been symbolic of this regime, and the focus of much activism around free speech and democracy. China monitors the Internet through extensive legal and administrative provisions, due to its claim to Internet sovereignty in a white paper issued in 2010. This has allowed it to regulate and control access and usage of the Internet within its borders, using an advanced mechanism of surveillance, filtering and blocking of content, with the large means at the disposal of the state. As a result, access to any information construed as politically sensitive is restricted, and dissent is easily suppressed, in effect imposing a condition of self-censorship wherein individuals and institutions willingly monitor and censor their online activity to avoid dire legal consequences. The Google controversy mentioned in the speech is perhaps the best example of the problematic idea of Internet sovereignty and self-regulation. Google entered the Chinese market in 2004 in compliance with the self-censorship regime with a filtered content search, but in 2010, following a barrage of cyber attacks on its infrastructure and loss of data, decided to move to an unfiltered version and redirected all search operations through Hong Kong instead of mainland China. Ostensibly, the restrictions on foreign players in the market has led to the growth of a thriving industry in China, with better access and innovation, which is often claimed to be based on the American model. In fact, as global social media sites like Facebook, YouTube and Twitter are blocked, their Chinese counterparts such as WeChat and Sina Weibo get to serve and innovate on the basis of a huge market protected from external competition. Blocking of global players, hence, does not stop in any way a large part of the Chinese population from being online and taking part in the 'social' web. The Internet has definitely bolstered the economy in several ways that were unimaginable before, especially with increased mobile phone access. According to a report by the Mckinsey Global Institute, depending on the speed and extent of industry adoption, the Internet could add 0.3 to 1.0 percentage points to China's GDP growth rate from 2013 to 2025. It is expected to change the very nature of growth by enabling GDP based on productivity, innovation and consumption, to develop a more sustainable model of economic growth.

The notion of Internet sovereignty, as contentious and problematic as it is, further complicates how we understand governance and regulation of the Internet. As Prof. Yong points out, the condition of a fragmented Internet with each country developing its own forms of regulation can actually be counterproductive to the goals of increased connectivity, sharing and access, as a result of which much of the democratic potential of the Internet would remain unrealised. Vint Cerf et al (2014) argue that Internet governance is a shared responsibility, because the Internet is "both a technology and a socio-economic space." it is a shared environment, and unlike a traditional commons "it is capable of growing at the will of those who use it and the entities that invest in its expansion". Its boundaries may therefore not be drawn as easily as with physical space, as the notions of space and community itself come into conflict due to the very fluid nature of the web. Stemming from this idea are several questions about regulation of speech online, dissent and activism itself, as citizens and particularly activists have always had to find innovative and sometimes insidious ways around the Internet police to communicate with each other and the rest of the world. A regularly used tactic is to actually publish politically sensitive material online and wait for it to be pulled down by authorities, because in the time that is taken down several people would have read and circulated the material. Another example is the famous meme on 10 mythical Chinese creatures featured on the interactive encyclopedia Baidu Baike, wherein vandalised and humorous contributions using profanity were made to the encyclopedia in an attempt to illustrate the uselessness of content filtering. As such, activism in the digital space can take various forms even in the face of several limitations.

As mentioned in the introduction, the Internet is still in some sense an aporetic idea, so models of governance and development need to keep in mind its expanse and immense potential for growth, with due consideration that democratic governance is incomplete without space for dissent.

References and Further Readings

2010. "The Internet in China." Information Office of the State Council of the People's Republic of China. Beijing. June 8. Accessed June 19, 2015. http://china.org.cn/government/whitepaper/node_7093508.htm.
2013. "A Giant Cage." The Economist. April 6. Accessed June 19, 2015. http://www.economist.com/news/special-report/21574628-Internet-was-expected-help-democratise-china-instead-it-has-enabled.
2014. "Baidu 10 Mythical Creatures." Wikipedia. November 30. Accessed June 19, 2015. https://en.wikipedia.org/wiki/Baidu_10_Mythical_Creatures
2015. "Internet Censorship in China." Wikipedia. June 18. Accessed June 19, 2015. https://en.wikipedia.org/wiki/Internet_censorship_in_China.
2015. "Internet in China, Twenty Years Later." CNN. Accessed June 19. http://www.cnn.com/2014/04/23/world/asia/china-Internet-20th-anniversary/index.html.
Barbrook R. & Andy Cameron. 1995. "The Californian Ideology." The Hypermedia Research Centre, Westminster University. Accessed June 19, 2015. http://www.imaginaryfutures.net/2007/04/17/the-californian-ideology-2/.
Barlow, J.P. 1996. "Declaration of the Independence of Cyberspace." February 8. Accessed June 19, 2015. https://projects.eff.org/~barlow/Declaration-Final.html.
Cerf, Vint et. al. 2014. "Internet Governance is Our Shared Responsibility." I/S: A Journal of Law and Policy. Volume 10, Number 1.
Johnny, R. & Stephan Halper. 2010. "Google vs China: Capitalist Model, Virtual Wall." OpenDemocracy. January 22. Accessed June 19, 2015. https://www.opendemocracy.net/johnny-ryan-stefan-halper/google-vs-china-capitalist-model-virtual-wall.
Tai, Zixue. 2006. The Internet in China: Cyberspace and Civil Society.Routledge Studies in New Media and Cyberculture. London: Routledge.

Woetzel, J. et al. 2014. "China's Digital Transformation: The Internet's Impact on Productivity and Growth." Mckinsey Global Institute. Accessed June 19, 2015. http://www.mckinsey.com/insights/high_tech_telecoms_Internet/chinas_digital_transformation

Yang, Guobin. 2011. *The Power of the Internet in China, Citizen Activism Online.* New York: Columbia University Press.

Old and New Media: Converging During the Pakistan Emergency
(March 2007 – February 2008)

Huma Yusuf

Introduction

On March 13, 2007, a few days after Pakistan's president General Pervez Musharraf suspended the Chief Justice of the Supreme Court, an online petition condemning the government's abuse of the independent judiciary was circulated via mailing lists and blogs.[1] But over the course of several weeks, the petition only attracted 1,190 signatories. Less than a year later, in February 2008, Dawn, the country's leading English-language media group, launched a citizen journalism initiative, inviting Pakistanis to submit images, ideas, news reports, and analyses that they wanted to share with the world.

In a matter of months, the Pakistani media landscape evolved from a point where a politically relevant online petition failed to gain momentum to one where a prominent mass media group felt the need to include citizen journalists in the process of news gathering. This paper aims to explain why this evolution occurred, how it was facilitated by both old and new media, and what impact it had on the political process and civic engagement.

To that end, the paper describes how certain communities – for example, university students – came to use digital technologies and new media platforms to organize for political action and report on matters of public interest. In *The Wealth of Networks: How Social Production Transforms Markets and Freedom*, Yochai Benkler advances the concept of a networked public sphere. With reference to the internet and online tools, he argues that the networked information economy produces a public sphere because "the cost of being a speaker ... is several orders of magnitude lower than the cost of speaking in the mass-mediated environment"[2]. He adds, "the easy possibility of communicating effectively into the public sphere allows individuals to reorient themselves from passive readers and listeners to potential speakers and participants in a conversation." In Benkler's words, then, this paper shows how some Pakistanis became "speakers and participants" in the political process. Enabled to create a networked public sphere, they began in the spring of 2007 to participate, reciprocate, and engage in many-to-many rather than one-to-many communications.

Interestingly, a networked public sphere emerged during a time of heightened political instability that has been colloquially termed the 'Pakistan Emergency' (March 2007-February 2008).[3] Digital technologies that were harnessed during this time for political advocacy, community organizing, and hyperlocal reporting include cellphones, camera phones (mobile-connected cameras), SMS text messages, online mailing lists, and internet broadcasts (live audio and visual streams). Meanwhile, popular new media platforms utilized during the Pakistan Emergency include blogs (live blogging), YouTube, Flickr, Facebook and other social networking or sociable media sites.[4]

Writing about mass-mediated markets that are slowly inundated with new media tools, Benkler points out that a transition occurs "as the capabilities of both systems converge, to widespread availability of the ability to register and communicate observations in text, audio, and video, wherever we are and whenever we wish"[5]. During the Pakistan Emergency, a similar convergence of old – that is, traditional broadcast – and new media occurred. In a time of turmoil and censorship, Pakistanis were driven by a desire to access information and thus turned to multiple media sources when the mainstream media was compromised. One could say the media landscape became hydra-headed during the Pakistan Emergency: if one source was blocked or banned, another one was appropriated to get the word out. For example, when the government banned news channels during the November 2007 state of emergency, private television channels uploaded news clips to YouTube and live streamed their content over the internet, thus motivating Pakistanis to go online. In this context, the mainstream media showed the ability to be as flexible, diffuse, and collaborative as new media platforms.

A combined use of digital technologies and new media tools also helped bridge the digital divide in a country where only 17 million people have internet access and the literacy rate is less than 50 percent. In "Democracy and New Media in Developing Nations: Opportunities and Challenges", Adam Clayton Powell describes how the internet can help open up developing democracies:

> Many argue that in much of the world, the Internet reaches only elites: government officials and business leaders, university professors and students, the wealthy and the influential. But through Net-connected

elites information from the Internet reaches radio listeners and newspaper readers around the world, so the Internet has an important secondary readership, those who hear or are influenced by online information via its shaping of more widely distributed media, outside of traditional, controlled media lanes of the past.[6]

No doubt, traditional broadcast media relay information from the internet to the Pakistani public. But the national "secondary readership" was established in a far more dynamic and participatory way during the Pakistan Emergency thanks to the prevalence of cellphones and the popularity of SMS text messaging. Indeed, this paper shows how citizen reporting and calls for organized political action were distributed through a combination of mailing lists, online forums, and SMS text messages. Emails forwarded to net-connected elites containing calls for civic action against an increasingly authoritarian regime inevitably included synopses that were copied as SMS text messages and circulated well beyond cyberspace. This two-tiered use of media helped inculcate a culture of citizenship in Pakistanis from different socioeconomic backgrounds. In other words, the media landscape witnessed a convergence of old and new media technologies that also led to widespread civic engagement and greater connection across social boundaries.

Despite such multivalent uses, this paper shows that the overall impact of digital and new media tools in Pakistan has been nebulous. After all, General Musharraf's dictatorial regime retained control over access to the internet and other communications infrastructure throughout the period of widespread civic engagement. As an increasing number of Pakistanis turned to YouTube, Flickr, Facebook, and SMS text messages as alternate media portals, the government clamped down on these sources. Between March 2007 and February 2008, cellphone networks were jammed, internet service providers were instructed to block the YouTube website, internet connectivity was limited or shut down, and blogging softwares were banned. Moreover, the authorities came to monitor the public's use of new media platforms: images of anti-government rallies posted to Flickr were used to identify and arrest protesters.

The only antidote to the government's control of digital and new media tools, this paper shows, was the widening of the networked public sphere to include Pakistanis in the diaspora and global media sources. For example, when the government blocked news channels and jammed cellular networks in November 2007, young Pakistanis across the globe continued to plan and organize protest rallies via the social networking site Facebook. Similarly, when university students demanding the restoration of an independent judiciary realized that security officials had prevented journalists from covering their protest, they submitted self-generated video clips and images to CNN's iReport, an online citizen journalism initiative. Indeed, as Pakistan's media landscape became a hybrid model in which professional and amateur journalists generated and disseminated news by whatever means possible, international mainstream media outfits such as CNN, the BBC, and the UK-based Channel 4 increasingly sought out hyperlocal reporting posted to local blogs, YouTube, and Facebook.

Ultimately, this paper identifies how the means of communication in Pakistan became dispersed, accessible, and decentralized, leading to a freer flow of information during the Pakistan Emergency. By focusing on how Pakistanis have harnessed digital technologies and new media platforms, the paper aims to illuminate the way for Pakistan to become a full-fledged digital democracy... By analyzing digital technologies in the context of existing technologies and social practices in Pakistan, the paper emphasizes the importance of real-world deployment. It shows that users adopt and adapt tools in a way that responds to local needs. As such, the paper can be considered a call for members of the civic media community to design tools that bridge the digital divide, adapt to local circumstances, and are flexible enough that different communities can use them in creative and relevant ways. After all, as Benkler puts it, "the networked public sphere is not made of tools, but of social production practices that these tools enable"[7].

Media Vacuum: Blocking Independent Television in Pakistan

November 3, 2007: State of Emergency Declared

President Musharraf's declaration of a state of emergency on November 3, 2007, arguably had a greater impact on Pakistan's media landscape than on its political history. The manner in which the government handled media outlets during the emergency, which ended on December 15, 2007, demonstrated the vulnerability of mainstream media and created an opportunity for the systematic, sustained, and nationwide use of new media platforms. Indeed, barely five years after independent television stations were established as the go-to medium for news and infotainment for one-third of Pakistan's 150-million strong population,[8] Musharraf's crackdown on news channels during the emergency demonstrated how easily the boom could go bust. During emergency rule, a media vacuum was created that allowed for the rise of new media outlets as viable alternatives for information dissemination and community organizing. Mediated practices that facilitated civic engagement and citizen journalism during the six-week-long emergency continue to be widely adopted and refined.

On November 3, soon after proclaiming emergency rule in a televised address, Musharraf demanded that cable television operators block the broadcasts of all local and foreign news channels, except those of the state-owned Pakistan Television Corporation. Nearly 30 privately owned channels were promptly taken off the air. The next day, policemen raided the Islamabad offices of Aaj TV, an independent news channel, and attempted to confiscate the channel's equipment. The telephone lines of Pakistan's first independent news channel Geo TV were cut and their broadcasters were threatened with long jail terms...[9]

Tightening Control in the Run-up to Emergency Rule

Ironically, the very media freedom that Musharraf stifled was one of the hallmarks of his rule until the emergency declaration. After coming to power in 1999, he increased freedom for the print media and liberalized broadcasting policies to mitigate the perception that military rulers are authoritarian. In March 2002, the Pakistan Electronic Media Regulatory Authority (PEMRA) was established to induct the private sector into the field of electronic media. Since then, 56 privately owned television channels have been licensed in Pakistan[10] and 48 were fully operational as of May 2008. Geo TV became Pakistan's first private news channel in 2002.

The recent proliferation of independent television channels is a marked departure for the Pakistani media landscape, which had been dominated by the state-owned channel Pakistan Television (PTV) until the early 1990s. In the previous decade, access to international satellite television channels, via illegal satellite dishes, had many Pakistanis tuning in to Indian channels such as Zee TV and other regional offerings via Star TV, the Asian news and entertainment network owned by News Corp. These illegal channels gained popularity as they circumvented the censorship and religiosity that defined Pakistani media throughout the 1990s.

Since 2002, independent news channels had been operating with unprecedented freedom as per Musharraf's directives. Cable television thus become the fastest growing media property in Pakistan: subscribers increased from 1.5 million to 3.27 million from July 2004 to July 2007, meaning that one-third of all Pakistanis had access to private news channels in 2007.[11] News content was increasingly investigative and often openly critical of the government. However, signs that the mainstream media remained vulnerable to the government's whims began appearing well before the emergency declaration of November 2007.

The freedom of the newly empowered broadcast media was first questioned in October 2005, when a deadly earthquake struck the country's northern areas. As a reporter for The Christian Science Monitor put it: "Pakistan's earthquake, while at once a story of national tragedy, is also the coming of age story of the country's fledgling private television channels. Their unflinching coverage of the disaster... showcases an era of unparalleled media freedom and influence. But it has also, by creating rifts with the government, underscored the very limits of that newfound freedom"[12]. Media coverage of the government's response to the disaster – often featuring angry villagers criticizing the Pakistan Army's inefficient or corrupt relief efforts – highlighted official shortcomings and portrayed the true extent of the disaster that the government was slow to acknowledge. The regularity with which the government was criticized in the months following the earthquake established the electronic media's watchdog role and approach to news coverage, which was biased toward analysis rather than objective reporting...

From Small Screen to Satellite and YouTube

... After most channels were blocked during the emergency, two independent news channels made every effort to continue live broadcasts. Geo TV and ARY One World, another independent station, transmitted live broadcasts from their bureaus in Dubai. The news that some independent news channels were continuing to broadcast prompted Pakistanis across the country to obtain illegal satellite dishes – which had declined in popularity since the 1990s – so as to continue receiving independent coverage of the unfolding political crisis from their favorite news anchors and broadcast journalists. Despite a prompt government ban on the purchase of satellite dishes, they sold like "hotcakes"[13].

The fact that Pakistanis resorted to satellite dishes in the wake of the government ban indicates that broadcast media were considered the most important form of news delivery in Pakistan (the English- and Urdu-language print media was not censored during the emergency, nor did they see an increase in sales). Interestingly, it was this desire to seek out live television broadcasts that also drove many Pakistanis to the internet, in many cases, for the first time.

Geo TV, ARY One World, and Aaj TV live streamed their coverage on the stations' websites.[14] As soon as Geo TV initiated live streams, its website registered 300,000 simultaneous users, up from 100,000 before the emergency. Through November, the site received as many as 700,000 hits after breaking news. News broadcasts featuring important updates were also uploaded both by station producers and users to YouTube to allow for easy circulation.[15] Moreover, websites such as Pakistan Policy compiled streaming audio and video content from the independent news channels to allow users across the country and diaspora to enjoy uninterrupted news reporting on political events.[16] Initially, then, broad Pakistani interest in finding news online was an example of old and new media colluding: content was produced by traditional media outlets and intended for consumption along the one-to-many model. But the distribution of that content was diffuse and collaborative...

The weeks during which all independent electronic news outlets were completely shut down or censored by the government marked a significant turning point in the Pakistani media landscape. It was in this media vacuum that other alternatives began to flourish: the public realized that to fulfill its hunger for news in a time of political crisis, it had to participate in both the production and dissemination of information. Activist communities established blogs and generated original news coverage of hyperlocal events, such as anti-emergency protests on university campuses. Civilians increasingly used SMS text messages to keep each other informed about the unfolding political crisis and coordinate protest marches. Young Pakistanis across the diaspora created discussion groups on the social networking site Facebook to debate the pros and cons of emergency rule.

Overheard: FM Radio and Public Participation

The Pakistani public's ability to use both old media and new digital technologies to ensure communications flow was demonstrated before the imposition of emergency rule. Indeed, before citizen journalists turned determinedly to blogs and social networking sites, citizens had been using FM radio broadcasts and cellphones as a way to organize and disseminate information. The emergent, ad hoc, and hyperlocal networked public spheres thus created served the public well under emergency rule.

Despite the burgeoning popularity of FM radio stations – by July 2008, there were nine operational FM radio stations in Karachi and 162 licensed stations nationwide[17] – the medium did not emerge as a site for civic engagement or community building. This is because unlike television, all FM radio stations – whether state- or privately-owned – were forbidden even before the Emergency from broadcasting news, current affairs shows, or any time-bound content with political implications...

Unable to provide news updates, Karachi's most popular community radio station, Apna Karachi FM 107, negotiated violent flare-ups in the city by issuing regular "traffic reports" which followed the law but signaled the real situation. On May 12, 2007 – when Karachi was affected by violent rallies, widespread gun battles, and the indiscriminate torching of vehicles after Chief Justice Chaudhry was prevented from properly visiting the city – the station punctuated its programming at five-minute intervals with these special "traffic updates."

Throughout the tumultuous afternoon, the station's radio journalists – reporting on the move via cellphones – called to indicate which roads were heavily congested, which were blocked, and which were seeing only sporadic traffic. Karachiites accustomed to urban conflict understand that the density of traffic hints at the relative safety of a road or neighborhood – after all, traffic thins out in areas where gunbattles are underway.

At 11:57 a.m. that day, the reporter Mohammad Qayyum stated: "the roads to the airport are empty. Public transport is at a standstill and the few taxis and rickshaws operating in the area have inflated their fares." Just after noon, he alerted drivers, "although we had earlier told you that Mai Kolachi Road was seeing normal traffic, we are now suggesting that you take a diversion and choose an alternate route." At 12:22 p.m., his colleague Waqarul Hasan reported, "buses have been torched near Karsaz, so people wanting to come to Drigh Road shouldn't head in this direction because traffic is bad." Later in the afternoon, the radio journalist Waqar Azmat advised drivers to avoid the area known as Gurumandir, "because the conditions there are not good, there is no traffic in the area." A few minutes later, at 2:26 p.m., he returned to the airwaves to say, "traffic on Shaheed-e-Millat Road is very bad, as it is on Sharah-e-Faisal. There's madness all the way until Tipu Sultan Road. Drivers should choose their routes carefully so that they don't become *victims of bad traffic*."

In its efforts to stay within the law while also providing coverage of violence throughout the city, Apna Karachi FM 107 was aided by Karachiites themselves. Throughout the day, hundreds of people called the station, from their cars, homes, and workplaces, to report on the traffic situation – and thus the security situation. For example, at 3:15 p.m. the station broadcast this call: "I'm Akhtar calling from my office on Shahrah-e-Faisal Road. I cannot leave right now because there are no buses on the road. They say buses will resume here by 5 p.m." Calls such as these helped Karachiites keep each other informed about which spots in the city were dangerous at any given time...

Subsequently, a similar combination of FM radio broadcasts, landline phones, and cellphones were used by Karachiites to create a networked public sphere and monitor protest rallies through the cities during emergency rule and general elections. This shows how people empowered by creativity and a commitment to aiding their community can use old and new media technologies to make a difference, even on an ad hoc basis.

Disconnected: Jamming Cellular Networks

November 6, 2007: Chief Justice Iftikhar Muhammad Chaudhry Addresses the Nation

As the public adopted alternative media platforms, the government escalated its efforts to control communication and news dissemination. On November 6, the ousted chief justice of the Supreme Court, who had been placed under house arrest when emergency rule was declared, chose to address the nation via cellphone. In his talk, he called for mass protests against the government and the immediate restoration of the constitution. Justice Chaudhry placed a conference call to members of the Bar Association, who relayed his message via loudspeakers. That broadcast was intended to be further relayed by members of the crowd who had planned to simply hold their cellphones up to the loudspeakers to allow remote colleagues and concerned citizens to listen in on the address. More ambitious members of the crowd planned to record the message on their cellphones and subsequently distribute it online.

However, most mobile phone services in Islamabad went down during Chaudhry's address, prompting suspicions that they had been jammed by the government.[18] In the first few days of the emergency, sporadic efforts to cut telephone lines and jam cellphone networks were common, even though the telecommunications infrastructure in Pakistan is privately owned. Mobile connectivity at the Supreme Court, protest sites, and the homes of opposition politicians and lawyers who were placed under house arrest was jammed at different times. In off-the-record interviews, employees at telecommunications companies explained that the government had threatened to revoke their operating licenses in the event that they did not comply with jamming requests.

The government's attempts to jam cellphone networks during the emergency demonstrates that, much like television, cellphones had become an integral medium of information dissemination and community organizing across Pakistan. This is not surprising given that cellphones have been the most rapidly adopted – and adapted – technology in Pakistan's history.

Between the late 1990s and July 2006, mobile penetration in Pakistan increased from 0.2 percent of the population to an unprecedented 43.6 percent.[19] Months before the emergency declaration, in August 2007, there were 68.5 million mobile phone users across Pakistan, which amounts to 60 percent of the total potential cellphone market in Pakistan...[20]

SMS text messaging also played a large role in helping communities organize protests during the emergency. Owing to the low literacy rate and the non-availability of mobile platforms in local languages, SMS traffic has remained low. That said, 2007 saw a marked increase to 8,636 million text messages exchanged from 1,206 million in 2006.[21] On July 20, 2007, when the Justice Chaudhry was first reinstated, 400 million SMS messages were sent nationwide. According to the PTA, that is the highest number of SMS generated in one day in Pakistan. But mobile service providers claim that a record number of SMS messages were exchanged in the five days after emergency rule was declared (statistics to support this fact are not available). No doubt, in the absence of independent news channels, text messaging emerged as an instantaneous way for people to update each other on developments such as protest rallies and the numerable arrests of lawyers, journalists, and activists. In the early days of the emergency, SMS text messaging was lauded across the Pakistani blogosphere as the savior of communication in a time of crisis.

Student Activism / Digital Activism

November 7, 2007: Police Surround the Lahore University of Management Sciences

In the media vacuum created by the censorship of television channels, Pakistani university students turned to new media platforms such as YouTube, Flickr, Facebook, and blogs to facilitate hyper-local reporting, information dissemination, and community organizing against emergency rule. As such, student activism during the Pakistan Emergency was synonymous with digital activism.

On November 7, over 1,000 students of the privately owned Lahore University of Management Sciences (LUMS) – Pakistan's most prestigious business school based in Lahore – gathered to protest the imposition of emergency rule. Students at universities across Pakistan had begun protesting and organizing vigils immediately after Musharraf's televised emergency announcement on November 3. But the gathering at LUMS was among the largest of the civil movement launched by lawyers, journalists, and students against the emergency. (By contrast, about 90 students attended a protest the same day at Lahore's National University of Computer and Emerging Sciences, FAST-NU, a federally chartered university.)

The protest took place amidst heavy police presence. Prior to the gathering, policemen warned LUMS students that they would be baton charged and arrested in the event of civil agitation. On the morning of the scheduled protest, police surrounded the campus, while plainclothes officers patrolled its grounds. Still, students managed to march through the campus grounds and eventually staged a sit-in at the main campus entrance, in front of the dozens of police officers. Broadcast journalists for Geo TV and other stations that were continuing to provide live coverage of emergency-related events via satellite and internet streams were present to cover the LUMS protest. However, police officials successfully prevented media personnel from entering the LUMS campus and eventually confiscated their cameras and other recording equipment. After successfully removing all journalists from the premises, the police ramped up their presence on the campus grounds.

Creating the News, Organizing the Community

Once LUMS students realized that major Pakistani news networks had not been able to cover their protest, they took it upon themselves to document the authorities' intimidation tactics and their own attempts at resistance. Midway through the day-long protest, a student narrated the morning's events in a post on The Emergency Times blog[22], which had been established to help students express their opinions about democracy and organize against emergency rule. This post was then linked to by other blogs, such as Metroblogging Lahore, that are frequented by Pakistani youth.[23] The Emergency Times blog also featured pictures of the protest.

Within an hour of the LUMS protest commencing, a Karachi-based blogger Awab Alvi, who runs the Teeth Maestro blog, also helped those behind The Emergency Times blog set up an SMS2Blog link, which allowed students participating in the protest to post live, minute-by-minute updates to several blogs, including Teeth Maestro, via SMS text message.[24] Students availed of this set up to report on police movement across campus, attempts to corral students in their hostels, the deployment of women police officers across campus, and the activities of LUMS students to resist these actions.

On the night of November 7, students posted video clips of the protest that were shot using handheld digital camcorders or cellphone cameras to YouTube.[25] These videos showed the students gathering to protest, confronting the university's security guards, and the heavy police presence at the university's gates. Many clips focused on protest signs that students were carrying in an attempt to convey their message in spite of the poor audio and visual quality of some of the video clips. Anti-emergency speeches delivered by students were posted in their entirety.

Some students uploaded their video footage of the protest, shot on cellphone cameras, to CNN's iReport website, which solicits contributions from citizen journalists across the globe in the form of video, photos, or blog posts.[26] Footage from iReport was then used in a regular CNN broadcast about the student protests. That CNN broadcast was then posted to YouTube for circulation amongst Pakistanis who no longer had access to the channel because of Musharraf's blanket ban on news programming.[27] Through this confluence of citizen reporting and the international broadcast media, Pakistanis – and a global audience – were informed about the LUMS protest.

Interestingly, between November 3-6, video clips of protests and gatherings at LUMS had been posted to YouTube. But none of these were as well produced or contextualized as those uploaded on November 7. In the days after the emergency, posted videos up to 10 minutes in length were not clearly titled for easy searchability, nor did they provide any explanation of the events portrayed in the footage.[28] In contrast, November 7 video clips were clearly titled and tagged. In many cases, the clips included captions that dated the event, identified the location, and contextualized the students' activities.[29] This difference suggests that university students were aware within days of the emergency that their collectively generated coverage of the campus protests was the primary source of information for those looking for coverage of responses to the political crisis, including local and international journalists. For example, Dawn News, Pakistan's first English-language news channel, first broadcast news of the student protests on November 10 in a clip that was made available via satellite and YouTube.[30]

It is worth nothing that university students became savvier in their use of new media platforms over the course of the emergency. On December 4, policemen and intelligence agents once again surrounded and barricaded the LUMS campus to prevent students and faculty from attending a daily vigil for civil liberties. As soon as police appeared at the LUMS campus, a post warning students that traffic in and out of the university was being inspected appeared on The Emergency Times blog...[31]

In all emergency-related demonstrations between November 3 and December 15, university students posted images from the events to Flickr.[32] However, security forces soon began using these images to identify student activists and subsequently arrest them. In an attempt to one-up the authorities, students began blurring the faces of protestors in images before uploading them to Flickr and other blogs.[33] The fact that the authorities were monitoring new media platforms such as Flickr is an indication of how quickly alternative resources gained influence in the media vacuum created by the television ban.

Meanwhile, young Pakistanis who were unable to join university protests and youth across the diaspora turned to the social networking site Facebook to express solidarity and oppose emergency rule. Within three days of the emergency declaration, a Facebook group titled "We Oppose Emergency in Pakistan" boasted over 5,000 members.[34] The group's homepage featured links to online petitions, up-to-date news reports from the Pakistani print and broadcast media, and blogs with original news content, such as The Emergency Times. Embedded video clips of messages by detained opposition leaders were also uploaded to the Facebook site. The group's discussion board quickly became the site of lively discussion, with teenagers and twenty-somethings – who previously did not have a voice in the Pakistani public sphere – debating the implications of Musharraf's decision. As the emergency dragged on and the movement to restore the judiciary gained momentum, Facebook was harnessed by diaspora communities as a tool for organizing protests.

...It is not surprising that university students were amongst the first Pakistanis to turn to the internet as a venue for information dissemination in the wake of the television ban. Owing to low literacy rates and high service costs, the internet has not been as widely adopted in Pakistan as cellphones. In December 2007, there were 70 internet service providers covering 2,419 cities and towns in Pakistan, but only 3.5 million internet subscribers. Owing to the popularity of cyber cafes, however, the total number of internet users was estimated by the PTA to be closer to 17 million. Pakistani universities are among the few venues where internet saturation is high: by 2005, over 80% of all university libraries had internet access. And in July 2007, the Higher Education Commission of Pakistan enhanced bandwidth four-fold at public sector universities – at private universities, bandwidth was doubled – to facilitate video conferencing and other online communications. Private institutions such as LUMS boast two internet access nodes in each double- or triple-occupancy room.

In times of emergency, The Emergency Times

...The Emergency Times (ET) blog and newsletter exemplify the collision and collusion between old and new media that helped shape civic action against increasingly authoritarian rule. What began as an informative on-campus handout quickly evolved to become the mouthpiece and major news resource for the Student's Action Committee (SAC), the umbrella organization that rallied student activists across Pakistan and the diaspora against Musharraf and his policies.

Launched online on November 5, 2007, ET described itself as "an independent Pakistani student information initiative providing regular updates, commentary, and analysis on Pakistan's evolving political scenario." An early experiment in youth citizen journalism and digital activism, ET became one of the most regular and reliable sources of information about the Pakistani civil society's movement against the government between November 2007 and June 2008. At its height, the blog claims to have reached over 150,000 people in over 100 countries.

Although many students were involved in generating the blog and its accompanying online mailing list, Ammar Rashid, a LUMS student who served as editor-in-chief for the blog, and Samad Khurram, an undergraduate at Harvard University who managed the mailing list, led the initiative. Khurram explains that Musharraf's crackdown on news channels during the emergency motivated his and Rashid's work: the blog was conceptualized as a daily newspaper while the mailing list was meant to emulate the one-to-many distribution model of traditional broadcast mediums. "Providing these were important to us," says Khurram, "since all the private TV channels were banned and the print media faced serious curbs." The choice of a blog and mailing list was further motivated by the fact that these mediums are "simple, reliable, and cost-effective."

Khurram, Rashid, and other SAC members initially experimented with a web-based television channel titled Freedom TV, but dropped the idea owing to time constraints and the lack of resources. The idea of launching an online radio station was also floated, but rejected. Eventually, Khurram and Rashid determined that the combination of a blog and mailing list would be the most effective in terms of disseminating information about the political crisis and organizing community action. While Rashid compiled and edited news, Khurram focused on coordinating and mobilizing different groups that included lawyers, journalists, and politicians in addition to students. This combined use of a blog and mailing list suggests that at the time of the emergency, Pakistanis with internet access were not yet accustomed to the interactive, collaborative, and user-generated culture of the blogosphere. Instead, they were seeking a broadcast alternative to the independent television channels that had come to dominate the media landscape in recent years.

Initially, the ET blog was limited in scope, catering primarily to the Lahore-based community of student activists. Anti-emergency vigils and protest marches demanding the restoration of the judiciary were documented on the blog through original images, video clips, and first-person testimonies posted by university students.[35] As the SAC movement gained momentum, the blog became the go-to website for information about the campaign, upcoming meetings and protests, and related events such as a lecture series featuring leading activists. Politicians and lawyers hoping to woo, inspire, or advise student activists also used the ET blog as a communications platform. Moreover, students who had the opportunity to meet or speak with leaders of the movement for democracy – such as deposed judges, detained lawyers, or opposition politicians – would share notes from their conversations with the SAC community at large through the blog.

Significantly, the ET blog was one of the few resources for original reporting on the government crackdown on student activism. Reports of students being harassed or arrested were regularly posted.[36]

After emergency rule was lifted and Musharraf surrendered his post as chief of army staff, the blog shifted its focus to campaign for the restoration of an independent judiciary. Broadening the ET's mandate in this manner kept it relevant and timely in the context of the unfolding political crisis, but resulted in a reduction of original content. Since most students were not directly involved in what came to be known as the "lawyers' movement" – a campaign to restore the independent judiciary that was in office on November 3 under Chief Justice Chaudhry – the ET blog increasingly featured news articles and opinion pieces from the mainstream print media, both Pakistani and international...

The mailing list, meanwhile, gathered momentum and gained credibility as it expanded to serve the activist community at large, particularly in the context of the lawyers' movement. By March 2008, during Black Flag Week, a week-long protest against the lawyers' deposition, the mailing list reached over 50,000 people. Khurram explains that he initially pushed his e-mails to prominent journalists, columnists, bloggers, newspaper editors, and political party leaders. The list was then forwarded by these 'influentials' to wide networks that were eventually incorporated into the original mailing list.

Thanks to the regularity of updates and its distribution of original content – posts from the ET blog or forwarded correspondence from high-profile lawyers, activists, and politicians – the ET mailing list came to be seen as a credible news source by most of its recipients. In a big moment for alternative news sources, Chief Justice Chaudhry chose to circulate a letter responding to allegations against him by Musharraf's government via the ET mailing list. Indeed, news items and statements originally circulated on the ET list were eventually cited by publications such as The New York Times and The Washington Post. The mailing list's credibility also allowed it to function as a fund-raising resource: "When I made a call for donations for the SAC long march [in June 2008] we were able to raise over USD 1,000 with one email," says Khurram.

Interestingly, both the ET blog and mailing list relied on their audience using SMS text messaging to push their content and community organizing efforts well beyond the limited online audience. For example, the blog coordinated a "mass contact campaign": readers were asked to forward protest messages and campaign demands to politicians via SMS text message. The coveted cellphone numbers of relevant recipients, including top-level politicians, diplomats, and army personnel, were posted to the blog.[37] For his part, when forwarding e-mails with logistical details about protest marches, Khurram would also make sure to circulate SMS text messages containing the same information. "We had a few key people in each segment of the population on an SMS list: a couple of lawyers, a couple of students, a few civil society activists, and some journalists," he explains. "They would then [forward the message] and inform others [in their network]. Text messaging was a primary source of communication and the mailing list was a close second."

Despite its success during the Pakistan Emergency, the ET blog suspended operations on June 25, 2008. In his final post, Rashid indicated a lack of time and resources to maintain the blog. As such, the fate of the ET blog raises questions about the sustainability of new media platforms beyond times of emergency. Can tools of digital activism also be harnessed as tools of expression? Can young Pakistanis overcome the participation gap and use new media platforms to enact democratic and participatory practices on an everyday basis and not only as tools for community organizing during crises? More importantly, is it necessary for new media platforms to be used in a sustainable way, or is it adequate that developing nations muster 'silent armies' of networked citizen journalists and community organizers who can mobilize during crises?

Citizen Journalism: Redefining Media and Power

December 27, 2007: Benazir Bhutto Assassinated

... In Pakistan, the assassination of former prime minister Benazir Bhutto on December 27, 2007, redefined Pakistani news media as a hybrid product generated by professional and amateur reporters and disseminated via old and new media sources. Bhutto's death shocked and enraged Pakistanis as well as the international community, heightening the sense of political instability across the country. By the time of Bhutto's death, Musharraf had lifted his ban on news channels and the incident received 24-hour news coverage for several days. The assassination was also extensively covered by the international press and broadcast media. In fact, Pakistani FM radio stations, which are legally prevented from broadcasting news, also spread word about Bhutto's death and its fallout with impunity. Anecdotal evidence suggests that most Pakistanis were glued to their television screens for information about Bhutto's last moments and the perpetrators of the attack. And yet the assassination marked a turning point in Pakistan's media landscape and ushered in a new era of citizen journalism...

Soon after Bhutto's death had been verified, its cause was contested. Eyewitnesses in Rawalpindi reported hearing gunshots before an explosion. Members of Bhutto's entourage and her colleagues in the Pakistan People's Party (PPP) claimed that the leader had been shot. In the immediate wake of the attack, a team of doctors examined her body and stated in a report that she had an open wound on her left temporal region. A day after the assassination, government officials claimed that Bhutto had died when her head hit the lever of the sunroof of her car as she ducked to avoid an assassin's bullets and/or in response to the sound of a blast caused by a suicide bomber. The question of whether Bhutto died of gunshot wounds or a head injury riveted the nation because the truth would have implications on allegations about lax security and government complicity in the assassination.

An important piece of evidence to help settle this debate came in the form of images and an amateur video generated by a PPP supporter at the rally where Bhutto was killed and subsequently circulated by a popular Karachi-based blogger. By making the footage and images available to the mainstream media and public at large, these citizen journalists sparked an accountability movement that eventually forced the Pakistani government to revisit its account of Bhutto's death.

The Teeth Maestro Blog: From Online Diary to Citizen Journalism

The blogger who initially circulated the key images and video clip is Dr. Awab Alvi, a dentist by day who runs a blog called Teeth Maestro. Alvi also contributes and cross-posts to Metroblogging Karachi, an English-language blog maintained by a community of Karachi-based bloggers. Alvi came to blogging early, launching Teeth Maestro in 2004 and signing up as part of the Metroblogging Karachi team in April 2005, soon after the launch of the group blog. Alvi is aware of the trajectory of his blogging career: "It started with me keeping an online diary. Then it became a serious hobby."[38] Since playing a significant role in the coverage of Bhutto's death, Alvi describes himself as a citizen journalist. His posts are regularly featured by Global Voices Online, an international blog aggregator.[39]

...Interestingly, Alvi did not primarily consider blogging as a means to community organizing and political advocacy. For example, when Bhutto was first targeted by a suicide bomb attack that killed 134 people in Karachi on October 18, 2007, Alvi chose not to acknowledge the violence in his posts. "When all these bad incidents were happening," he says, "I thought we should cover Karachi in a positive light and so I went to Flickr and picked up all these inspirational pictures and for several days I just kept a photo blog. I wanted to Karachi to remember its beauty and how it is really a good place."

During the emergency, however, Teeth Maestro – motivated much like The Emergency Times by the media vacuum created by Musharraf – emerged as a go-to blog for information about the students' activist movement. Alvi also proved to be one of the most technologically forward bloggers in Pakistan. He was the first to introduce the SMS2Blog feature for live updates and helped others covering anti-emergency protests install the technology as well. At the time of Bhutto's assassination, Alvi was arguably the most prominent Pakistani blogger and his interests had clearly shifted from cultural observations to political commentary, advocacy, and community organizing. This is evidenced by the fact that on the day of Bhutto's death, he posted four blogs on Teeth Maestro, including live updates via SMS. The next day, he posted 12 times: his own updates from the streets of Karachi and links to important news items and insightful commentary from the global print media were supplemented by contributions from other bloggers and citizen journalists. For example, he posted an eyewitness report of the violent response across Karachi to Bhutto's death that he received via email.[40]

Hybridity: Citizen Journalists Inform Mainstream Media Coverage

Two days after the assassination, someone contacted Alvi claiming to have obtained images and a video clip that confirmed that Bhutto was shot by an assassin, and therefore did not succumb to a head wound as government officials were suggesting. These images and video footage had been posted by a PPP supporter to his home page on the social networking site Orkut. However, after being inundated with questions and comments about the new evidence, the original source removed the images and clip from Orkut. Luckily, Alvi's contact was able to grab screen shots of those uploaded images before they were taken down.

Alvi then contacted the original source, the PPP supporter, and convinced him to share the images and video. Soon after, Alvi had obtained four images indicating that Bhutto had indeed been shot. However, the video clip proved harder to obtain. The PPP supporter was based in Islamabad and only had access to a dial-up internet connection. Since the video was a 56MB file, he was having trouble uploading and electronically forwarding it to Alvi. At that point, Alvi contacted two employees at Dawn News, an independent, English-language Pakistani news channel, and arranged from them to collect the video from the PPP supporter's house the next morning. The goal, after all, was to make the images and video clip available to the public as soon as possible, whether via the Teeth Maestro blog or a mainstream media broadcast. After a late-night phone call with Alvi, the PPP supporter agreed to share the video clip with the Dawn News team. But the next morning, the original source could not be reached on his cellphone, and the handoff of the video clip did not occur.

In the meantime, by the end of the day on December 29, Alvi had posted the four images he received from the PPP supporter to his blog.[41] Teeth Maestro was thus the first media outlet to circulate images of Bhutto's assassination that could help clarify whether she died of gunshot wounds or a fatal head injury. "The moment I saw these images, I knew I had to get them out publicly as soon as possible," says Alvi. "I quickly edited the posts, published them online on my blog and circulated the link far and wide, letting the dynamics of the free and open internet protect me and the [original] source."

The images were soon cross-posted on other Pakistani blogs, such as The Emergency Times.[42] Alvi also contacted CNN iReport with his story about fresh evidence and forwarded the images to the Dawn News channel. But these mainstream media outlets were slow to pick up on the story. Dawn News first broadcast the images in the context of an interview with a security analyst at 3 p.m. on December 30...

New Media and Citizenship

February 18, 2008: General election in Pakistan

After Bhutto's assassination, general elections, initially scheduled for January 2008, were postponed until February 18, 2008. It was widely understood that the outcome of the elections would be pivotal for restoring democratic norms in Pakistan. After all, since the official election period began in November 2007, Pakistanis had seen the independent judiciary dismissed and the constitution undermined emergency rule. They had also seen their most popular politician, Bhutto, assassinated. While Pakistanis struggled to imagine who could possibly replace Bhutto – a shoo-in to be elected to her third term as prime minister – they were adamant that the decision be theirs alone, as reflected in a free and fair election.

However, in the run-up to the election it became clear that election rigging and campaign misconduct were rampant. On February 12, the New York-based Human Rights Watch reported that the Pakistani election commission charged with managing polling was under the control of pro-Musharraf officials.[43] Opposition politicians across the country complained that the police and representatives of Musharraf's governing party were harassing them, illegally removing their billboards and banners, and obstructing their campaign rallies. Citizens demonstrating support for any other than the ruling party were either being intimidated by police into changing their vote or bribed.

After being subject to new restrictions during emergency rule, the mainstream media was in no position to expose these dire circumstances. Journalists, particularly those in rural areas, reported that they were being prevented from covering news stories and campaign rallies, threatened with arrest, and regularly having their equipment confiscated. The mainstream broadcast media, meanwhile, was prohibited from covering election rallies and protests and from airing live news broadcasts, live call-in shows, or live talk shows.[44] Moreover, the government kept specific restrictions on election coverage deliberately vague in order to put the onus of caution and restraint on media outlets...

Mailing Lists, Monitors, and Mobilization

In this environment, citizen journalists took it upon themselves to monitor the elections armed with little more than camera phones. According to The Wall Street Journal, the Free and Fair Election Network (FAFEN), an independent coalition of non-governmental organizations, enlisted over 20,000 civilians to observe polling stations and pre-election campaigning in more than 250 election zones. Such recruitment was unprecedented in FAFEN's history. Speaking to The Wall Street Journal, Ahmed Bilal Mehboob, the executive director of the Pakistan Institute of Legislative Development and Transparency, another election monitoring group, said, "Never before has there been such large-scale mobilization for a Pakistani election… The role civil society is playing has been a real positive"[45]…

Mailing lists became the main form of communication between activists and Pakistanis in the days before the election. Samad Khurram, the manager of The Emergency Times mailing list, which at the time of the election boasted over 50,000 recipients, explained that mailing lists had particular appeal because content circulated remained among existing networks of trust. Since the goal was to organize the surreptitious monitoring of the polls by civilians, Khurram pointed out, it would make little sense to use a more open and accessible media platform such as YouTube or a blog. Activists learned the hard way during emergency rule that pro-Musharraf officials and security personnel would monitor new media content, particularly Flickr images and YouTube video clips, to identify and arrest protestors and democracy advocates. Relying on similar platforms during the election would have made volunteer monitors targets for harassment by election commission delegates and police officers…

It is important to note that activist groups did not rely on mailing lists alone to mobilize Pakistanis on election day. Each email included a cellphone number that volunteers could contact via SMS text messages with questions and to indicate the specific timeslots during which they were available to monitor polling. In most cases, emails included short messages that were meant to be copied and further circulated via SMS text message. The parallel use of SMS text messages allowed activists to reach a wider audience while continuing to keep information about their monitoring activities restricted to trusted recipients.

On the day after the election, activist groups and volunteer monitors used the mailing lists to distribute their observations from the polling booths. First-hand accounts of election rigging at specific polling stations were widely circulated by civilian monitors. For example, on February 19, Ahmed Mustafa, a student at the Sindh Muslim Law College in Karachi sent out the following email with the subject "100% rigging at polling station NA250 and NA24":

> I was … on my field visits [at] polling station of SM Law College NA250. Presiding officer stamped 400 fake ballot papers in favor of [political party] MQM in front of our team…. When we approached NA 242 in Federal B. Area, people said that when they entered the polling booth

to cast votes, a person with a badge of the MQM blocked everyone and snatched [their] ballot papers.

Mainstream media journalists and non-governmental organizations such as Human Rights Watch used such brief emails to evaluate the prevalence of election rigging.

Live Blogging the Vote

Although mailing lists were the preferred form of communication on election day, bloggers remained active in providing election coverage. In the run-up to voting, bloggers were regularly posting links to news reports about election rigging, voter intimidation, recommendations from international monitoring committees, and articles from the international print media analyzing the importance of the February 2008 elections. For example, on February 16, The Emergency Times blog ran a transcript of a phone call in which Pakistan's attorney general admits that the upcoming elections will be "massively rigged." The post included an audio clip of the phone conversation as well as background information about the attorney general and his political biases.[46]

Meanwhile, NaiTazi – with its slogan "Pakistani news. Powered by You!" – emerged as a leading source of information during election week. The blog featured comments by prominent journalists and news anchors against the government's restrictions on the media.[47] It also posted helpful analyses of previous elections and voting trends to orient young voters, who in many cases were heading to the polls for the first time in this historic election. For example, a post titled "Karachi: MQM sets yes on 18 out of 20 [National Assembly] seats from Karachi", uploaded on February 15, documented the electoral success of a prominent, Karachi-based political party, the Muttahida Qaumi Movement (MQM). The post included details about the party's campaign tactics, popularity level by location, and past performance when in office.[48]

On election day, bloggers were providing updates about polling results as they came in through the mainstream media, particularly independent news channels. The Teeth Maestro blog, for example, posted an update about which political parties were leading in the polls and included a summary about each party's stance with regards to seminal issues such as the restoration of the judiciary.[49]

More importantly, many young voters turned to popular blogs to post descriptions of their polling experience and, often, expose election rigging. For example, midway through election day, a student at the PECHS Girls College in Karachi documented explicit rigging at the NA251 polling station on the Teeth Maestro blog.[50] Her account described several irregularities in the way polling was being conducted as well as a ballot-stuffing incident. The post generated several responses that either discounted claims of election rigging at the same polling station or described similar election rigging efforts at polling stations in the jurisdictions of rival political parties.

YouTube and SMS Text Messaging: Motivating Civic Action

In addition to blogs, YouTube was used in innovative ways to mobilize Pakistanis. Since calls for civilian election monitoring could not be broadcast online, leading activists uploaded inspirational messages and mission statements to inspire action. For example, Aitzaz Ahsan, the head of the Pakistan Bar Association and leader of the movement for the restoration of an independent judiciary, posted a series of original poems, recited by himself, to YouTube. One poem, titled "Yesterday, Today, and Tomorrow" and posted on February 14, traced the history of Pakistan's democratic aspirations and civil society movements against the army and other forms of oppression.[51]

Mediated civic engagement was not restricted to activists, citizen journalists, and civilian monitors alone. On election day, average voters used SMS text messages to urge their friends, family, and colleagues to vote. One SMS that was widely circulated on the morning of the elections read: "With the elections, lets all light a flame of hope, that we will not let Pakistan be destroyed by people who are not part of us." Moreover, SMS text messages were used to counter widespread fear that there would be violence and bomb blasts at polling stations. For example, confident after casting her vote that there was no security threat at her appointed polling station, Tabassum Saigol, a Karachi-based voter, text messaged everyone in her cellphone directory. She assured them that the streets were safe, the polling stations well-guarded, and the voting process straightforward and efficient.

Sadly, despite such efforts, the 44.5 percent voter turnout remained lower than the 45% registered during the previous general elections in 2002. The use of new mobilizing tools was offset by a greater fear of violence. But there was a significant civic media success story: the civilian monitoring efforts proved that new media platforms could be used efficiently to coordinate civic action by specific communities.

Civilians with Camera Phones

February 21, 2008: Rigging during 2008 General Elections Exposed

On February 21, a civilian monitor posted a video documenting blatant election rigging to YouTube. The clip shows a woman in charge of conducting polling at the NA250 station in Karachi marking several ballots in favor of the

MQM political party with her thumbprint (owing to low literacy rates, this is a common way of casting a vote). The angle from which the video is shot, its quality, and duration indicate that the civilian monitor used a concealed camera phone to capture the incriminating footage.[52]

By February 22, the link to the YouTube clip was distributed via the mailing lists that had been established in the run-up to the election and posted to a handful of blogs. But the same day, users began to complain that they could not access the YouTube domain. Blogs such as PKPolitics[53] and Adnan's Crazy Blogging World[54] reported that YouTube had been banned in Pakistan. These reports prompted a range of responses from internet users nationwide: some claimed that they could still access the video-sharing site, others were convinced that the Pakistan Telecommunications Authority (PTA) had in fact banned YouTube. Eventually, it was determined by several bloggers that users relying on internet service providers that utilized the infrastructure – primarily phone lines – of the government-run Pakistan Telecommunications Limited (PTCL) were being prevented from loading the YouTube domain.

Since the Pakistani government had not officially announced a ban on the video-sharing site, bloggers began to speculate as to why access to YouTube was being limited. Adnan Siddiqi – who maintains Adnan's Crazy Blogging World – wrote:

> I ... don't know what's the actual reason [for the YouTube ban] but ... [people] say that there were some videos published on YouTube which were singing praises of free and fair election in Pakistan.[55]

...Pakistanis posting to online chat forums such as Shiachat also linked the government's attempt to block YouTube to the clips documenting election rigging.[56] Indeed, news of the government's attempts to suppress evidence of election rigging sparked a vibrant conversation throughout the Pakistani online community about the transparency of the 2008 elections, the frequency of polling violations, and the significance of rigging. The political party whose officials can be seen improperly marking ballots in the video was also maligned.

On February 23, the Pakistani government officially blocked access to the YouTube domain, claiming that the popular website hosted blasphemous content. No mention of the election rigging videos was made in the announcement... The BBC reported that the PTA had instructed Pakistani internet service providers to block the site because it featured the controversial Danish cartoons depicting the Prophet Muhammad as well as a trailer for a Dutch film that negatively portrays Islam...[57]

It is interesting to note that if the government had not blocked YouTube, the election rigging video would only have been viewed by activists, students, and volunteer monitors who subscribed to mailing lists. The YouTube block, however, created a buzz in the blogosphere and curiosity about the government's motivations, thereby attracting more attention to the election rigging clip and ensuring its broad circulation.

The incident also prompted an interesting collaboration between old and new media. Soon after reports about the YouTube ban surfaced online on February 22, the leading independent news station Geo TV broadcast the original video uploaded by the civilian monitor. However, as it became increasingly clear that the government was making an effort to suppress the video, the news channel, which had already been banned during the 2007 emergency, ceased broadcasting the clip.

Instead, the channel took a cue from the clip's content and, emboldened by the online response to the YouTube video, began broadcasting other footage that revealed irregularities at polling stations. Although Geo TV reporters had captured this footage on election day, February 18, they did not compile and broadcast it as an investigative report focusing on election rigging until February 22, the day the YouTube video was being circulated online.[58] The channel made sure to include any footage captured on hidden cameras in an effort to mimic the tactics of citizen journalists and civilian monitors who mobilized for the election.

Interestingly, some of the early viewer comments about the election rigging clip posted to YouTube betray skepticism about the video's authenticity, with one viewer asking why Geo TV has not broadcast the clip if it is genuine. This response shows that the primary trust of the public remained with mainstream media outlets, rather than citizen journalists, even at a time when new media tools were in wide deployment. While it cannot be explicitly documented, the fact that Geo TV did eventually broadcast the YouTube clip must have boosted the perceived credibility of citizen journalism. More importantly, the fact that Geo TV shifted the focus of its programming to accord with a civic media artifact indicates that the Pakistani media landscape is moving towards a hybrid model, where professional journalists take the work of citizen journalists seriously, while citizen media relies on the mainstream media for dissemination and legitimacy...

On February 24, the Pakistani government's attempts to block YouTube led to a worldwide shutdown of the website for several hours... [A] guest blogger on the Teeth Maestro website wrote:

> It seems illogical for the government of Pakistan to hinder their own people from using one very important tool of the modern era. Pakistan Internet Exchange is also advised to upgrade its filtering/censorship systems which can cater to URL-specific blocks and not take the entire country down a roller coaster of censorship.[59]

Owing to the global ramifications of the YouTube block, the Pakistani government was forced to lift the ban on February 27. Clips showing election rigging – those posted by the civilian monitor as well as subsequent broadcasts from independent news channels – continue to be available on the website.

Pakistani vs. Western New Media Use

In this paper, we have seen how new media platforms and digital technologies have been harnessed by citizen journalists and democracy advocates for hyperlocal reporting and community organizing. We have also seen how mainstream media outlets increasingly serve as distribution channels for citizen journalism, initially generated and circulated via blogs, YouTube, or SMS text messages. Within certain communities, then, the adoption of new media platforms in Pakistan resembles their use in developed democracies such as the United States.

There are, however, differences between Pakistani and western approaches to new media. In the developed world, new media platforms gained popularity as many-to-many communications tools that reoriented the public as media producers and participants in a conversation rather than passive consumers within the one-to-many broadcast model.

In Pakistan, however, access to information – rather than the desire to participate – has driven the adoption of new media platforms. When old media distribution channels were compromised, new media was harnessed to fill in the gaps and maintain a flow of news and information. As such, new media in Pakistan has helped old media survive. The result is a media amalgamation in which information is pushed to the public, promiscuously distributed across broadcast media, new media platforms, and various digital technologies to prevent being disrupted or corrupted by the authorities. Thanks to amateurs and activists, students and concerned civilians, a nugget of information can leap from local televised news broadcasts to YouTube to SMS text message to FM radio broadcasts to blog posts to international news reports – whatever it takes to go public.

It would be a mistake to conclude this paper with the impression that digital technologies and new media platforms are the exclusive preserve of educated and privileged activists and citizen journalists, used solely for information dissemination and community organizing. Indeed, some of the best uses of new media and digital technologies address highly localized issues and are emergent, ad hoc, and culturally specific. For example, the residents of Karachi occasionally create an ad hoc, networked public sphere using FM radio broadcasts, cellphones, and landline connections not only to negotiate urban violence, as they did during the Emergency, but also to navigate flash floods during the monsoon, negotiate bad traffic owing to construction, and monitor protest rallies through the city.

Endnotes

1. "Pakistanis Condemning the Mockery of the Judicial System in Pakistan." http://proud-pakistani.com/2007/03/13/sign-the-petition-now/
2. Benkler, Yochai. 2006. *The Wealth of Networks: How Social Production Transforms Markets and Freedom.* New Haven: Yale University Press. P. 213.
3. The paper describes the use of digital technologies and new media platforms in Pakistan between March 2007 and February 2008, a period colloquially referred to as the 'Pakistan Emergency'. In this time, the military ruler General Musharraf dismissed the Supreme Court Chief Justice Iftikhar Muhammad Chaudhry, thereby undermining the country's independent judiciary. Taking advantage of a weakened judiciary, General Musharraf continued to serve simultaneously as the country's president and chief of army staff, thus blurring the distinction between democracy and dictatorship. Between November 2007 and February 2008, Pakistanis learnt just how rocky the road to democratic rule can be: in that time, General Musharraf imposed a state of emergency and suspended the constitution, opposition parties called for elections, a popular politician – former prime minister Benazir Bhutto – was brutally assassinated, and general elections were held. Moreover, press freedom was drastically curtailed during this time – amendments promulgated by General Musharraf in the summer of 2007 made it impossible for the media to report on elections or investigate matters relating to the government or Pakistan Army.
4. Certain digital technologies and new media platforms such as wikis (server programs that allow users to collaborate in forming the content of a website) and Twitter are not described in this paper because they have yet to gain popularity in Pakistan owing to limited internet access, low literacy rates, and the non-availability of web content in the national Urdu language.
5. Benkler, p. 219.
6. Powell, Adam Clayton. 2003. "Democracy and New Media in Developing Nations: Opportunities and Challenges". In Henry Jenkins & David Thorburn (Eds.) *Democracy and New Media.* Cambridge: MIT Press. P. 173.
7. Benkler, p. 219.
8. Mufti, Shahan. 2007. "Musharraf's Monster". *Columbia Journalism Review.* November/December. http://www.cjr.org/feature/musharrafs_monster.php?page=1
9. 2007. "Musharraf Imposes Tough Curbs on Pakistani Media." VOA News. November 4. http://www.voanews.com/english/archive/2007-11/2007-11-03-voa20.cfm?CFID=58366452&CFTOKEN=88144752
10. 2008. "Eight TV and 10 Radio Channels Issued Licenses." The Daily Times. May 23. http://www.dailytimes.com.pk/default.asp?page=2008%5C05%5C23%5Cstory_23-5-2008_pg7_29
11. Precise television viewership statistics for Pakistan are not available. This pie chart showing advertising time shares on different private channels and the state-owned PTV is thus a good indicator of the relative popularity of different channels. (Source: MediaTrak Pakistan, http://www.travel-culture.com/pakistan/media/).
12. 2005. Montero, David. "Quake Emboldens Pakistani TV." The Christian Science Monitor. December 1. http://www.csmonitor.com/2005/1201/p04s01-wosc.html
13. 2007. "Top Judge Attacks Musharraf's Rule." BBC Online. November 6. http://news.bbc.co.uk/2/hi/south_asia/7080433.stm
14. 2007. McDowell, Robin. "Pakistan TV Fights Back." The Associated Press. November 8. http://www.internews.org/articles/2007/20071108_ap_pakistan.shtm

15 2007. "Pakistan Emergency Geo News." YouTube. November 3. http://www.youtube.com/watch?v=BqbJj2ZKDYM
16 "Live Pakistani Television." The Pakistan Policy Blog. http://pakistanpolicy.com/pakistan-television-live/
17 Dawn News article: http://www.dawn.com/2008/07/25/nat22.htm
18 2007. "Top Judge Attacks Musharraf Rule." BBC Online. November 6. http://news.bbc.co.uk/2/hi/south_asia/7080433.stm
19 2007. "PTA Annual Report 2007." Pakistan Telecommunications Authority. www.pta.gov.pk/index2.php?option=com_content&do_pdf=1&id=1033. In the 1990s, three telecom operators (Paktel, Ufone, and Mobilink) were present in Pakistan. However, exorbitant connection fees, airtime charges, and billing on incoming calls kept mobile penetration at 0.2 percent until the end of the decade. The Pakistan Telecom Authority (PTA) – a government agency founded in 1997 to regulate the telecom industry – introduced a calling party pays (CPP) policy in 2001, which resulted in industry competition that helped increase mobile penetration to 5.28 percent in 2004. The introduction of two new telecom operators in early 2005 led to fiercer competition, cheaper connections, and affordable handsets. By July 2006, overall teledensity in Pakistan stood at 46.9 percent, of which only 3.3 percent was due to fixed line services.
20 2007. "PTA Annual Report 2007." Pakistan Telecommunications Authority. www.pta.gov.pk/index2.php?option=com_content&do_pdf=1&id=1033. According to the PTA, the total target market for the cellphone users – excluding those living well below the poverty line and children under the age of 8 – is about 97 million people. In other words, over 60 percent of the potential Pakistani market was using cellphones when Musharraf suspended the constitution. Since 2003, telecom companies have invested over US$ 8 billion in Pakistan, with the mobile sector accounting for 73 percent of that expenditure. In the 2007 fiscal year alone, the mobile sector invested USD 2.7 billion. And the market is expected to grow: China Mobile has acquired one cellular network and contracted USD 500 million to companies such as Ericcson, ZTE, and Alcatel to roll out new networks. Meanwhile, existing mobile service providers are investing heavily in the industry. For example, Mobilink, the largest local network, invested US$ 500 million in the 2008 fiscal year to improve the quality of its service and expand infrastructure.
21 2007. "PTA Annual Report 2007." Pakistan Telecommunications Authority. www.pta.gov.pk/index2.php?option=com_content&do_pdf=1&id=1033.
22 2007. "Details of the LUMS Rally and Police Response." The Emergency Times. November 7. http://pakistanmartiallaw.blogspot.com/2007/11/details-of-lums-rally-and-police.html.
23 2007. "Protest at LUMS." Metroblogging Lahore. November 7. http://lahore.metblogs.com/2007/11/07/protest-lums-november-7th-2007/.
24 2007. "Update @ 13:40: Police Outside LUMS Lahore." Teeth Maestro. November 7. http://www.teeth.com.pk/blog/2007/11/07/update-1340-police-outside-lums-lahore.
25 2007. "2nd Major Protest Rally at LUMS." YouTube. November 7. http://www.youtube.com/watch?v=FbfD_xyN7Dw&feature=related.
26 CNN iReport. http://www.ireport.com/about.jspa
27 2007. "LUMS Protest on CNN." YouTube. November 7. http://www.youtube.com/watch?v=5zobFeyJ2Uc&feature=related
28 2007. "LUMS Protest." YouTube. November 5. http://www.youtube.com/watch?v=oVg_dHsghpI
29 2007. "2nd Major Protest Rally at LUMS." YouTube. November 7. http://www.youtube.com/watch?v=FbfD_xyN7Dw&feature=related
30 2007. "LUMS Student Protests in Pakistan – Newseye –Dawn News." YouTube. November 10. http://www.youtube.com/watch?v=fJYp-jPEPgU
31 2007. "LUMS Besieged by Police." The Emergency Times. December 4. http://pakistanmartiallaw.blogspot.com/2007/12/lums-beseiged-by-police.html
32 2007. "Essamlums Photostream." Flickr. November. http://flickr.com/photos/essamfahim/page2/

33 2007. "Update @ 21:13: Images from Today's Peace Rally at LUMS." Teeth Maestro. November 9. http://www.teeth.com.pk/blog/2007/11/09/update-2113-images-from-todays-peace-rally-at-lums
34 "We Oppose Emergency in Pakistan." Facebook. http://www.new.facebook.com/group.php?gid=5772092761
35 2007. "Pictures from the Islamabad Rally." The Emergency Times. December 18. http://pakistanmartiallaw.blogspot.com/2007/12/pictures-from-islamabad-rally.html
36 2008. "SAC Lahore Members Harassed and Beaten Up." The Emergency Times. February 2. http://pakistanmartiallaw.blogspot.com/2008/02/sac-lahore-members-harassed-and-beaten.html
37 2007. "Force MMA to Boycott." The Emergency Times. December 2. http://pakistanmartiallaw.blogspot.com/2007/12/force-mma-to-boycott.html
38 Awab Alvi in discussion with the author. December 31, 2007.
39 Global Voices Online. http://globalvoicesonline.org/.
40 2007. "Was Yesterday's Carnage in Karachi All PPP's Doing or Did MQM Have a Hand In It?" Teeth Maestro. December 28. http://www.teeth.com.pk/blog/2007/12/28/was-yesterdays-carnage-in-karachi-all-ppps-doing-or-did-mqm-have-a-hand-in-it-an-eyewitness-report.
41 2007. "Updated: Mobile pictures – Benazir Wad Definitely Shot Dead Before the Blast." Teeth Maestro. December 29. http://www.teeth.com.pk/blog/2007/12/29/mobile-pictures-benazir-was-defintely-shot-dead-before-the-blast/.
42 2008. "Mobile Phone Pictures Reveal Benazir Was Shot Before The Blast." The Emergency Times. December 31. http://pakistanmartiallaw.blogspot.com/2007/12/mobile-phone-pictures-reveal-benazir.html.
43 2008. "Pakistan: Election Commission Not Impartial." Human Rights Watch. February 12. http://hrw.org/english/docs/2008/02/11/pakist18034.htm.
44 2008. "Pakistan: Media Restrictions Undermine Election." Human Rights Watch. February 16. http://hrw.org/english/docs/2008/02/16/pakist18088.htm.
45 2008. "As Pakistan Election Nears, Citizens Fan Out to Combat Vote Rigging." The Wall Street Journal. February 16. http://www.naitazi.com/2008/02/16/as-pakistan-election-nears-citizens-fan-out-to-combat-vote-rigging/.
46 2008. "Pakistan's Tehalka!" The Emergency Times. February 16. http://pakistanmartiallaw.blogspot.com/search?q=pakistan+tehalka.
47 2008. "Hamid Mir Writes to Nations." NaiTazi.com. February 17. http://www.naitazi.com/2008/02/17/hamid-mir-writes-to-nations/.
48 2008. "Karachi: MQM Sets Eyes On 18 Out of 20 NA Seats from Karachi." NaiTazi.com. February 15. http://www.naitazi.com/2008/02/15/karachi-mqm-sets-eyes-on-18-out-of-20-na-seats-from-karachi/.
49 2008. "Election Roundup." Teeth Maestro. February 19. http://www.teeth.com.pk/blog/2008/02/19/election-roundup-0630-pst.
50 2008. "Beyond Belief: My First Pakistani Voting Experience." Teeth Maestro. February 18. http://www.teeth.com.pk/blog/2008/02/18/beyond-belief-my-first-pakistani-voting-experience-narration-from-a-voter.
51 2008. "Kal, Aaj, Aur Kal (Part One) – Poem by Aitzaz Ahsan." YouTube. February 14. http://www.youtube.com/watch?v=6Il4GO5sOXc.
52 2008. "Rigging by PPP in NA 250 Karachi Elections 2008." YouTube. February 21. http://www.youtube.com/watch?v=r693adEEGhQ.
53 2008. "YouTube Banned in Pakistan." PK Politics Blog. February 22. http://pkpolitics.com/2008/02/22/youtube-banned-in-pakistan/.
54 2008. "YouTube Banned in Pakistan." Adnan's Crazy Blogging World. February 22. http://kadnan.com/blog/2008/02/22/youtube-banned-in-pakistan/.
55 2008. "YouTube Banned in Pakistan." Adnan's Crazy Blogging World. February 22. http://kadnan.com/blog/2008/02/22/youtube-banned-in-pakistan/

56 2008. "YouTube Blocked in Pakistan by PTA's Orders, After Vote Rigging Videos Show Up???" ShiaChat. February 22. http://www.shiachat.com/forum/index.php?showtopic=234941366.
57 2008. "Pakistan Blocks YouTube Website." BBC Online. February 24. http://news.bbc.co.uk/2/hi/south_asia/7261727.stm.
58 2008. "MQM Rigging in Karachi." YouTube. February 22. http://www.youtube.com/watch?v=zqvXOkD5HYQ.
59 2008. "TWA Internet Backbone Link Blocks Only Blasphemous Video URL." Teeth Maestro. February 24. http://www.teeth.com.pk/blog/2008/02/24/twa-internet-backbone-link-blocks-only-blasphemous-video-url.

Annotation

Shobha S.V.

After reading Huma Yusuf's paper, "Old and New Media: Converging during the Pakistan Emergency (March 2007-2008)," what strikes the reader primarily is that the piece is rather dated. It is important to understand that the piece is set in 2007, when the tech-media landscape was different from the present. And it is funny that I use the word 'dated' to describe something that happened only about seven years ago. 2007 represents a time when blogs and email lists were used as a major channel of communication. Things are not the same now!

Events like the Arab Spring, the Shahbag protests at Bangladesh, and the Anna Hazare anti-corruption movement in India are evidence of the fact that activism by citizens looks very different now, especially with Twitter and Facebook playing a major role of mobilisation and information dissemination. Messaging services like Whatsapp are playing an important role as well. For instance, in 2012, people moved to Whatsapp en masse when the state of Karnataka in India, in a bid to counter rumour mongering, imposed a ban on telecom operators on sending text messages in bulk.

However, what hasn't changed for quite a significant amount of the population in South Asia is the issue of access to the Internet. While India is home to one of the largest populations/numbers of mobile phone owners in the world, it's only a relatively small group that owns smartphones. While the number of smartphone owners is on a rise, the majority still owns feature phones.

Radio is still the most easily accessible medium for the masses in the Indian sub-continent. Unfortunately, it is also one of the most regulated media. In India, news is banned on private radio channels. News is played only on the government-run All India Radio. Huma Yusuf beautifully demonstrates how, in the face of a news ban, radio stations used innovative ways of subversion to get news of their loved ones stuck in different parts of the city of Karachi with the active participation of Karachi residents. The ban on news on radio has also given rise to newer mediums like mobile radio in India. Jharkhand Mobile Vaani and CGNet Swara are some notable examples. It is also useful to note that mobile radio does not come under any government regulation in India.

Reading this piece gives a fascinating insight into the development of citizen journalism. Citizen journalism is a common phenomenon today. The popularity of social media and democratisation of media tools (which only media professionals had access to earlier) are some of the reasons for the popularity of citizen journalism all over the world. However, reading this paper brought some questions to the fore. Did the idea of citizen journalism flourish only in the face of a ban on mainstream media? Did it flourish only in the face of suppression and crisis? Answers to these questions will give rise to interesting insights on the emergence of citizen journalism in your community, your city, or your country.

Also, news media in the past followed the broadcast model, i.e., it relayed the news, and the readers consumed it. Apart from letters to the editor, there wasn't any other way for the general public to communicate back. With the advent of digital tools, what has crucially changed is the interactive element of media, where the consumer of the media is also an active participant. While traditional forms of media (radio, newspapers) are still thriving especially in the Indian subcontinent, they have incorporated the interactive element in various ways. News gathering and news consumption cannot be the same as it was in the past.

References and Further Readings

CGNet Swara, http://www.cgnetswara.org/.
Hicks Maynard, Nancy. 2000. "Digitization and the News." Nieman Reports. December 15. http://niemanreports.org/articles/digitization-and-the-news/.
"Jharkhand Mobile Vaani." Gramvaani. http://www.gramvaani.org/?page_id=343.
Matheson, Donald. 2014. "History of Citizen Journalism." In Patricia Moy (Ed.) *Communication*. Oxford Bibliographies. DOI: 10.1093/obo/9780199756841-0145. http://www.oxfordbibliographies.com/obo/page/communication.
Singh, Sanjay. 2012. "North-East Exodus: Telecom Firms Flout Bulk SMS Directive." Business Today. August 20. Accessed April 26, 2015. http://businesstoday.intoday.in/story/north-east-exodus-telecom-firms-flout-bulk-sms-directive/1/187317.html.
Shetty, Anuradha. 2012. "WhatsApp Messenger Records 10 Bn Messages in a Day." Firspost Tech. August 25. Accessed April 26, 2015. http://m.tech.firstpost.com/news-analysis/whatsapp-messenger-records-10bn-messages-in-a-day-36702.html.
Worstall, Tim. 2013. "More People Have Mobile Phones Than Toilets." Forbes. August 23. Accessed on April 26, 2015. http://www.forbes.com/sites/timworstall/2013/03/23/more-people-have-mobile-phones-than-toilets/.

Redefining Youth Activism through Digital Technology in Singapore

Weiyu Zhang

Introduction

Generational shifts in civic engagement are evident around the globe. In most of the liberal democracies of the western world this shift has been manifested among younger people as an increasing disengagement and disaffection with traditional participatory mechanisms. The mechanisms of representative democracy are no longer adequate to mobilize young citizens. Young people are involved less and less in voting, the fundamental participatory act of a representative democracy (Putnam, 2000). Party membership has dropped, and the nature of involvement with a political party has changed (Dalton and Wattenberg, 2002). Distrust of elected political figures, such as parliamentarians, has been found to be high among young people (Dalton, 2004). Youth have withdrawn from many traditional participatory acts, such as attending to news (Delli Carpini, 2000; Mindich, 2005). Instead, youth in the West seem to be attracted by a variety of new forms of civic engagement: issue-based activism, lifestyle politics, identity politics, and consumerist acts have become increasingly popular among the young (Bennett, 1998; Ward and de Vreese, 2011). These changes suggest a new political horizon. However, whether this horizon is shared by youth in other parts of world remains an open question.

Generational replacement also happens in countries that are in transition, or in the early years of democracy. However, the prevailing conditions are vastly different from those seen in mature liberal democracies. In many new democracies young citizens are fighting against historical barriers, such as fear-driven political cultures or repressive colonial laws. Furthermore, recent developments in liberal democracies, such as the decline of party politics and disenchantment with representative mechanisms, also influence the way in which young citizens in the new or still developing democracies interpret their future. Against this particular backdrop of political developments, youth activism in young or semi-democracies is expected to manifest through distinguishing patterns, creating unanticipated implications for their societies.

The introduction of information and communication technology (ICT) since the 1990s has played a significant role in the generational shifts. Children born into this era, and growing up with digital technology, are variously known as the Net generation (Palfrey and Gasser, 2008), Generation Y (Americans born after 1976), Millennials, or DotNets, as they are defined by their coming of age along with the Internet (Zukin et al., 2006). However, it remains unclear whether, and how, ICT reshapes politics. While Internet use can be linked to traditional political participation (Kim and Kim, 2007), scholars have also been drawn to the political potential of an online public sphere (Zhang, 2006). Both participatory democracy and deliberative democracy have been used as guiding models when looking at the impact of ICT. Such impact is supposed to be even more apparent among the young, as their everyday lives are organized around the new media. In addition, the promising role of ICT in promoting democratization has been confirmed by real life events, such as the Egyptian and Libyan revolutions. Scholars have documented the power of ICT to both reinforce dominating regimes and to challenge them (Yang, 2010; Zheng, 2008). When the younger generation seizes the power of ICT in their own hands, how will it affect their civic engagement, and how will their participatory acts change the political landscape? These are the thematic queries that mandate this investigation.

This article aims to examine the relationship between youth, ICT and civic engagement, within the context of an authoritarian democracy, Singapore. Youth, as describing an age group, without doubt includes a diverse collection of people. In order not to fall into the trap of over-generalization, this examination is focused on younger people who, not only have the access to ICT, but who also are involved in some form of civic activity. In-depth interviews with 23 young activists in Singapore were used to gather information about the emerging phenomenon of digital activism. The findings are presented in three parts. First, I explain how the concept of activism has been understood in the Singaporean context and how young activists have redefined, appropriated, or rejected this concept. Through this exercise of defining activism, we are able to see how ICT goes beyond functioning as a tool, to become an important component of their political lexicon. Second, I examine generational shift through the young activists' own accounts of their parents and seniors, including how the prominence of ICT differs between older and younger generations. Third, I explore the details of using ICT in activism, examining different forms of technology, with their advantages and disadvantages. I conclude with a discussion of the theoretical and political implications of the findings.

Activism in an Authoritarian Democracy

A basic definition of democracy suggests that the rulers have to be selected by the ruled. Singapore fulfills this definition, as it holds regular elections to select its legislative body and presidency. The elections have broad suffrage, as almost every citizen has the right to vote. In addition, the voting procedure is fair and does not involve fraud. However, in Singapore there is an effective single-party system, in which opposition parties have never overturned the domination of the ruling party. Singapore has held 11 general elections since its independence in 1965, and the People's Action Party (PAP) has continued to return to power, with an overwhelming majority, with the recent 2011 election yielding a 60% majority. Competitive party politics has been absent from most of the past elections, due to electioneering and legislative devices (Chua, 2004). For instance, the Internal Security Act (ISA) gives the government the power to detain anyone for a period of up to two years, without the need for a public trial. This Act has been invoked twice recently, in 1987 and 2001.

The hybrid nature of the Singaporean political system has, to a great extent, shaped the activism now occurring in the city-state. Political activism is narrowly defined as opposition party politics that challenges the dominance of the PAP (Chua, 2004). Civil society organizations are not allowed to affiliate with political parties, preventing coalitions developing between oppositional social forces. This means that many social entities that are not necessarily pro-opposition, but are critical of certain governmental policies, are unable to find an efficient means for exerting influence. Some scholars have therefore claimed that Singapore has a strong state, but a weak civil society (Lam, 1999; Ming, 2002).

Strong state intervention is evident in many areas, including its youth policies. The government has purposely cultivated young leaders. Many awards (e.g., a National Youth Achievement Award) and various government-funded scholarships are handed out to young Singaporeans who excel, and who are expected to pay back through their contribution to society. The average youth is not left out of the governmental plan, either. In fact, the government has been promoting charity-focused activities, as well as community-based volunteering, in the society as a whole, and particularly among the youth. The government has adopted the objective of providing Singaporeans with essential services, such as education, housing, and health care, while reducing the welfare burden on the state (Cheung, 1992). Therefore, the role played by local philanthropic organizations is crucial to Singaporean society. Citizens are also encouraged to contribute actively to charities, exemplified in the regular fundraising telethons. For younger citizens, co-curricular activities (CCAs) are compulsory, non-academic activities in which Singaporean students must take part. These CCAs often happen in groups, including clubs, societies, and associations. Such group activities are often linked to community-based volunteering, such as helping in the homes of the elderly. Both philanthropy and volunteering work are activities performed by many Singaporean youth. These group activities, although not aimed at political change, nevertheless foster social capital, and cultivate civic identity among young people. The causes supported through these activities are mostly collective, in contrast to personal interests, such as hobby groups. Therefore, it is inaccurate to say that the youth in an authoritarian democracy are given no chance of getting involved in social activism.

Young activists, growing up in such a political environment, are expected to be different from the older activists. The older generation of activists in Singapore, as represented by oppositional party leaders, carries the image of being radical, antagonist, and unsuccessful. For example, Tang Liang Hong, an electoral candidate affiliated with the Workers' Party, was sued for defamation, and fled as a fugitive to Australia after failing in his challenge of the ruling party. Joshua Benjamin Jeyaretnam, another opposition politician, was declared bankrupt after failing to keep up his payments for damages owed to PAP leaders as result of a libel suit. These examples illustrate how the older activists have been presented to Singaporeans. The youth activism as seen today thus both inherits and differentiates itself from this tradition of oppositional politics. The spirit of promoting social change is maintained, but the practicalities of being oppositional are neutralized. In short, a new wave of activism is emerging among Singaporean youth.

ICT, Youth, and Civic Engagement

Singapore has enjoyed high ICT penetration since the government initiated a master plan of developing the city-state into an 'intelligent island'. The computer ownership rate was 84% in 2010 (Infocomm Development Authority, 2010). Internet access had increased to 78% in 2010, as compared to a mere 6% in 1996. Mobile phone penetration in 2009 had reached 137%, meaning that many Singaporeans use more than one phone. These figures not only exceed the regional average, but also put Singapore among the most developed ICT countries in the world.

Considering the prominence of ICT in Singaporeans' everyday life, it may be expected to have a significant impact on civic engagement. However, the reality shows otherwise. The political culture under an authoritarian democratic system (Skoric, 2007) has rendered the majority of the population either apathetic, or afraid of getting involved in politics (Tamney, 1996). A media system closely controlled by the government presents the prevailing political culture. Nation-building is considered the primary function of local press (Lee, 2000: 217-218, 225). Mass media are supposed to inform and educate citizens rather than provide a platform for all kinds of political expression. Publishers and journalists who have neglected this primary goal have been punished under the Newspapers and Printing Presses Act, or the Defamation Act (Lee, 2002; Seow, 1998). The regulations relating to the Internet service are similar to those of the mass media. For example, all Internet service providers (ISPs) must be licensed by the Media Development Authority (MDA). Another example is that the MDA maintains a symbolic list of 100 blocked sites to showcase their authority in censoring online content. An apathetic and fearful citizenry, along with careful control of media, makes some scholars think that any kind of organized resistance, even online, would be fraught (Rodan, 2003).

However, it is worth discussing whether the lack of influence of ICT on civic engagement holds true among the younger section of the population. There were 818,500 Singaporeans who fell into the category of youth (20-34 years old) in 2010, which comprised around 22% of the total population (Singapore Department of Statistics, 2010). These younger people were socialized in an environment where poverty is a remote memory, and all the post-Second World War chaos has been dealt with. They do not necessarily buy into the nation-building argument, because the need for strong intervention by the government does not seem to be as urgent as before. They are also very much influenced by more liberal countries, such as the UK and US, as Singapore shares the same official language, English, and Singaporeans are exposed to many cultural products from the liberal West. The political culture forged in the earlier years of the nation is thus not that applicable to the younger generation. Instead, they are better educated, exposed to wider worldviews, and feel more comfortable with voicing their concerns and demanding to be heard.

The introduction of ICT accompanied the socialization of this younger generation. Young people use ICT for various purposes, including both social and political. A recent survey (Lin and Hong, 2011) shows that during the 2011 General Election, people aged between 21 and 34 were far more actively involved in online politics, such as writing about the elections on blogs, Facebook, or Twitter (28% youth vs 10% total population), and forwarding or sharing online content (20% youth vs 10% total). In addition, among those who agreed to reveal their voting decisions, 16% of younger respondents said they supported the opposition, in comparison to an overall rate of 11%. These numbers show that younger Singaporeans not only are less likely to share with their seniors an apathetic and fearful culture, but also are more likely to express their political views through online platforms. This present article is thus motivated to examine how young activists in Singapore, socialized in an ICT-saturated environment that is increasingly distanced from political apathy and fear, engage in civic activities.

Method

A snow-ball sampling method was used to recruit interviewees. An age limit of 18-34 years old was set. There was an average age of 24 years old among our 23 interviewees. The recruitment of interviewees was conducted with a clear intention of reaching both demographic and opinion diversity. In order to make sure that various types of young activists, as well as various perspectives, were included in our interviews, informants were recruited from three communities: student volunteers, who are mainly involved in charity work and community volunteering; issue activists, who are motivated by specific issues, such as the environment and human rights; and political activists who are engaged in party politics. An effort was made to ensure that both genders were equally represented in the sample (12 males and 11 females) and that racial minorities were included as well (1 Malay, 3 Indians, 1 Caucasian, and 1 Eurasian).

Our sample showed an average of 15 years of education, which equates to a college degree in Singapore. The interviewees reported that they were somewhat, or very, interested in politics (M 1⁄4 3.5 on a 1-4 point scale) and they paid quite a bit (M 1⁄4 3.76 on a 1-5 point scale) of attention to political and governmental news. On two or three days every week they watched TV news, read newspapers, and talked with others about political and governmental issues. All these numbers confirmed that our sample was not a sample of average youth, but was more skewed toward the active members of society. In addition, our sample was also an ICT-experienced group. They had an average 10-year history with the Internet, which meant that they had started using the Internet in their teenage years. On average, they surfed the Internet for news on politics and government on five days a week, which is clearly higher than their use of other media channels, such as TV and newspapers, for the same purpose. These figures suggest that our sample is indeed a group of young people growing up with digital technology.

The potential interviewees were first contacted through either personal ties or emails. The interviewers scheduled the interviews at a time and place convenient to the interviewees. Some of the interviews were conducted in a university meeting room and others were in public spaces, such as coffee shops. Each of the interviewees was provided with a document that introduced the project in detail, and they signed a consent form before proceeding to the actual interview. The interviews took from one to two hours, and except for two interviews (one email and one instant messaging), all were conducted face-to-face. The interviews were conducted between September 2009 and February 2010.

All interviews were audio-recorded (with the interviewees' permission) and transcribed by qualified personnel. A three-step analysis was carried out. First, an overall reading of all transcripts was done, and various notes were added to the margins. Second, a number of themes were identified by combining and comparing the notes. Finally, different themes were organized under the three major topics: contesting activism in a digital age; a Net generation of activists; and the pros and cons of ICT in activism. These are presented below, as the main findings of this analysis.

Contesting Activism in a Digital Age

Activism, by definition, emphasizes action. However, there are numerous ways to take action on varying issues. For this reason, activism becomes a highly debatable concept. Through an exploration of the meaning of activism we can see how political contexts, as well as ICT, can play their roles in influencing young Singaporean activists' perceptions and identifications. Although all of our interviewees were involved in one or more activities that advocated certain causes, their interpretations of the simple identification of being an activist were quite diverse. Some dedicated youths saw this identity as very true to their hearts, and considered activism to be a crucial characteristic defining who they are. C.[1] is a human rights activist and she answered:

> I would identify myself as an activist. It's ingrained in my personality. I find it sometimes hard not to be political, even when in normal conversations.

G., another student activist who focuses on human rights issues, said:

> I would say it's very much a part of me, as in how I am, what I believe. It drives me in a sense because of my interest in it, so that's why what I'm studying now actually, I feel, gives me a better understanding of civil society.

Some interviewees even felt that they were not doing enough to qualify as activists, although they were eager to become one. S., a university year-4 student, who advocates for animal rights, expressed her feelings:

> OK, to be very frank, I wouldn't consider myself an activist now, because of my level of commitment to work. But before, in my year 1, year 2, year 3, I could say I was really involved. I really had a voice. I really could channel my voice. And I really tried to do things that would change the environment, even in the university environment, or the larger environment. But I don't think that with my lack of initiative at the moment, it's not fair to say

that I'm an activist. But what I really hope to do in the future – I definitely cannot, as in – to me, a real activist, is the people who work in these NGOs like chose to put themselves there and they chose to fight for different things.

On the other hand, some young activists denied being an activist up-front. For instance, Z., a member of several environmental groups, said:

> I am not too sure if I am considered an activist. I tend to do things on a very sporadic level as in I don't tend to get involved in too many things. As in I don't tend to specialize too much I tend to be very generalist . . . I will just simply say I am a concerned citizen who just wants to make the world better.

The distance Z. put between himself and the title activist probably reflects the political context in which activism is defined. It is mainly due to the perception that activism has negative connotations. Z. explained this perception and its formation very well:

> Activists in Singapore tend to [be connoted] more in the negative light. Because people will think that you are neglecting your commitments just because of this cause, or you are just an attention seeker. Or people will say that being an activist is being anti-establishment, or you just trying to get yourself into more trouble, you know.

S.N., a member of a migrant worker NGO, shared the view that activism is linked to oppositional party politics, and therefore denied being an activist:

> I don't know if I can be called an activist, 'cause I don't know what it means. In Singapore we don't get an education about what activism means. And I think the forms of activism we have, it doesn't seem like, it just seems like it's that and there's nothing more. And if there's more, it would be to take a political position into an opposition party. But that is not so desirable for me.

Activism in Singapore is often narrowly understood as political opposition that is against the establishment. The methods that have been used by the older-generation activists are often antagonist and radical. Therefore, the media portrait of such behaviors shapes a perception of activism as civil disobedience. Such a perception has inevitably influenced young activists, and how they plan to approach the initiation of social change. One approach, in contrast to the oppositional style of activism, emphasizes a cooperative relationship between activists and government. K., a leader of volunteer work, stated how he engaged with the ruling powers:

> I'd say that the way the activists [who try] to bring the messages across is rather [a] confrontational method, through demonstration, rally, riot

to bring the message in a hard way to the government to some extent, that people might be affected, arrested. To me, I don't agree with the way they do things. Yes, we want to provide feedback to the authority, but that should be done in a proper mode of communication, which is the consultation mode.

Another interviewee, R., works on environmental issues. She termed her activities awareness building, rather than activism. She said:

I haven't personally gone hard core online to actively protest. It's a very aggressive way. At the end of the day, what we need is a conducive environment for both parties, if you were to introduce tension and restriction over there, it's just gonna create more resistance, so I tend to call it not activism but awareness.

The role of ICT in this debate over activism is to function as efficient tools in building awareness and recruiting participants. L.J., a mental health activist, described how his activism was prompted by the Internet:

I don't think I would be so interested in going into activism if not because a lot of what I've read is online, even though now I've started reading some books as well. And then, how do I volunteer for Maruah [a human rights NGO]? I did it online. How do I reach out to people? I do it online. How do I find out about events? I do it through Facebook.

In addition, the recruitment is not always intentional. For instance, one of our interviewees, S., described how she 'bumped into' an activity that interested her:

I was writing a happy birthday message on my friend's wall and I saw it under the groups she just added. I clicked on it because the name sounds cool, you know 'vibrant colors'. Actually I heard about it before, they [had been] to my secondary school to promote the program.

The recruiting of young people into advocating public causes is not limited to local activities: several of our interviewees had engaged, via the Internet, in international causes, such as those run by the United Nations, or even issues that were local to other countries. S.L, for example, had participated in the Free Burma campaign in Singapore, mostly through online means, such as reading Burmese news websites.

Some activists went a step further in defining their activism as being through ICT-based activities. If activism emphasizes actions, online actions qualify as online activism. In other words, it seems to them that online involvement is no less active than offline engagement. A., a prominent local blogger, said:

> If you look at our website, we call ourselves bloggervists, not just bloggers or activists. It's a combination of both. Sometimes we just blog, sometimes we become activists fighting for a cause ...

According to our young activist interviewees, they argued against the negative connotation of activism in Singapore, either by proudly identifying themselves with activism, or by tactically denying being an activist in the sense of opposition party politicians. Furthermore, they seemed to be open to various means of advocating social change. They not only accepted the method of cooperating with the ruling power, but also valued basic activities, such as awareness building, no less than those activities that aim for immediate and real effects, such as petitions, protests, rallies, and so on. ICT supports this expanded understanding of activism by facilitating information dissemination and participant recruitment. Some young activists assigned to their online activities equal importance with offline activities by calling themselves 'bloggervists', a term that illustrates a new form of activism. This new form of activism, emerging in the Singaporean context, is distinguished from the confrontational approach of opposition party politics, and also incorporates ICT-based activities as part of its repertoire.

A Net Generation of Activists

Young activists in Singapore are different from the older generation in many ways. For one, they are offered more opportunities to engage in public matters than their parents were. For instance, one interviewee, S., mentioned that the civic education young people receive forges them into a new generation of civic-minded citizens. In addition, chances to visit parliament, and other political institutions, are provided to the youth, which were not available in previous eras. These new opportunities expand the possibilities for civic activism among younger people.

These changes in opportunities for activism should be seen in the larger context of the nation's developmental stage: Singapore was still a developing country when independence was declared. The living conditions under which the older generation grew up were very different from those today. Therefore, the kind of activism that the older generation got involved in was different, too. O., a sportsman who later became an environmental activist, pointed out that:

> They [his parents] fundamentally thought about how to survive. When you don't have enough money, when you have to go to hospital, let's put together enough money for your hospital bill. When you don't have a house, come, let everybody contribute. Now we're different. Now we have different system whereby you should have enough money to live on your own, beautifying the house, what level you want.

The improvements in living conditions have given activists time and resource to work in activism, as their basic needs are no longer urgent. The nature of the causes that attract people to take action have also changed. The survival issues have already been solved, and sporadic cases of need can be taken care of by existing institutions. However, precisely because of this situation, O. felt that his generation is not as civic minded as his parents' generation was. He said:

> We're on a thin line, we cannot call it civic. Achieving civic is a challenge because civic means an ideal whereby I will act socially because I want to help you naturally. But for us, we're going further from this. We all want something better, which is directly opposite from civic.

Another difference the young activists observed, is a difference in challenging authority. The political culture in Singapore, established through making known the failed cases of political activists, is marked with fear and apathy (Rodan, 1998; Tamney, 1996). While older generations were busy surviving, and the authorities thought controlling the citizenry was necessary for nation-building, the widespread attitude was to avoid getting into trouble through being silent, or by turning one's back on certain issues. However, this is no longer the case. N., an active community volunteer, stated the difference quite clearly:

> The main difference you would see is that the younger generation is more willing to speak up. We fear the government less, maybe. My grandmother thinks if you say anything, [the] police will get you and you'll die. My mom thinks if you say things responsibly, it's OK. For me, I think you can say anything as long as you have facts to back it up responsibly, it shouldn't be a problem.

There were a few interviewees who came from families with an activist tradition. However, even in cases like this, our interviewees still saw differences in perspectives, priorities, and experience. For instance, Y.W., an environmental activist, pointed out that he does not necessarily share his father's perspective, as his father used to be in the socialists' organization. Nevertheless, the influence of the older generation is evident. Although parents and children do not always agree upon causes and methods, their values and beliefs with regard to activism and good citizenship are held in common. R. commented on this:

> Since young they [her parents] already infused us with values, attitudes. I don't see myself thinking very much differently from my parents, which is why some of my fellow peers often said that my way of thinking tends to be old-fashioned. It's about how you preserve these values or beliefs. They have never proved to be the wrong ones, and often, new solutions

> are not always the best solutions, so it's always good to be on the same track with those who have gone [along] the path.

L.J. expressed appreciation of his parents:

> I have a good fortune to have my parents talking about politics at the dinner table. I think not [all] parents talk about politics to their children. It got me interest[ed] even though I'm not very interested in politics. I know that my father generally talks about it, but he actually does not do anything about it, and my mother was a civil servant so it's not entirely her fault.

Despite a continuation of activist values and attitudes, there are clear variations between the generations in understanding and actually 'doing' activism. The reasons for these differences are many. As discussed before, the opportunities presented to younger people to access civic activism are broader now. Compared to their parents, who by necessity had to focus on bread and butter matters, younger people today have a more supportive environment, allowing them to engage in various activities. The civic education they receive in schools also helps them to get past the mentality of fear and apathy. ICT serves as another important information source and engagement platform, for potential young activists.

The Pros and Cons of ICT in Activism

When talking about the differences between the younger and older generations, S. thought one big difference is that younger people do not read newspapers as much as older people. Instead, younger people rely heavily on online media to access and disseminate information.

Mailing lists, as one of the oldest online media, remain important in disseminating information. Most of our interviewees subscribed to mailing lists belonging to various organizations, and received event notifications and other information from those organizations. Blogs have increasingly become another major information source. When asked where they get their information, most interviewees referred to local blogs and social network sites. A., an influential local blogger, has used blogging as his major approach to activism. He emphasized the importance of laying the foundation of a credible online information source, which is judged by intelligent readers who pass on the information to more citizens. He said:

> Once people know that you're credible, they're fine. They're the ones who will tell their friends about this, and I know it, because I know teachers, lecturers have been passing it on. I know there was a teacher who happened to find us on the Internet, she emailed us and said, 'I'm recommending this to the whole class when they're doing their social

studies.' This is great. From one person to a whole class, 30–40 students. When they find it credible, the opinion makers, people who can influence others, they can pass it on.

However, not all the young activists felt comfortable voicing their opinions online. The political culture still seemed to influence a few of our interviewees, and made them practice self-censorship. S. explained why she did not get involved in blogging about serious stuff:

> No, because I wouldn't want to say the wrong thing. And because there are newspaper reports of some people writing political stuff and getting sued for it. So that one I try not to touch, but for example, when I went for the parliament thing, I just said something like 'It's a good experience', a generic thing.

The contribution of these blogs or websites is recognized by young activists as primarily providing an alternative voice that cannot be heard in the traditional mass media that are controlled by the government. G., for instance, commented:

> I would say so because a lot of times alternative media carry a lot more interesting information that may not be reported in The Straits Times (the major daily newspaper in Singapore).

However, this recognition is not accepted without caution. Many of our interviewees were conscious about the potential biases of online sources. K., an active volunteer, pointed out:

> In terms of a disadvantage, the level of trust or credibility of the information published on the website, there [are] still some doubts over it. As an Internet user, sometimes when we blog about articles, we input our own personal thoughts that might be quite subjective. To me, that's the disadvantage of the new media.

In addition to blogs, social network sites, such as Facebook and Twitter, are also widely used in activism. Many of our interviewees mentioned that they use Facebook to gather information, to broadcast their events and activities, as well as to participate in activist groups, and to get in touch with fellow activists. A. relied on Facebook as a source, not only for personal information, but also for news gathering. He said:

> Every morning you go to Facebook and see news, something you don't know. Sometimes my friends have their own sources. If they find something interesting, they also post on Facebook, and I see it, then I post it on my blog, then 5000 people see it, then it gets passed on. Going viral is very useful that way, for news gathering as well as for news dissemination.

G. is responsible for the Facebook account affiliated with her organization. She explained what she did when managing the Facebook account:

> Actually what I do is just add people, update the events, photos, advertisement or whatever platform that we have. That's mainly what we do for Facebook. . . . Because it offers us the convenience of inviting people, because it's a very central platform that a lot of youths use, from there we decided that's the best way to reach out to our friends. Unless you go directly and ask your friend face to face, 'Can you come to this event?' you just need to do a Facebook invite. It's just that with the Facebook invite, some people may say that they're attending, but they may not turn up.

In addition to information exchange, blogs and social network sites also support debates and dialogues among Internet users. H. made this point clearly:

> Facebook – mainly for commenting on people's links, notes, and status updates – and the comments threads on TOC, KRC, etc. . . . Besides Facebook, I participate in online debate and discussion on current affairs news sites such as The Online Citizen, SG Daily and the Kent Ridge Common.

The role of ICT has also been incorporated into the everyday running of activist groups. Several interviewees mentioned that they use Google groups and Google documents to organize their activities. They relied on ICT to the extent that online communication can replace some of the offline meetings. L.J. said:

> I guess it's quite important because in the organizations where I'm in, we don't really meet that frequently. Much of the things we do are online, so it's kind of more informal. A lot of stuff is organized online. It makes things more convenient and it also compresses the time we need to discuss things. You don't have to meet at a specific time. I guess it helps in the organization of events and discussion on whether to proceed with certain things.

The capacity of ICT in facilitating organizations is particularly crucial for activists who work internationally. Young activists all over the world are able to collaborate on common issues, thanks to ICT. V., who has run an international project, was technologically savvy enough to take full advantage of the Internet. He used Google documents creatively to share information, as well as to organize voting (with an online spreadsheet). He also used a content management system to put up agendas for real-time online meetings. Real-time reports of such meetings were also published through this system. V. concluded:

The Commission on Sustainable Development, the one that I work with the UN for. By the very fact that I'm the only one who is from Singapore, from Asia actually, for the CSD 17 that I'm coordinating, we had to gather inputs from across the world, across various people who spoke different languages, who had different time zones, definitely the Internet turns to be a huge thing.

Twitter, another social network tool, is reported to be less important than Facebook. Most of the time our interviewees synchronized their Facebook, blog, and website activities with their Twitter accounts. Twitter only functions as another dissemination channel. The reasons given for not fully utilizing Twitter include its 140-character limit, the fragmented nature of the tweets, and the lack of popularity of Twitter among both activists and the general public. It was also observed that online forums, a typical Web 1.0 social platform, are not very much used by these young activists. Lack of interaction in online forums was cited as the major reason for their not being used.

While the significance of the Internet in information exchange was fully acknowledged by our interviewees, they were not blind to the shortcomings, or inherent disadvantages of ICT. Information overload was one of these shortcomings. L.J. used the exact term in referring to his difficulty with Facebook:

> Information overload, definitely! It shows you all [this] supposedly interesting stuff but I mean you have so many friends on Facebook, this whole list of update, even though it's not important, I don't really care what other people are doing anyway. Sometimes people send out mass invites, I'm guilty of that too, such as application invites. Recently I just make sure that I ignore all app invites.

A concern about the homogeneity of online communities was also voiced. H., a social worker on food issues, pointed this out, after complimenting Facebook on being instantaneous:

> The downsides are that I am exchanging views with people I regularly speak to already, as well as a particular demographic group, such as students/social activists/social media people, etc. rather than a wide spectrum of the affected population.

Loss of privacy was named as another side effect of using a Facebook personal account to raise awareness and organize activities. N., after listing the benefits of online channels, said:

> As much as I love how much it reaches everyone, I think your own personal privacy . . . When you do projects like, all the more you want to focus on it, not on you, but people tend to link both together. You don't want that.

A major frustration facing many interviewees was how to turn online support into offline action. A. had organized quite a few real life actions, but they had not drawn a sufficient number of supporters. He described one of the events:

> One of the downsides is people prefer to stay online, and it's proved through all the events we organized at the Speakers' Corner. For one event, the Facebook group has 5000 members but only 200 people turned up on the actual day. I think mostly social networking platforms are good for dissemination and like I said, gathering news. It's not very effective from what we can see in organizing people to come out in real life.

C. made a similar comment by recognizing the role of ICT in raising awareness, but not in translating into real action:

> I think ICT has been very useful to raise awareness, at least to put it in the consciousness of the people, just to let them know that the issue exists. I think the challenge is how to translate it into real action. Anyway, signing an online petition is very easy, but at the end of the day, does it actually influence decision-makers? That's where we have to find this link.

While how to activate online support remains a challenge to almost all activists in the world, one contextual reason should not be ignored, and that is the lack of responsiveness from local politicians to online sentiments. G. mentioned that:

> For us, I don't think we use ICT to influence a politician because this is Singapore and they don't really recognize [ICT] . . . They always say that alternative media is there, but maybe not significant enough to create a great impact, so they don't really care. Even though they monitor, they don't really care a lot.

Although mobile phones enjoy complete penetration among the Singaporean population, they are generally not used for most activist purposes, with a few exceptions. The first exception is that mobile phones are used to keep in touch with fellow activists, just as with interpersonal communication with friends. Another exception is that a migrant worker organization used a helpline to assist migrant workers. S.N. introduced the topic:

> This mobile number is alternating among staff members. We have a social worker who handles the calls, it's a separate mobile. But if she's not around, I take over.

However, in most cases mobile phones are not used for activist work. The short message service (SMS) has never been used in coordinating large-scale offline gatherings in Singapore, whereas the Philippines, a neighboring country, has exploited SMS in its public demonstrations, such as People's Power. One of the reasons is that mobile phones are often considered to be personal devices, meant for private use, not for public communication. A. explained why mobile phones were not used in his news gathering:

> The other time we were thinking about having a hot line. We were to get a phone card with a number. If people have a news tip, they could SMS us. After I thought about it, it's going to bring a lot of hassle, people will just give us wrong information, we will have to spend time running around, when we are there, we realize that people play us up, it's a false alarm, it's going to be a lot of waste, so no.

Despite the different extents to which ICT is used in activism, all of our young activists had made use of at least one or two ICT tools to help them with their activities. The best use of ICT was found to be for accessing and disseminating information. As a result, the information is able to reach a broader readership and mobilize interested individuals to participate, especially when some online-based activities are effortless to participate in. The scope of the reach sometimes goes beyond national boundaries, which clearly facilities international collaboration regarding certain widely shared causes (e.g., environmental issues). However, concerns over ICT-based activism were expressed. These ranged from issues of credibility and information overload, to homogeneity and privacy. A major challenge is to translate online activities into offline actions that have a real impact on government and policy-making.

Conclusions and Discussion

This study's findings suggest that in contrast to the declining political participation among youth in many liberal democracies, Singaporean young activists are not less actively engaged in activism than the older generations. Rather, they seem to be active in both the old (e.g., community volunteering) and the new (e.g., issue-based activism)arenas of activist work. However, the accepted definition of activism, or the popular type of activist work, does show a generational shift: whereas most of the older generation of Singaporean activists were either intentionally or unintentionally involved in opposition party politics, most of our interviewees did not show any interest in joining opposition parties. They are instead attracted to a variety of social issues that do not directly challenge the ruling power, but, nevertheless, require work to raise awareness and obtain support from the general public. ICT has been highly effective in serving the goal of information dissemination, both among the young activists themselves, and to the public they want to reach.

Weiss (2011) claimed that, in Singapore, '[a]ccessing information becomes, in effect, activism'. She went on to explain that the very act of engaging online is, in itself, a form of protest. The significance of accessing information through ICT has to be understood within the context of the Singaporean information infrastructure. As mass media are controlled by the authorities, and the physical space allowed for debate and discussion (e.g., Speakers' Corner) is limited, there are almost no alternative venues for acquiring information, except via the Internet. Going online to get alternative viewpoints is an expression of activism because these alternative views are not readily available in the dominant public sphere (i.e., through mass media). What the activists have done is to exploit the tools of ICT to seek for, as well as to supply, such alternative viewpoints from the Internet. This purpose has been, to a large extent, successful, according to the interviewed activists.

What is challenging is how to build a link between online activism and actual policy making, which still largely happens offline. First, the convenience and ease of use of ICT for activist work do not change the inconvenience and difficulty of participating in those offline activities that could bring pressure to bear on policy makers. Therefore, an increasing engagement with online activism does not necessarily mean that people will be motivated to take offline actions that can influence policy makers – the demands associated with such activities are considered to be too onerous. Second, the existing decision-making structure has yet to incorporate online forms of participation into its regular routines. In other words, day-to-day policy making remains offline, and if online actions are not extended into the offline mechanisms (e.g., through protests or appeals to members of parliament) the system seems to disregard what is being done in cyberspace. Due to these two reasons, ICT-based activism has not been successful in directly influencing policy making and governmental decisions in Singapore.

Our analysis shows that the role that ICT can play is shaped by contextual factors. The extent to which ICT can make an impact is also constrained by contextual factors. The Singapore situation suggests that how young activists perceive the contribution of ICT to their work is limited by the historical trajectory of political development, and the current arrangement of institutions. If there is a new horizon in youth activism, it is definitely the increasing prominence of ICT. However, the exact impact of using ICT varies. I would argue that the difficulty facing young activists in Singapore is not disengagement or disaffection; indeed, we have witnessed a peak of youth engagement in the recent elections (Zhang and Lim, 2012). But the challenge facing young activists in Singapore is how to take advantage of ICT while avoiding the disadvantages of this technology, in order to promote democratization in the light of various barriers, be they historical, institutional, or psychological.

This article ends with a few policy implications. First, the findings suggest that complete control over information flow is almost impossible in the Internet era. Formal institutions, as well as social organizations, should not shy away from joining the flow, and need to actively promote their messages through cyberspace. This has to be done effectively, rather than half-heartedly.

Otherwise, the backlash effect would put these efforts into a negative light, and harm the institutions and organizations that set up the channels and send the messages. An effective means for engaging citizens online is to provide constant and interactive communication. Not only should messages be broadcast, but conversations with Internet users should also be held in a timely manner. Second, although our young interviewees are all online, policy makers should not ignore the fact that a large number of the older population is not online. The situation is particularly tricky when mainstream on the Internet equates with alternative to the offline world. In other words, if young people receive their information largely from alternative online sources, that hold very different positions compared to the national mass media, the risk of seeing a polarized nation becomes real. Those who rely on mass media would perceive the country's situation quite differently from those who rely on online alternative media. Policies are needed to bridge the digital gap as well as the perceptual gap, and thereby to facilitate integration.

Acknowledgments: The author wants to express thanks for the excellent assistance provided by the following students: Catherine Candano, Jodie Luu, Mao Chengting, and Yoke Hian Chan.
Funding: This research received grant from the Youth, ICTs, and Political Engagement in Asia project, funded by the International Development Research Center, Canada through Ideacorp Inc. in the Philippines.

Endnotes

1   Interviewees' initials are used for the purpose of protecting their identity and privacy.

References

Bennett, W.L. 1998. "The Uncivic Culture: Communication, Identity, and the Rise of Lifestyle Politics." Ithiel de Sola Pool Lecture, American Political Science Association. *Political Science and Politics*. Volume 31. Pp. 41–61.
Cheung, P.P.L. 1992. "The Development of Private Philanthropy in Singapore." In K.D. McCarthy, V.A Hodgkinson, and R.D. Sumariwalla (Eds.) *The Nonprofit Sector in the Global Community*. San Francisco: Jossey-Bass. Pp. 454–465.
Chua, B.H. 2004. "Communitarianism without Competitive Politics in Singapore." In B.H. Chua (Ed.) *Communitarian Politics in Asia*. London: Routledge Curzon. Pp. 78–101.
Dalton, R.J. 2004. *Democratic Choices: The Erosion of Political Support in Advanced Industrial Democracies*. Oxford: Oxford University Press.
Dalton, R.J. & M.P. Wattenberg. 2002. *Parties without Partisans: Political Changes in Advanced Industrial Democracies*. Oxford: Oxford University Press.
Delli, Carpini MX. 2000. "Gen.com: Youth, Civic Engagement, and the New Information environment." *Political Communication*. Volume 17. Pp. 341-349.
Infocomm Development Authority. 2010. *Annual Survey on Infocomm Usage in Households and by Individuals*. Accessed October 10, 2011. http://www.ida.gov.sg/doc/Publications/Publications_Level3/Survey2010/HH2010ES.pdf.

Kim, K.S. & Y-C Kim. 2007. "New and Old Media Uses and Political Engagement among Korean Adolescents." *Asian Journal of Communication*. Volume 17, Number 4. Pp. 342–361.

Lam, P.E. 1999. "Singapore: Rich state, Illiberal Regime." In J.W. Morley (Ed.) *Driven by Growth: Political Change in the Asia-Pacific Region*. Armonk, NY: ME Sharpe. Pp. 255–274.

Lee, K.Y. 2000. *Memoirs of Lee Kuan Yew, From Third World to First: The Singapore Story: 1965–2000*. Singapore: Times Media Pty Ltd.

Lee, T. 2002. "New Regulatory Politics and Communication Technologies in Singapore." *Asia Pacific Media Educator*. Volume 12, Number 2. Pp. 14–25.

Lin, T. & A. Hong. 2011. "Youth, New Media and Political Participation in the Election." In Impact of New Media on General Election 2011 Conference, Singapore.

Mindich, D.T.Z. 2005. *Tuned Out: Why Americans Under 40 Don't Follow the News*. Oxford: Oxford University Press.

Ming, S. 2002. "Civil Society in Southeast Asia: Cases of Singapore and Malaysia." In R.K.H. Chan, K.K. Leung & R.M.H. Ngan (Eds.) *Development in Southeast Asia: Reviews and Prospects*. Aldershot: Ashgate. Pp. 17–36.

Palfrey, J. & U. Gasser. 2008. *Born Digital: Understanding the First Generation of Digital Natives*. New York: Basic Books.

Putnam, R.D. 2000. *Bowling Alone: The Collapse and Revival of American Community*. New York: Simon and Schuster.

Rodan, G. 1998. "The Internet and Political Control in Singapore." *Political Science Quarterly*. Volume 113, Number 1. Pp. 63–89.

Rodan, G. 2003. "Embracing electronic media but suppressing civil society: Authoritarian consolidation in Singapore." *Pacific Review*. Volume 16, Number 4. Pp. 503–524.

Seow, F.T. 1998. *The Media Enthralled: Singapore Revisited*. Boulder, CO: Lynne Rienner.

Singapore Department of Statistics. 2010. *Census of population 2010: Advance Census Release*. Accessed October 10, 2011. http://www.singstat.gov.sg/pubn/popn/c2010acr.pdf.

Skoric, M.M. 2007. "Is Culture Destiny in Asia? A Story of a Tiger and a Lion." *Asian Journal of Communication*. Volume 17, Number 4. Pp. 396–415.

Tamney, J.B. 1996. *The Struggle over Singapore's Soul: Western Modernization and Asian Culture*. Berlin: Walter de Gruyter.

Ward, J. & C. de Vreese. 2011. "Political Consumerism, Young Citizens and the Internet." *Media, Culture and Society*. Volume 33, Number 3. Pp. 399–413.

Weiss, M.L. 2011. "New Media, New Activism: Trends and Trajectories in Malaysia, Singapore, and Indonesia." In Workshop on Asia's Civil Spheres: New Media, Urban Public Space, Social Movements, Singapore, September.

Yang, G. 2010. *The Power of the Internet in China: Citizen Activism Online*. New York: Columbia University Press.

Zhang, W. 2006. "Constructing and Disseminating Subaltern Public Discourses in China." *Javnost / The Public*. Volume 13, Number 2. Pp. 41–64.

Zhang, W. & J. Lim. 2012. "Social Media and Elections in Authoritarian Democracies: The Cases of Malaysia and Singapore." In 62nd Annual Conference of the International Communication Association, Phoenix, AZ.

Zheng, Y. 2008. *Technological Empowerment: The Internet, the State and Society in China*. Stanford, CA: Stanford University Press.

Zukin, C. et al. 2006. *A New Engagement? Political Participation, Civic Life, and the Changing American Citizen*. Oxford: Oxford University Press.

Annotation

Sarah McKeever

When approaching a new article, case study, or even dataset, it can be helpful to first examine the origins of the piece, in order to adjust our expectations accordingly. Our academic backgrounds and schools of thought deeply influence the way we are trained to read a piece, the questions we expect to be asked and answered, and the way in which we evaluate research. The piece in question, a case study on digital youth activism in Singapore, was originally published in a communication studies journal. Therefore it answers different questions than would a piece published in an anthropology or political sciences journal. Academia is not a monolithic entity, but full of deeply ingrained theoretical biases, critiques, and practices which act as points of contention between different fields.

When reading a text, it is also helpful to examine the sources cited and examine the origin of other case studies and theories present in any work. As this case study examines Singapore, it is helpful to examine how many of its cited texts directly relate to the Singaporean, or even Asian, context. How many sources are regional case studies, and what type of theory shapes the argument? The author references a number of Singapore-specific case studies and historical research to base the case study on. Unfortunately, most of the core theoretical texts within the evolving and interdisciplinary field of social media studies are based solely on American or European case studies, including many referenced in this case study. Many academics, myself included, feel forced to cite these core works when their relevance to other contexts is deeply problematic, and this is an issue which needs to be challenged.

Examining the methodology of the study can also provide additional insight into a case study. In this case study, the author uses personal contacts and "snowball" interview techniques to approach participants, and meticulously notes a variety of participant personal information, including the gender, education, and age of participants. While the author is very clear about the type of participants involved in the study, one must always be cautious of sampling bias creeping into any study, or at least acknowledge its existence. The relatively high level of education among the Singaporean participants could skew the relative importance of digital mobilisation. Many of the participants appeared disenchanted with traditional political mobilisation (or strictly oppositional politics), working on issues of the environment, mental health, and even a "Free Burma" campaign. However, issues of class, education, gender, language, and access to digital spaces must be considered when making claims to representativeness within a society as diverse as Singapore.

Bringing history and context into focus, Singapore represents an interesting challenge to what has historically been considered "activism." Many of the participants rejected the label as being linked to historical oppositional politics, which they appeared to feel very little affinity with, in spite of the fact that some of their parents had participated in earlier political movements. Active civic participation is encouraged, but appears to be linked to the state. The consequences of protesting the state may be potentially severe, which could lead to an understandable reluctance to report dissent in the digital and offline world in Singapore. The much-touted benefits of digital activism are the ease with which activism can be accomplished. When the consequences of these "easy" actions are fairly severe, how does this challenge our understanding that digital activism somehow requires less of us than activism on the ground?

To summarise, it is helpful when approaching any text to be aware of its methodological and theoretical origins and to evaluate any work bearing our own personal and academic biases in mind. It is additionally crucial to be aware of the applicability of theory outside of its geopolitical context. This case study is a good entry point into the use of ICT among youth activists in Singapore and encourages us to make further enquiries into the complex historical, political, social, and geographical context of the country.

References and Further Readings

Earl, J. & K, Kimport. 2011. *Digitally Enabled Social Change: Activism in the Internet Age*. Cambridge, MA: MIT Press.

Gerbaudo, P. 2011. *Tweets and the Streets: Social Media and Contemporary Activism*. London: Pluto Press.

Kozinets, R. 2010. *Netnography: Doing Ethnographic Research Online*. London: Sage Publications.

Acknowledgements

This Reader owes intellectual, infrastructural, and affective debt to a whole range of people and institutions who made it possible: The knowledge partners at Hivos, Amis Boersma, Josine Stremmelar, and Remko Berkhout, who helped in conceptualising this project and supported it generously and with care; the administrative team at Leuphana University, Goetz Bachmann, Samantha Gupta, and Sara Morais, who made it all seem so smooth and easy even as we worked across continents and time-zones; my fellow principal investigators Clemens Apprich and Oliver Lerone Schultz at the Post-Media Lab at the Centre for Digital Cultures, without whom none of this would have ever been possible; the Meson Press and the faith and trust of the colleagues at The Hybrid Publishing Lab at Leuphana University, especially Mercedes Bunz and Marcus Burkhardt; the entire group of change actors who have become a part of the making-change network (https://makingchangeblr.wordpress.com/); the annotators who have contributed generously to this book, sharing their perspectives and ideas with us; Anirudh Sridhar, Denisse Albornoz, and Verena Getahun for their critical help in gathering and editing the materials; and the incredible team at the Centre for Internet and Society that has worked tirelessly to put together the entire process.

> Nishant Shah
> Co-Founder, The Centre for Internet and Society, India.
> Knowledge Partner, 'Making Change Project', Hivos, The Netherlands.
> Visiting Professor, Centre for Digital Cultures, Leuphana University, Germany.

Contributors

Denisse Albornoz is Ecuadorian and resides in Toronto. She worked for 11 months at the Centre for Internet and Society as a program associate for the Making Change project, looking at methods for change at the intersections of art, technology and activism. She continued her research back in Toronto exploring how trans-media storytelling practices are used in Bangalore to challenge dominant discourses and strengthen citizenship habits. She graduated from the International Development Studies program at the University of Toronto in 2015.

Esra'a Al Shafei is the founder and director of Mideast Youth, a network of online platforms that amplify under-reported and marginalized voices throughout the Middle East and North Africa. She is a recipient of the Berkman Award from Harvard University's Berkman Center for Internet and Society for "outstanding contributions to the internet and its impact on society," and is currently a Shuttleworth Foundation Fellow. Previously, she was an Echoing Green Fellow and a Senior TED Fellow. In 2011 she was featured in Fast Company as one of the "100 Most Creative People in Business" and awarded the Monaco Media Prize, which acknowledges innovative uses of media for the betterment of humanity. In 2014, she was featured in Forbes' "30 Under 30" list of social entrepreneurs making an impact in the world. The same year, Mideast Youth received the Human Rights Tulip, awarded annually to an organization which promotes and supports human rights in innovative ways.

Maesy Angelina works on research and social innovation for women empowerment and poverty reduction in Jakarta, Indonesia. Her weekends are spent running POST, an independent bookshop and creative space that she co-founded in a traditional market in Jakarta.

Htaike Htaike Aung is the Programme Manager at Myanmar ICT for Development Organisation, or MIDO. She is interested in Internet culture, and has been involved in Internet propagation events in Myanmar since 2006. She is a computer privacy and circumvention activist. Htaike Htaike conducts trainings on Internet and digital security for the human rights defenders in Myanmar. She is one of the founders of the Myanmar Bloggers Society, and is an organizer of the Barcamp Yangon, http://www.barcampyangon.org/index.html, considered one of the biggest Barcamp gatherings in the world. She has also worked with several international NGOs to provide ICT training to grassroots activists and workers.

Anat Ben-David is a lecturer in the department of Sociology, Political Science and Communication at the Open University of Israel.

Nandini Chami is Senior Research Associate at IT for Change http://www.itforchange.net/, a Bangalore-based NGO, working on information society theory and practice from the standpoint of gender equality and social justice. Her research interests are: democracy and citizenship in the digital age and community informatics.

Sumandro Chattapadhyay is Research Director at the Centre for Internet and Society, India. He leads the open data activities at CIS, and also the Researchers at Work (RAW) programme. His academic interests span over topics of history and politics of informatics in India, new media and technology studies, and data infrastructures and economies; and is also keenly interested in questions and techniques of digital humanities.

Tracey Cheng was born in the U.S. and raised in Taiwan. She received both her Bachelor's degree in Comparative Religion and her degree in Master of Communication in Digital Media (MCDM) from the University of Washington. She currently resides in Taiwan.

Armand Hurault has been working on the Middle East since 2008 and on the political dynamics and forms of dissent of the Arab Spring since 2011. He is currently deputy coordinator at ASML, a Syro-French organization supporting the emergence of an alternative and professional media landscape in Syria. Armand holds a first master's degree from Sciences-Po, France, and a second in Middle East Politics from the School of Oriental and African Studies (SOAS), University of London.

Rachael Jolley is the editor of Index on Censorship magazine. Having started as a news reporter on a local newspaper, she moved on to writing for magazines, newspapers and websites in the UK and internationally (including The Times, the Financial Times and The Guardian). She has been editorial director at think tank British Future, managing editor for monthly magazine Business Traveller, and editor of Business Traveller Middle East, and commissioning editor (online) for the Fabian Society. She also launched the quarterly magazine Public Health Today.

Youngmi Kim is an associate professor at the department of International Relations / Public policy at Central European University. She received her PhD from the University of Sheffield (UK) in 2007 and joined CEU in 2009. Youngmi was previously a Leverhulme Trust Early Career Fellow and an ESRC Post-Doctoral Fellow at the University of Edinburgh, and has also taught at University College Dublin, Ireland. Her main interests are in comparative politics, especially in the study of political parties and party systems in new democracies, online politics, and comparative regionalism. Her current research explores online political participation and its relationship with offline activism, and the impact of political culture on political behavior.

Merlyna Lim is a scholar studying ICT (Information and Communication Studies), particularly on the socio-political shaping of new media in non-Western contexts. She has been appointed a Canada Research Chair in Digital Media and Global Network Society in the School of Journalism and Communication Carleton University in 2014. Formerly she was a Visiting Research Scholar at Princeton University's Center for Information Technology Policy and a Distinguished Scholar of Technology and Public Engagement of the School of Social Transformation Justice and Social Inquiry Program and the Consortium for Science, Policy and Outcomes at Arizona State University. She previously held a Networked Public Research Associate position at the Annenberg Center for Communication at the University of Southern California, Los Angeles. She got her PhD, with distinction (cum laude), from University of Twente in Enschede, Netherlands, with a dissertation entitled "@rchipelago Online: The Internet and Political Activism in Indonesia."

Sarah McKeever graduated from the University of Chicago in 2010 with a degree in International Studies, focusing on contemporary Indian politics and society. She was a Fulbright-Nehru English Teaching Assistant from 2010-2011, working in a government school in New Delhi to assist in English language comprehension and verbal skills. After working in Washington, D.C. on Sino-Indian relations, Ms. McKeever graduated with an MSc in Contemporary India from the University of Oxford in 2013. She is currently working on her PhD in Contemporary India Studies at the India Institute at King's College London. Her work focuses on the impact of social media on contemporary political movements.

Subhashish Panigrahi is an an educator and open source activist based in Bangalore, India. He is a long time Wikimedian and is involved in India's first GLAM project. Currently he is working at the Access To Knowledge program of the Centre for Internet and Society. In the past, he has worked on building partnerships with GLAM institutions, universities, language research organizations, government departments and individuals for bringing more scholarly and encyclopedic content on language, culture and history under free licenses. He has learning interests in building collaborative GLAM projects that operate in low cost and bring institutions, resourceful experts and scholars under one roof. He has been involved in various language related conferences and spoken in both policy and implementation discourses around open knowledge and open source.

Prabhas Pokharel is a practitioner using technology for social development in the developing world, focusing on Nepal. He is currently working as a Product Design Fellow at the Kathmandu Living Labs, responding to the Nepal earthquake with information products utilizing technology and crowd intelligence. He has worked in roles ranging from the very technical (software developer) to the the very non-technical (researcher / blogger) in places ranging from

Nepal, India, Kenya, Kosovo, Nigeria, Peru and the United States. Some examples of his work include: the development of technology infrastructure to support local-level grant-making in Nigeria, and helping establish the UNICEF Innovations Labs in Kosovo. Prabhas is a native of Nepal. Starting in the fall of 2015, he will be a student at the Product Design program at Stanford University.

Puthiya Purayil Sneha is Programme Officer with the Researchers at Work programme at the Centre for Internet and Society (CIS), India. Her training is in humanities, and she has previously worked with a research programme on higher education in India at the Centre for the Study of Culture and Society, (CSCS) Bangalore. At CIS she is presently engaged with a project on mapping the emergent field of Digital Humanities in India, and is also interested in questions on changing modes of knowledge production in the humanities with the advent of the internet and new digital technologies.

Padmini Ray Murray joined the Srishti Institute of Art, Design and Technology, Bangalore in January 2015. Ray Murray is one of the founders of the South Asian Digital Humanities Network and currently serves as vice-chair of Global Outlook::Digital Humanities, as editor-in-chief at SHARP news, and on the editorial board at Technoculture. Her research interests span the history of the book, public history, comics, videogames and literary studies. Ray Murray received her PhD in 2008 from the University of Edinburgh.

Urvashi Sarkar is a freelance journalist with an interest in politics, gender and culture. She currently works in the development sector and is a former reporter with The Hindu.

Nishant Shah is Professor of Culture and Aesthetics of New Media at the Leuphana University Lüneburg, Research Associate at Common Media Lab, Affiliate at Digital Cultures Research Lab, and International Tandempartner at Hybrid Publishing Lab. He is the co-founder and former-Director-Research at the Centre for Internet and Society, India. In his varied roles, he has been committed to producing infrastructure, frameworks and collaborations in the global south to understand and analyse the ways in which emergence and growth of digital technologies have shaped the contemporary social, political and cultural milieu. His Ph.D. thesis titled "The Technosocial Subject: Cities, Cyborgs and Cyberspace" builds a framework to examine the technosocial identities that are produced at the intersection of law, digital technologies and everyday cultural practices in emerging information societies like India. Nishant was an Asia Research fellow looking at the cost and infrastructure of building IT Cities like Shanghai. He is the author of a recent thought-piece titled "Whose Change is it Anyway? – Towards a future of digital technologies and citizen action in emerging information societies" that seeks to revisit the debates around digital activism and change in the global context. His current interests are in critically intervening in debates around Digital Humanities and conditions of change mediated by technologies.

Shobha S V is a digital media professional working in India. She is a trained journalist with an experience of working with media organisations viz. Daily News and Analysis, Times group and Mid-Day. A sociologist by training, she currently works for a women's rights organisation working on issues relatyed to violence against women. She has experience in researching women's experiences on social media, managing digital content, and designing and implementing projects related to crowd sourced knowledge and social justice.

YiPing (Zona) Tsou is a language and intercultural educator as well as creative learning entrepreneur. She holds a degree in Foreign Languages and Literatures from National Taiwan University and an M.A. in Cultural Studies from National Central University and has presented her poetic and scholarly work internationally. A translator, lecturer, and frequent collaborator, Tsou co-founded Becoming, the first crowd-learning community for cross-cultural creatives in Taipei. She also started a creative center in Kaohsiung called InBetween to bring together cultural literacy and language learning.

Hu Yong is a professor at Peking University's School of Journalism and Communication, and a well-known new media critic and Chinese Internet pioneer.Before joining the faculty of Peking University, Hu Yong has worked for a number of media sources for over 15 years, including *China Daily*, *Lifeweek*, *China Internet Weekly* and China Central Television. He is active in industry affairs as he is co-founder of the Digital Forum of China, a nonprofit organization that promotes public awareness of digitization and advocates a free and responsible Internet. In 2000, Hu Yong was nominated for China's list of top Internet industry figures. Hu Yong is a founding director for Communication Association of China (CAC) and China New Media Communication Association (CNMCA). His publications include *Internet: The King Who Rules*, the first book introducing the Internet to Chinese readers, and *The Rising Cacophony: Personal Expression and Public Discussion in the Internet Age*, documenting major transformations in the Chinese cyberspace.

Huma Yusuf is a freelance media researcher and a Global Fellow of the Woodrow Wilson International Center for Scholars in Washington, DC. She holds a master's degree from MIT's Comparative Media Studies program and a bachelor's degree from Harvard University. She was a research associate at the MIT Center for Future Civic Media during the 2007-2008 academic year. Her academic research at MIT examined how new media platforms and mediated practices help shape urban identity and negotiate street violence. As a print and online journalist based in Karachi, Pakistan, she reports on Pakistani politics, media trends, development, and violence against women. She is the recipient of the European Commission's 2006 Natali Lorenzo Prize for Human

Rights Journalism and the UNESCO / Pakistan Press Foundation 2005 Gender in Journalism Award.

Weiyu Zhang is an Associate Professor at the Department of Communication and New Media, National University of Singapore. She graduated from the Annenberg School for Communication, University of Pennsylvania. Her research interests are in New Media and Civic Engagement, Social and Cognitive Psychology of New Media.

Publication Details and License Information

We are deeply grateful to the authors and the original publishers of all the readings in this compilation for allowing republication of the same. Please give close attention to the copyright and license details of these readings before reusing or redistributing them. In case of doubt, please contact the author and/or the publisher of the material concerned.

All media associated with the readings are shared under the same copyright and license conditions as the reading concerned, unless mentioned otherwise.

The annotations in this book are all owned by the Centre for Internet and Society, and are shared under the Creative Commons Attribution-ShareAlike 4.0 International (CC-BY-SA 4.0) license. So you are free to reuse and redistribute them in any way you want, provided you mention the original source of the work (that is, 'Attribution'), including the name of the author and the URL to this book, and use the same license to distribute the work or any of its derivatives (that is, 'ShareAlike').

Albornoz, Denisse. 2014. "From Taboo to Beautiful - Menstrupedia". The Centre for Internet and Society. April 30. Accessed June 10, 2015. http://cis-india.org/digital-natives/making-change/menstrupedia-taboo-beautiful.

> This post was originally published on the website of the Centre for Internet and Society, Bangalore. Copyright is retained by the author, and CIS retains the right to partial or full republication of the post. Please contact the author if you want to republish the post with an altered title or significant editing.

Angelina, Maesy. 2011. "Digital Natives' Alternative Approach to Social Change." In Nishant Shah & Fieke Jansen (Eds.) *Digital Alternatives with a Cause: Book 2 - To Think*. The Centre for Internet and Society, Bangalore, India and Hivos Knowledge Programme, The Hague, The Netherlands. Accessed June 10, 2015. http://cis-india.org/digital-natives/blog/dnbook.

> Copyright to the text is held by the Centre for Internet and Society and Hivos, and is shared under Creative Commons Attribution-Non-Commercial-ShareAlike 3.0 Netherlands License. You are free to share and make derivative works of this publication only for non-commercial purposes and under the conditions that you appropriately attribute it, and that you distribute it only under a license identical to this one.

Aung, Htaike Htaike. Personal interview with Sumandro Chattapadhyay. May 15, 2015.

> This article is an edited transcript of an interview with Htaike Htaike Aung, Program Manager, MIDO. Please contact the Centre for Internet and Society for any potential reuse or redistribution of the text.

Ben-David, Anat. 2011. "Digital Natives and the Return of the Local Cause." In Nishant Shah & Fieke Jansen (Eds.) *Digital Alternatives with a Cause: Book 1 - To Be*. The Centre for Internet and Society, Bangalore, India and Hivos Knowledge Programme, The Hague, The Netherlands. Accessed June 10, 2015. http://cis-india.org/digital-natives/blog/dnbook.

> Copyright to the text is held by the Centre for Internet and Society and Hivos, and is shared under Creative Commons Attribution-Non-Commercial-ShareAlike 3.0 Netherlands License. You are free to share and make derivative works of this publication only for non-commercial purposes and under the conditions that you appropriately attribute it, and that you distribute it only under a license identical to this one.

Cheng, Tracey. 2014. "Taiwan's Sunflower Protest: Digital Anatomy of a Movement." Flip the Media. Accessed June 10, 2015. http://flipthemedia.com/2014/07/social-media-taiwan/.

> This article was originally published on Flip the Media, http://flipthemedia.com/, and has been reproduced with permission from the author, who retains all the rights to the work.

Hurault, Armand.2013. "Digital Revolution in Reverse: Syria's Media Diversifies Online." Rising Voices, Global Voices. October 30. Accessed June 10, 2015. https://rising.globalvoicesonline.org/blog/2013/10/30/digital-revolution-in-reverse-syrias-media-diversifies-offline/.

> This post was originally published on Rising Voices, https://rising.globalvoicesonline.org/, and shared under Creative Commons Attribution 3.0 license.

Jolley, Rachael. 2013. "India Calling." *Index on Censorship*. September 26. Volume 42, Number 3. DOI: 10.1177/0306422013503065. http://ioc.sagepub.com/content/42/3/62.

> This article was first published in Index on Censorship Magazine, http://www.indexoncensorship.org/magazine, in Volume 42, no 3, 2013. Please contact Index on Censorship for any potential reuse or redistribution of the text.

Kim, Youngmi. 2008. "Digital Populism in South Korea: Internet Culture and the Trouble with Direct Participation." KEI Academic Paper Series. Volume 3,

Number 8. Accessed June 10, 2015. http://www.keia.org/sites/default/files/publications/APS-YoungmiKim.pdf.

> This chapter was originally published as part of the Korea Economic Institute of America's (KEI) Academic Paper Series: Youngmi Kim, "Digital Populism in South Korea? Internet Culture and the Trouble with Direct Participation," Academic Paper Series, (Korea Economic Institute of America (KEI)), November 2008, at http://www.keia.org/publication/digital-populism-south-korea-internet-culture-and-trouble-direct-participation. For permission for partial or full republication of the article or any other usage of this content please contact Nicholas Hamisevicz at nh@keia.org.

Lim, Merlyna. 2013. "Many Clicks but Little Sticks: Social Media Activism in Indonesia." *Journal of Contemporary Asia*, 43:4, 636-657, DOI: 10.1080/00472336.2013.769386.

> This article has been originally published in the Journal of Contemporary Asia by Taylor and Francis http://www.tandfonline.com/, and is being reprinted here under appropriate permission from the same. Please refer to the Terms and Conditions of the publisher, http://www.tandfonline.com/page/termsand-conditions, and contact the publisher for any potential reuse and redistribution of the text.

Panigrahi, Subhashish. 2015. "Indigenous Language Digital Activism." Edited transcript of presentation at Global Voices Citizen Media Summit 2015, Cebu City, Philippines. January 25. Directly collected from the author.

> This transcript is reproduced here with permission from the author, who retains all rights to the work.

Pokharel, Prabhas. 2011. "Towards 2 Way Participation." In Nishant Shah & Fieke Jansen (Eds.) *Digital Alternatives with a Cause: Book 3 - To Act*. The Centre for Internet and Society, Bangalore, India and Hivos Knowledge Programme, The Hague, The Netherlands. Accessed June 10, 2015. http://cis-india.org/digital-natives/blog/dnbook.

> Copyright to the text is held by the Centre for Internet and Society and Hivos, and is shared under Creative Commons Attribution-Non-Commercial-ShareAlike 3.0 Netherlands License. You are free to share and make derivative works of this publication only for non-commercial purposes and under the conditions that you appropriately attribute it, and that you distribute it only under a license identical to this one.

Sarkar, Urvashi. 2014. "Wikipedia, Bhanwari Devi and the Need for an Alert Feminist Public." Kafila. March 27. Accessed June 10, 2015. http://kafila.

org/2014/06/27/wikipedia-bhanwari-devi-and-the-need-for-an-alert-feminist-public-urvashi-sarkar/.

> The post was originally published on Kafila, http://kafila.org/, and no permission is required for its partial and full republication. Please contact the author if you want to republish the post with an altered title or significant editing.

Shafei, Esra'a Al. 2014. "Keeping Our Voices Loud - the Evolution of CrowdVoice.org." Medium. August 18. Accessed June 10, 2015. https://medium.com/@ealshafei/keeping-our-voices-loud-the-evolution-of-crowdvoice-org-6ee8c837ba3e.

> This post was originally published on Medium, https://medium.com/. It is reproduced here with permission from the author, who retains all rights to the work.

Tsou, YiPing (Zona). 2011. "Digital Natives in the Name of a Cause: From Flash Mobs to Human Flesh Search." In Nishant Shah & Fieke Jansen (Eds.) *Digital Alternatives with a Cause: Book 2 - To Think*. The Centre for Internet and Society, Bangalore, India and Hivos Knowledge Programme, The Hague, The Netherlands. Accessed June 10, 2015. http://cis-india.org/digital-natives/blog/dnbook.

> Copyright to the text is held by the Centre for Internet and Society and Hivos, and is shared under Creative Commons Attribution-Non-Commercial-ShareAlike 3.0 Netherlands License. You are free to share and make derivative works of this publication only for non-commercial purposes and under the conditions that you appropriately attribute it, and that you distribute it only under a license identical to this one.

Yong, Hu. 2014. "Three Forces Acting behind the Development of the Internet." Speech at Consensus and Spring Luncheon, Consensus Media Group. Xia Baiyan (Ed.) 21ccom.net. April 16. Accessed June 10, 2015. http://www.21ccom.net/articles/dlpl/gswp/2014/0416/104503.html.

> This article is a transcript of a speech delivered by Prof. Hu Yong at 'Consensus and Spring Luncheon', and was published first on Consensus Net, and reproduced on 21ccom,net. The title has been given by Xia Baiyan, the Editor-in-charge of the website. The speech has been translated into English and published here with permission from the author, who retains all rights.

Yusuf, Huma. 2009. "Old and New Media: Converging during the Pakistan Emergency (March 2007 - February 2008)." MIT Center for Civic Media, MIT. January 12. Accessed June 10, 2015. https://civic.mit.edu/blog/humayusuf/

old-and-new-media-converging-during-the-pakistan-emergency-march-2007-
-february-2008.

> The text republished here is a long extract from the original report published by the MIT Center for Civic Media under Creative Commons Attribution-ShareAlike 3.0 United States license. Please contact Andrew Whitacre, Communications Director, Comparative Media Studies/Writing and MIT Center for Civic Media, MIT, <awhit@mit.edu>, for any communication regarding possible usages of the text.

Zhang, Weiyu. 2013. "Redefining Youth Activism through Digital Technology in Singapore." *International Communication Gazette*. Volume 75, Number 3. Pp. 253-270.

> This article was originally published in the International Communication Gazette by SAGE Publications Inc. http://gaz.sagepub.com/, and is being reprinted here under appropriate permission from the same. For permission for partial or full republication of the article or any other usage of this content, please see http://www.sagepub.com/journalsPermissions.nav.

www.ingramcontent.com/pod-product-compliance
Lightning Source LLC
Chambersburg PA
CBHW031145020426
42333CB00013B/521